Lucius N. Wheeler

The Foreigner in China

Lucius N. Wheeler

The Foreigner in China

ISBN/EAN: 9783743338777

Manufactured in Europe, USA, Canada, Australia, Japa

Cover: Foto ©ninafisch / pixelio.de

Manufactured and distributed by brebook publishing software (www.brebook.com)

Lucius N. Wheeler

The Foreigner in China

REIGNER
IN CHINA.

L. N. WHEELER.

FOREIGNER IN CHINA.

BY

L. N. WHEELER, D.D.

WITH INTRODUCTION BY PROF. W. C. SAWYER, PH.D.

CHICAGO:
S. C. GRIGGS AND COMPANY.
1881.

COPYRIGHT, 1881,
BY S. C. GRIGGS & COMPANY.

TO

THE HON. S. WELLS WILLIAMS, LL.D.

WHOSE STERLING CHRISTIAN CHARACTER

AND EMINENT SERVICES

IN DIPLOMACY

AND IN VARIOUS DEPARTMENTS OF ORIENTAL LEARNING

ENTITLE HIM

TO THE GRATITUDE AND ADMIRATION ALIKE

OF HIS COUNTRYMEN;

AND WHO IS WARMLY REMEMBERED

AS FRIEND AND NEIGHBOR

DURING FOUR YEARS' RESIDENCE IN THE

CHINESE CAPITAL,

THIS VOLUME IS

RESPECTFULLY INSCRIBED BY

THE AUTHOR.

CONTENTS.

INTRODUCTION 11

CHAPTER I.
EARLY DATES.

Origin of the Chinese — Progress of the empire — The mythical Fuh-hi — The first emperors — The prodigious labors of Yu — The population 2,000 B.C. — The Hia, Shang, Chaou, and Tsin dynasties — The Great Wall — The burning of the books — The modern period in Chinese history — Introduction of Boodhism — A popular religion — An illustrious monk — An ignoble priest — A period of persecution — The faith established. 23-33

CHAPTER II.
THE EAST AND WEST.

The arts and inventions common to all countries — Chinese astronomy borrowed from India or Bactria — Paper and printing — Gunpowder — Jesuits teach the Chinese the manufacture of cannon — The knowledge of iron comes from the West — Silk manufacture — The mariner's compass — The Old Testament and the Shoo-king — Chinese travelers visit Persia — Rome and Peking — Arabian travelers — The marvelous career of Marco Polo — China and the discovery of America — Portugal, Great Britain, and Russia, in contact with China — Mohammedanism — A Jewish colony. 34-46

CHAPTER III.
TROUBLOUS TIMES.

Tendency to a war of races — Native arrogance — The Portuguese outrage — Freebooting expedition of Mendes Pinto — The first Portuguese embassy — Alfonso de Melo — The

Macao settlement — Spanish oppression of the Chinese in Manila — The Dutch established in Formosa — Their exclusive policy — The struggle with Koshinga — A modern Regulus — The abandonment of Formosa — English broadsides in Canton river — English grievances — Strife among Europeans — Turbulent sailors. . . . 47–59

CHAPTER IV.

THE FORTUNES OF DIPLOMACY.

The unsuccessful attempt of Great Britain — Dutch commissioners at the court of the first Manchoo emperor — No adequate consular authority — Trade in peril — Col. Cathcart's mission — Earl Macartney sent to Peking — The imperial dignity — Court ceremonials — His Excellency declines to perform the *kotow* — The embassy a failure — The Batavian commission — The American consulate — The East India Company negotiate with the governor — Lord Amherst appears at Peking — His exit — Provincial intrigues successful — An imperial letter to the Prince Regent of England — Important epoch. 60–72

CHAPTER V.

ORIGIN OF THE OPIUM WAR.

The question of free trade — Appointment of Lord Napier — Unique character of his mission — Injudicious conduct of the superintendent — His death — Chinese and English characteristics — Origin and progress of smuggling in opium — Memorials to the throne on the subject of opium — The emperor resolves to execute the laws against that drug — Foreigners at Canton interfere with a public execution — Captain Elliot — Commissioner Lin — The demand for the surrender of opium — Its destruction by the government — Trade interdicted — The appeal to arms. . 73–87

CHAPTER VI.

THE WAR AND ITS RESULTS.

The capture of Ting-hai — The blockade — Negotiations at Canton — The proposed sacrifice to the god of war — The disgrace of Lin—Canton ransomed from the English—Fall of Amoy, Chin-hai, Ningpo, and Cha-pu—Valiant Tartars—Two Chinese generals in contrast—Native *sang-froid*—The assault on Chin-kiang-fu—A scene of horror—Nanking invested—The treaty—A conference on the subject of opium—Honors from the Queen—The imperial displeasure—The stipulations ratified and carried into effect—A remarkable state paper—Supplementary treaty—Various nations seek intercourse with China—Mission of Caleb Cushing—The French treaty—Recovery from the effects of the war—Barriers broken down—A peace offering. 88–103

CHAPTER VII.

RENEWAL OF HOSTILITIES—THE NORTH CHINA CAMPAIGN.

Foreigners excluded from Canton—The British flag insulted—Anglo-French alliance—Attitude of Russia and the United States—The Capture of Canton—A foreign squadron at the mouth of the Pei-ho—The negotiations of Tien-tsin—Defeat of the allies at Ta-koo—The breath of Mars—Capture of the outer forts—A sharp battle—Curious Chinese documents—The fall of Ta-koo and Tien-tsin—A foreigner's opinion of Chinese prowess—"San-ko-lin-sin's folly"—The desolations of war 104–118

CHAPTER VIII.

THE BELEAGUERED CAPITAL.

Its early history—The environments—The city walls, temples, palace, etc.—The allies' approach—Treatment of a funeral procession—Flight of the emperor—Storming of the summer palace—The work of spoliation—Scenes in the grand imperial reception hall—The emperor's bed-room—Wanton destruction of property—Sale of an emperor's effects—Preparations for the attack—Surrender of the An-ting gate—Indignation in the camp—The summer palace laid in ashes—Exchange of ratifications—A banquet—The *Te Deum* 119–133

CHAPTER IX.
ROMAN CATHOLIC MISSIONS.

The ascetic Tamo — Monks and the silkworm — Nestorianism — Francis Xavier — Valignano — Ricci — Paul Siu and Candida — The first persecution — Schaal — The Manchoo dynasty — A Chinese Constantine the Great — A Jesuit becomes president of the astronomical board — The second persecution — Verbiest — The missions prosperous under Kang-hi — The fatal controversy — The glory of the Jesuits departed — Martyrs of the faith — Catholic and pagan idolatry — The sciences and propagandism — Papal assumption — Modern success — The old antagonisms to be renewed in China 134–150

CHAPTER X.
PROTESTANT MISSIONS.

Robert Morrison — His call and preparation — Arrival in China — The difficulties encountered — Becomes translator to the East India Company — His labors and death — William Milne — E. C. Bridgman — Father of the American mission — Dr. Lockhart — The great missionary movement of 1842 — Caleb Cushing's tribute to missionaries — S. Wells Williams — The Chinese Repository — The delegates' version of the Bible — Other versions — Extensive circulation of the Scriptures — Improvement in the printing art — Christian Chinese literature — Christian schools — Medical missions — Public preaching — The Pauline method 151–169

CHAPTER XI.
HINDRANCES TO EVANGELISM.

Nature of the language — Embarrassments in communicating evangelical thought — A question of terms — The national vanity — Influence of modern civilization overrated — An obtuse mandarin — The universal ignorance — "A Death-blow to Corrupt Doctrines" — "Expulsion of the non-human species" — Popular stories about the adherents of

Christianity — Popular superstition — A city struck with terror — Missionary with a bottle full of demons — Characteristics of Chinese superstition — The gospel preacher misunderstood — Foreign vices — Native estimate of foreign character — Debate in a chapel — An emperor's view of the opium question — The famine — Dr. Legge's discussion with a mandarin — The political view — An Englishman's arraignment of his country 170–199

CHAPTER XII.

PROTESTANT MISSIONS NOT A FAILURE.

Criticism from a mercenary standpoint — The standard of success — "A patient pursuit of results" — Three classes of foreigners in China — The merchants — Their unsuccessful attempts to introduce new articles of trade — The golden days of commerce in the past — The officials — The failures of diplomacy — The famous revision controversy — The legations at Peking — The missionaries — Pioneer work — Church organizations — The Synod of China — The first annual conference of the Methodist Episcopal Church — North China mission of the American Board — Tract Society — Shanghai Missionary Conference — "Living Boodhas" — Too late to discuss a question of success or non-success — Confucianism tried and found wanting — The time of the evening sacrifice 200–220

CHAPTER XIII.

THE TI-PING INSURRECTION.

Origin of the movement — The God-worshipers — Hung as a seeker after truth — A zealous convert — Development and growth of fanaticism — The Eastern and Western princes — Iconoclasm — Takes on a politico-religious character — A British squadron and the pirates — The Pun-te and the Kih-kea — Union of the pirate and rebel forces — Divine right of rebellion — Decadence of the empire — Proclamation of the Ti-pings — Female rebel chiefs — Accessions from the Triad Society — Sublime courage of the leader — Progress of the insurrection — The Bible adopted as a sacred book — Religious practices and organizations — Morning devotions — Occupation of Nanking — Movement toward the northern capital — Disastrous end of a brilliant campaign — Foreigners take part against the Ti-pings — The last hope of the Heavenly Dynasty expires — The rebel chief commits suicide — His son put to death — The imperial edict 221–237

CHAPTER XIV.

OCCIDENTAL LIFE IN THE ORIENT.

The "Paris of China" — A cathedral — The foreign settlement — The island of Hong-Kong — Harbor and shipping — A mixed population — Street scenes — Sources of culture and amusement — Exiles from home — The last resting-place — Shanghai — The foreign city — Various open ports — A barbarous Anglo-Chinese dialect — Unhappy breach between merchants and missionaries — The imperial customs under Robert Hart — Light-houses — The arsenal at Kiang-nan — Government works under foreign direction at Foo-chow — Account of their origin and remarkable progress — The foreign drill-master — The civil service reform — Government schools at Canton and Shanghai — The imperial college — The educational mission to America — Introduction of various western improvements — A progressive mandarin — Origin of the Burlingame Mission — The foreign ministers admitted to audience — The strength and future progress of Western ideas — Our Chinese policy 238–261

INTRODUCTION.

CIVILIZATION, in its westward march from the old Asiatic home, has at last compassed the entire globe, and the youngest nation is now next neighbor to the oldest. Centuries after China had attained to about its present advancement, our fathers were still nomadic and barbarous, sacrificing human beings to the sun and moon, or worshiping Wodan and his wife Frea and Thor and Tyr—whom we commemorate in our names of the days of the week. But ancestor-worship has held the Chinese people stationary for more than two thousand years, nothing higher than the standard already attained by their fathers seeming to them desirable or possible. In the meantime, the tribes that migrated from the cradle of mankind into Europe, carrying with them very little besides their rude weapons and an uncultivated language, have set up and overthrown empires, and formed new languages, philosophies, and faiths, some of which endure to our own day, and some of which have perished from the earth. So that, notwithstanding this early superiority of the Chinese, it is said that they are now our moral as well as geographical antipodes. A large probability of the former contrast we could view complacently, if we were only assured that the actuality of the latter would be permanent. But when our ears are growing familiar with "Pigeon-English," and our eyes with the queue and flowing robes of the Mongolian, we are forcibly admonished to investigate the merits of this oriental civilization and its relation to our own.

Questions into which politics enter are usually discussed with so much partizan feeling in this country as to afford the people very little trustworthy information. Of this character are the discussions of the merits of presidential candidates, of the policy of protecting native industries, and notably of the duty of our government toward the Chinese who come to our shores.

To escape as far as possible from that partizanship which vitiates so much of our reasoning, we must go to China for our witnesses upon some of the chief questions that here concern us, though the Americans are but few who know anything about China from personal observation. Our witnesses should also have considerable familiarity with the Chinese language; for a language mirrors forth the mind of its framers, and we study a people to a great disadvantage if we do not both read their literature and commune with them by the living voice. The literature is the ultimate appeal concerning intellectual development and the higher forms of thought. Of similar importance is the oral communication with the people themselves. Even prolonged residence and travel in a country yield but meager and often mistaken views and impressions, provided the queries constantly arising at the sight of strange places and strange customs can find no expression and no solution save in the random guess so often indulged in and published to the astonishment of everybody acquainted with the facts. Upon this kind of writing by tourists must Sir Henry Maine rest his objections to the tales of travelers, against which he warns the public.

As regards the above qualification, the author of the work before us, Mr. Lucius N. Wheeler, is thoroughly qualified to speak on all Chinese matters. He was appointed missionary to China in 1865, and remained there until 1873, when failing health compelled his return. Soon after his arrival in China he took charge of the Methodist Episcopal Mission Press at Foochow. In 1867 he founded "The Missionary Recorder," a monthly paper containing a wide range of original miscellany touching the character and history of the native languages, the moral and physical condition of the people, and the various methods of propagating truth. This publication afterward changed its name to "The Chinese Recorder and Missionary Journal," and has continued until this day under the editorial supervision of able men. It circulates among English readers in the various open ports of China and Siam, as also in Japan and India. Shanghai is its present place of publication. Soon after the establishment of this paper, Mr. Wheeler removed to Peking, where he was the first representative of his Church in the capacity of missionary to that important center, serving four years as superintendent of the Mission. He preached in the native language, edited and published a "Directory of Protestant Missions in China," also the "Anglo-Chinese Almanac and Miscellany," translated a catechism into the Court dialect, and assisted in the preparation of the first Methodist Episcopal hymn-book in the same dialect.

Under the excellent opportunities thus afforded him, Mr. Wheeler studied not only the Chinese people, but also, by means of both the written and spoken language, their history and traditions, together with the history of all the forces that have penetrated China from the outside world. He gives us here the mature fruit of that study, embracing considerable matter of interest and historic value which has never before been given to the general public. Though we might expect the story of "The Foreigner in China" to be very short on account of the proverbial exclusiveness of the race, yet we find here not only numerous chapters of the record of his doings, but thrilling interest as well, tending to rouse feelings of indignation or sympathy, — and the indignation is not always against the conceited Celestials. Nevertheless, the following pages show every evidence of candor and fairness, even where the feelings might be sufficiently moved to affect the correct working of the judgment.

The light contributed in this work finds practical application beyond the pleasure of the reading and the mere acquaintance with a new race, which is at the same time a very old one, in the adjustment of the relations of the Chinese foreigner in the United States.

A cry has been raised that "myriads of millions" in China threaten to overrun our western continent, degrade our blood, corrupt our morals, and leave us no room to develop our ideals of government, of science, and of religion. In 1879 these perils seemed so imminent that a large majority of our congressmen, for the sake of rescuing a supposed birthright, were willing to violate the stipulations of the treaty between the United States and China. Treaty obligations without doubt should be sacred in the eyes of all citizens who would not themselves violate a promise to pay to which they have appended their signatures. From a breach of faith of this nature, and the consequent national disgrace, we were saved by the timely veto of President Hayes. We have thus gained time to reconsider the grounds of the panic on the Pacific coast, and to secure by a change of treaty the right to regulate the immigration of the Chinese.

The right of expatriation was solemnly affirmed by both parties to the Burlingame treaty, and our congress, at about the same time, declared that any impairment or questioning of the right would be "inconsistent with the fundamental principles of the Republic." The Angell treaty, or the new treaty, grants to our timidity the *privilege of impairing* the Chinaman's right of expatriation.

But while this stipulation is valuable chiefly in what it saved us of possible violations of international law, another article of the same treaty commits us to the support of a plain moral principle which will cost us some commercial losses, but which in the past has been trampled upon for the sake of commercial advantages by the unchristian representatives of christian states. The history of the opium trade with China, as fairly presented in this volume, places the opium war among the greatest outrages that disgrace the christian name. The new treaty engages that we will not transport opium to China or sell it there. Some of our merchants complain of this provision, the possibility of which complaint indicates how sore was the need of the stipulation. The whole christian world, however, will be profoundly thankful that at last the treaty making regarding the opium traffic with China has fallen into the hands of "men unused to business," provided all the merchants, like those who have thrust upon China the opium curse, are unable to do right in full view of an opportunity to get great gain by doing wrong. It will at least be impossible for any reader of this book to repeat the injustice of a misinformed American writer, who added to the injury of forcing opium upon the Chinese with bayonets and batteries the insult of charging upon their government that "all the pretended virtue and horror for its use is put on for political effect."

The feature of the recent treaty, however, which specially meets the public interest among Americans, is concerning the right to regulate Chinese immigration. Since this right has been conceded to us, it is now incumbent upon us to address ourselves to the task of discovering the bearings of this immigration upon our national prosperity. We need not, for this purpose, enter upon any questions that bear with equal or greater force upon the immigration from Ireland or Germany, for these are not in the indictment brought against the Chinese, though it is not impossible that some charges of this class might be urged with even greater justice and force than those which we hear oftenest.

The desire on the part of the sand-lotters and hoodlums to have all the Chinese who have come to the United States go home and stay there is heartily reciprocated by the Chinese, with the single and not unreasonable provision that the Americans who have gone to China should do the same. The following are the exact terms of a part of a proposition laid before the Board of Supervisors of the City of San Francisco in 1873:

"We propose a speedy and perfect abrogation and repeal of the present treaty relations between China and America, requiring the retirement of all Chinese people and trade from these United States, and the withdrawing of all American people and trade and commercial intercourse whatever from China." Somewhat similar is a passage in the memorial of the presidents of the Six Companies to President Grant:

"But, if the Chinese are considered detrimental to the best interest of this country, and if our presence here is offensive to the American people, let there be a modification of existing treaty relations between China and the United States, either prohibiting or limiting further Chinese immigration, and, if desirable, requiring also the gradual retirement of the Chinese people, now here, from this country. Such an arrangement, though not without embarrassments to both parties, we believe, would not be altogether unacceptable to the Chinese government, and doubtless it would be very acceptable to a certain class of people in this honorable country."

The political inconsistency and moral cowardice of this

opposition on the part of about fifty millions of Americans from all parts of the globe, to the hundred thousand of peaceable and industrious Chinese that have come to earn a livelihood in our midst, is entirely overshadowed by the economical rashness of the measure. What people in history ever drove away any number of their laboring class without suffering conspicuously for their folly? The Chinese are not much like the Huguenots, but if we expel them from our country, the people of San Francisco will better understand the value of the Huguenots to France, of the Puritans to England, and of the emancipated negroes to the South.

The very matter-of-fact plaintiff in this case is not disturbed by any Chinese fondness for ancestral cemeteries, or by their peculiarities of tailoring and of sprinkling clothes. I think I may add, without any injustice, that he is not generally impatient at the slowness with which they take on our education or our religion. His chief alarm seems to be caused by the fact that the yellow man will work for lower wages than the white man, and that thus the price of labor is depressed.

What would be the consequence of a reduction of say thirty per cent. in the price of labor in this country? Evidently the employer will have larger profits, and consequently more capital, and will then seek more laborers so as to employ his increased capital. When he thus reduces the excess of laborers, he will have to pay more wages in order to secure laborers enough to employ all his capital. The increased wages will in turn reduce the profits of his business, and thus maintain an equilibrium between the supply and demand in labor, as in anything else. There is no evidence that the Chinaman will refuse to profit by the capital he has created or the skill he has acquired.

But will not the white competitor suffer in his personal interests during the temporary depression? If he did, it would do him no injustice, for he came here and depressed wages in the same way himself. But it is demonstrated as a good answer to the above complaint, that there is no cheap labor in California, and that the urgent need of the manufacturing interests of the Pacific coast is cheaper labor, so that they can manufacture their own products instead of sending them east to a point where labor is cheaper. The facts go to show that the white man's wages are not depressed, nor the difficulty of finding employment increased, by the presence of the Chinese. In the construction of the Southern Pacific railroad, we are assured by the vice-president of the road that as Chinamen were not good teamsters or bridge builders or overseers, white men were given those employments at twice the pay of the Chinamen — no white laborer who wanted work being refused. Such pay would have been impossible if the Chinese had not taken the brunt of the work. The superintendent of construction of the Central Pacific testified before the congressional committee that when sufficient white labor could not be employed he hired a large force of Chinese, and after that three times as many white men were hired as could be found before. We are reminded of the cry, when railroads were first introduced, that horses would be thrown out of use and become almost worthless on our hands. Whatever excuse may then have existed for such ignorance of economical science, there can be very little now.

If, however, this plea against the Chinese from the standpoint of the laborer will not hold, will not this other, so much used by the "statesmen" of the Pacific coast, namely, that the Chinaman tends to impoverish the country by carrying a portion of his earnings to China? Is it not still true that half a loaf, or any other fraction, is better than no bread? Suppose one of these men should remain but a single day in this country, and at night should take his dollar, more or less, and pay twenty-five cents for his board, and start for China? Has he then robbed us of seventy-five cents? Let us see. The man who employed him and paid him one dollar was not actuated by love for the laborer, but by love of gain, and for the dollar paid out he received of real wealth the equivalent of a dollar and a quarter. The boarding-house keeper gained something also, having received twenty-five cents for what cost him fifteen. The account therefore between the parties will stand as follows:

John Chinaman, in account with the United States.

DR.

To cash for labor	$1 00
To actual cost of food	15
	$1 15

CR.

By one day's labor	$1 25
By cash paid for board	25
	$1 50
Balance left in the United States	35

It appears, therefore, that instead of the Chinaman's having taken seventy-five cents out of the United States, leaving no equivalent, the United States has taken thirty-five cents out of the Chinaman, and is at least that much better off for his having come. If, however, beyond the simple transactions supposed, the laborer purchases clothing, rides on the railroad, provides himself a home, or deposits his savings in a bank, every transaction is sure to increase the advantage of the United States, and this regardless of the question whether the man has grown rich by his industry and frugality, or expended his earnings for beer and whisky like so many of his whiter enemies.

It should also be noted that the Chinese, by their greater sobriety, and by their fashion of returning to China to die, when no longer able to labor, add almost nothing to the cost of our penal and charitable institutions, while at the same time they pay their taxes and all other obligations much more faithfully and promptly than white laborers.

We have long endured the immigration of Celts and Teutons at a rate fifty times more rapid than the coming of the Celestials, and no political economist would dare to say that we should be better off without them, though they have made it almost impossible to govern New York and some other cities even respectably. Strange to say, these very Celts and Teutons are the men whose minds are most exercised lest we shall be overrun by an inferior race, and their hoodlum sons, not the Chinese, are the disturbing element in San Francisco.

When our statesmen dare not further continue the experiment of free government, much as we have conducted it hitherto, let them adopt a rational protective principle, and apply it impartially,— such, for instance, as an educational suffrage qualification. For if we could reduce the power of the very ignorant and the vicious over our legislators, they would perhaps devote their attention to the real wants and dangers of our country instead of those that are imaginary.

W. C. SAWYER.

LAWRENCE UNIVERSITY,
    Appleton, Wis., August 1881.

THE FOREIGNER IN CHINA.

CHAPTER I.

EARLY DATES.

THE "black-haired race," whose habitat in the south-eastern portion of Asia abounds in beautiful scenery and natural wealth not exceeded by any other land under the sun, connect their history with times almost fabulously distant; and European writers on oriental subjects, although rejecting the evidently vague and improbable in their chronology, do not hesitate to concede them a very high degree of antiquity.

It is said that more than a thousand years before the founder of Rome reared his hut on the banks of the Tiber, China had fixed the seat of her empire and had laid the foundations of her future greatness. While Greece was yet divided into petty and hostile states, with as many monarchs as there were cities, China possessed a government whose imperial head extended his sway over a united people; and when Europe was a battle-field for barbarian hordes, China presented many of the aspects of a great and enlightened nation pursuing the arts of peace. It is probable, however, though we confess it reluctantly, that even these more moderate claims concerning the Chinese chronology are somewhat enthusiastic and extravagant.*

---

* See "Origin of the Chinese," by John Chalmers, A.M., pp. 63-7; also, "China and the Gospel," by Rev. William Muirhead, pp. 292-5.

The original possession of the Chinese people, so far as we are able to ascertain, was the southern portion of Chih-li, the province in which the present capital is situated, together with a part of Shan-si. How the founders of the nation came to be in that locality is one of those questions connected with the origin and spread of mankind about which we can only conjecture. A parallelogram, extending two degrees north and two degrees south of the 35th line of north latitude, thus measuring approximately north and south 250 miles, and east and west 600 miles, will include almost all that part of China where we have reason to believe letters were cultivated in the beginning of the Chaou dynasty, 1000 B.C. Confined to this area, not much greater than that of the British Isles, or scarcely one-sixth part of the present eighteen provinces, the civilized people of this Middle Kingdom were hemmed in on all sides by aboriginal tribes. These untutored sons of the soil, as time progressed, were mixed up with the more cultivated and ruling races, sometimes as servants, sometimes as disagreeable neighbors, and sometimes as allies. A native historian describes them as "mean and degraded barbarians, who held no communication by writing with superior states"; but he excepts the Tsinites on the west, whose ballads have a place in the Book of Poetry — an important and significant exception, when we come to look for the origin of Chinese civilization. By the processes of military conquest and colonization the vigorous and united people of the northwest slowly extended their territorial possessions; but not until about two hundred years before Christ was the southern portion of what we call China proper brought under subjection, and the bulk of the population continued to be aboriginal, or non-Chinese, for a long time after. The beginning of the Tang dynasty, or the year of our Lord 618, marks the period of substantial and final conquest.

A succession of dynasties, with varying fortunes, illustrious for great achievements or infamous for oppression and cruelty, arose and fell during the ongoing ages. Fuh-hi appears as the first imperial character; but we must relegate him, with his mythical deeds, into the unwritten past. Yaou and Shun were doubtless real men, chiefs of the earliest immigrants into China, although we see them through the mists of legend and of philosophical romance. Confucius adopted them as his favorite heroes, endowed with all the princely virtues.* Concerning Shun's accession to power, the following data are gathered from the Shoo-King. When Yaou had been on the throne for seventy years, finding the cares of government too oppressive for his advanced age, he proposed to resign in favor of his principal minister, the "Four Mountains." That worthy declared his virtue unequal to the office, but recommended to the favor of his august master "Shun of Yu, an unmarried man among the lower people." Of a family in which the parents were obstinately unprincipled and insincere, and associated with a brother whose arrogance was a perpetual provocation, he had been able by his filial piety to live harmoniously with them, and bring them to a considerable degree of self-government and good conduct. The monarch was delighted, but resolved upon a preliminary trial before investing Shun with the highest honors. He accordingly gave him his own two daughters in marriage, declaring that he would test his fitness for the throne by witnessing his behavior with his two wives. We are to suppose that Shun stood the test, for he was soon appointed

* "The Chinese Classics," by James Legge, D.D., vol. iii. pt. ii. pp. 52-80

"General Regulator" of the empire, and subsequently succeeded to the superior dignity.

Various incongruities of historical statement respecting this period give to much that is said the character of legendary tales. The stories of regal pomp, extensive empire, divine intelligence, and exalted virtue — the galaxy of brilliant ministers — the arts of astronomy, surveying, legislation, and various feats of men who are clearly entitled to the rank of demigods — will be regarded as akin to such works of imagination as "Plato's Republic" or "More's Utopia."

Concerning the successor of Shun, Bunsen says: "Yu the Great is as much an historical king as Charlemagne; and the imperial tribute-roll of his reign in the Shoo-King is a contemporary and public document just as certainly as are the capitularies of the king of the Franks." To this Dr. Legge, the eminent oriental scholar, replies: "That Yu is a historical king is freely admitted; but that the tribute-roll of his reign which we have in the Shoo-King was made by him, or is to be accepted as a genuine record of his labors, must be as freely denied." It is probable that the reign of this monarch marks the point of time when the rule of petty chiefs gave place to one united and absolute sovereignty.

The ancient annals speak of the condition of the surface of eastern Asia as one of disorder and desolation when he entered upon his heaven-appointed task. He is made to appear from the west, "tracking the great rivers, here burning the woods, hewing the rocks, and cutting through the mountains which obstructed their progress, and there deepening their channels, until their waters are brought to flow peacefully into the eastern sea. He forms lakes, and raises mighty embankments, until at length the grounds along the waters were everywhere made habitable; the hills were cleared of their superfluous wood; the sources of the streams were cleared; the marshes were well banked, and access to the capital was secured for all within the four seas. A great order was effected in the six magazines *of material wealth;* the different parts of the country were subjected to an exact comparison, so that contribution of revenue could be carefully adjusted according to their resources. The fields were all classified with reference to the three characters of the soil, and the revenues for the Middle Kingdom were established."* One might suppose that the time required for the completion of so vast an enterprise would extend beyond the period of one man's life; but, if we are to credit the commentators, Yu is to be regarded as a supernatural being, who could lead the immense rivers of China as if he had been engaged in regulating the course of feeble streamlets. Having thus "traveled and toiled and subdued the face of nature," it is presumable that the possessions of Yu were widely extended; but we have no trustworthy means of ascertaining their boundary. The population, also, becomes a question of interest. One of the older writers placed it at 13,553,923. As the statement was first made, so far as known, about two thousand five hundred years after the date to which it refers, we can hardly receive it with much credence. The number of one million which Sacharoff would allow for the Chinese of Yu's time is, in the opinion of Dr. Legge, abundantly large. The house of Hia, which is to be regarded as the first Chinese dynasty, was founded by this illustrious ruler, whose descendants maintained their supremacy for about

* Legge's Classics, vol. iii. pt. ii. p. 58.

four hundred years, from 2000 to 1600 B.C.* Among the contemporary events of importance are the call of Abraham, Jacob's flight to Mesopotamia, and Joseph's elevation in Egypt.

The Shang dynasty, under twenty-eight sovereigns, characterized by wars among rival princes, and the Chaou dynasty, continuing for eight hundred and seventy-three years, under thirty-five monarchs, the longest of any in history, bring us down to an eventful epoch. Among the feudal states under the house of Chaou, that of Tsin, on the northwest, had long been the most powerful. One of the princes, Chaou Siang-wang, carried his encroachments into the imperial possessions, and soon became master of the whole empire. The son crowned with complete triumph his father's rebellious career, and assumed the name of Chi Hwang-ti (*i.e.* First Emperor) of the Tsin dynasty. He divided the country into thirty-six provinces, over which he placed governors, made progress through his dominions with a splendor hitherto unknown, opened roads and canals to facilitate intercourse between the provinces, besides performing other distinguished acts. Having repressed the incursions of the Huns, and driven them into the wilds of Mongolia, he conceived the idea of extending and uniting the walls which the subject northern states had erected on their frontier into one grand fortification, stretching across his wide domain from the sea to the desert. Such was the origin of the far-famed Great Wall of China, which gigantic undertaking was completed in ten years, or about 200 B.C. With a vain ambition to destroy all records written previous to his own reign, that he might be regarded

---

* Chalmers' "Origin of the Chinese," p. 65; "The Middle Kingdom," by S. Wells Williams, LL.D., vol. ii, p. 210.

by posterity as the first emperor of the Chinese race, he issued an order for the total destruction of the works of Confucius and Mencius, and other classic writings. "The burning of the books" was attended by the slaughter of many of the literati, upward of four hundred and sixty of whom were buried alive in pits for a warning to the empire. This Chinese event has been compared to the proceeding ascribed to Edward I of England, who is said to have assembled, in A.D. 1284, all the Welsh bards, and caused them to be put to death. This attempt to efface the history of former times, and to blot out from the memory of mankind the names which had been held in reverence for hundreds and thousands of years, failed of complete success, thanks to the marvelous memory of devoted scholars, and the recovery of a few copies of the ancient records in a better or worse state of preservation; albeit a shade of doubt has been thrown upon the venerated classics.

The successor of the sanguinary and impolitic Chi was soon displaced by a soldier of fortune, who, under the name of Kaou-tsu, founded the Han dynasty. From this commencement of modern Chinese history we are speedily brought to an event of signal importance in the religious world.

Boodhism, one of the three powerful religions in China, not only originated in a foreign country, but was first disseminated by foreign propagandists. During the first century of the Christian era, there was a spiritual dearth in the land. Although Confucius has been too hastily condemned as an atheistical philosopher, it being altogether probable that his confession of ignorance as to the powers above nature and in nature, and as to the hidden and mysterious life of man, was entirely ingenuous, it cannot be denied that his system completely failed to meet in any measure, and much less to satisfy, the immortal longings of the people. The charms, incantations, and magic arts of Taouism — the knowledge of letters, and the craft of state, — even the effort to turn the great master into a god by raising tablets to his memory and temples for his worship, — did not answer the crying necessity of the age. About 60 A.D. the Emperor Ming-ti, influenced, as it was thought, by a dream, or, as others have supposed, by a saying of Confucius — "In the West there are great sages," — or, as still others have imagined, by a rumor of Him who was "born king of the Jews," dispatched embassadors on an errand similar to that of the Wise Men of the East, who followed the light of Bethlehem's star. Proceeding as far as India, the embassy there met with Boodhist priests; and, supposing that the deity whose fame was thus brought to their attention was the divine person they had been sent to seek, they returned home with the new god, accompanied by a number of religious teachers. These priests of Boodha were received by His Majesty with signal marks of favor. A succeeding emperor sent to India for more of their order, and no less than 3,000 went to China, where they were inducted into a temple of one thousand rooms, built expressly for them. This strange religion, shorn of all the indecencies and fanatic madness of Indian worship, appealing to the hopes and fears of men by its doctrine of future rewards and punishments, and pleasing their imaginations with a pompous ritual and splendid pictorial scenes of far-away worlds, under imperial patronage and protection, spread rapidly among the masses. The hostility conceived on the part of the literati upon its introduction into the country has continued to the present; but as these astute critics have been unable to offer anything better, the result is, as Dr. Morrison has observed, " Boodhism in China is decried by the learned, laughed at by the profligate, yet followed by all." The seventh maxim of Kang-hi, pointed against all strange religions, presents that monarch in the attitude of a defender of the orthodox faith as taught in the classics, while he was himself a daily worshiper at the shrine of Boodhist idols.

During the early part of the seventh century a monk flourished who is perhaps the most famous of all his co-religionists in the Far East. Leaving his native place, Yuan-chwang traveled westward in search of the books and doctrines of his faith. He spent sixteen years abroad, five of which were passed in the great religious establishment of Nalanda, in Magadha, where he mastered the Sanscrit language, and pursued with devout zeal his studies in sacred learning. According to one authority, he translated, or helped to translate, six hundred and fifty-seven works under the auspices and command of the Emperor. He also wrote an "Account of Western Countries," which is a very interesting volume, but disfigured by improbable statements, and gross absurdities imposed on him from Indian sources. His unconquerable will, his dauntless courage, his genius and scholarship, and above all his unswerving faith, his fervent spirit, and his purity of life, commend him to our highest admiration. Such examples of unselfish and sublime devotion to imperfect forms of truth must have had their inspiration from a superhuman source; and they indicate to us the probable fact that Boodhism, containing less of gross and fatal error than any other of the pagan religions, is destined to exercise a propædeutic office for Christianity.

It must be confessed, however, that all professed believers were not like this master of the law. Many of the foreign priests practiced necromantic arts, and imposed on the people by pretended drugs for conferring long life; and numbers of them, in 657, were sent back to their native country. During the reign of the Empress Woo, Boodhism was popular and powerful, but cannot be said to have made an honorable use of its good fortune. The profligate character of the Empress, and the vices of her favorite, the priest Huai-yi, disgraced religion in the palace, and became a source of corruption in all departments of political and social life.

A severe reverse of fortune came to the adherents of the Indian deity in the middle of the ninth century. Under a fanatical Taouist influence, the lands and other property attached to religious houses were appropriated by the government; the images, bells, and all other metallic articles, were melted down and made into coin, and the wood and stone of the sacred structures were taken to make and repair public buildings. Of the first grade monasteries 4,600, and of the smaller establishments 40,000, were in this manner destroyed; and over 260,000 monks and nuns were sent adrift in the world. This was by far the severest blow ever inflicted on Boodhism in China, and perhaps the world has never seen a religious body disendowed and secularized on a more magnificent scale.*

Since that time the religions of the country have con-

---

* "Boodhism in China," by T. Watters, in the "Chinese Recorder," July 1869; also the numerous authorities there cited.

tinued their triangular contest, but with varying fortunes; until, in these latter days, each maintains its ascendency, — Confucianism for the state, Taouism for the philosopher, and Boodhism for the ignorant, struggling, aspiring people.

CHAPTER II.

THE EAST AND WEST.

THAT the present occupants of the soil of China are not identical as to race with the first inhabitants, appears to be a fact beyond all reasonable doubt. Coming from a remote west and northwest region, they doubtless brought with them to their new country the rudiments of the arts and sciences. Whether they possessed many independent inventions and discoveries, is a question not easily determined. Various implements and arts which have existed among them from the earliest historic times are common to nearly all countries of great antiquity,—such as pottery, brick-making, archery, swords, spears, shields, plows, carriages, harps, wind instruments, statuary, drawing or painting, drums, bells, spinning, weaving, embroidery, mail-armor, standards, flags. To imagine that all these are so natural and easy that each nation might have separately fallen upon them, is by no means a scientific or satisfactory conclusion. It is more consistent with reason and revelation to suppose that they, for the most part, were invented only once, when mankind were all together in one place.

Notwithstanding the adverse opinion of some writers, we are inclined to favor the view that the Chinese acquired their astronomy from the West before the Christian era. The sudden appearance, in Sze Ma-tsin's History, of the Calippic cycle — a method far in advance of anything known before in China, which was familiar to Aristotle, whose pupil, Alexander, carried his conquests to the East as far as the Punjaub, B.C. 328–325,—and the common expression, *chih ching*, or "the seven directors," to be taken in the sense of sun, moon and five planets, and applied to days, point them out as imitators of the Hindoos or Bactrians; and the Hindoos, certainly, in their turn, borrowed from the Greeks.*

China has long had the credit of having invented writing, paper, printing, gunpowder, and the mariner's compass, with perhaps no better claim than her own arrogant pretensions, and the general tendency among Europeans to assign to that nation anything the origin of which is unknown or obscure. It is probable that paper and ink were introduced from the West. These necessary accompaniments of even a rude civilization were in common use in Europe from the time of Alexander the Great, but were unknown in China until about the beginning of the Christian era, when the paint-brush gradually assumed the form of the modern pencil, and the cumbrous tablets of bamboo were exchanged for paper manufactured from hemp, flax, and old cloth. The Chinese long employed a coarse paint in writing their characters. Ink is first mentioned in the third century, and was made of soot and resin. It is a singular fact that the Romans used precisely these constituents, as Pliny informs us. As to printing, we are not so well enlightened; although, as it has been significantly remarked, "the seal or 'signet' used by the sons of Jacob was a printing instrument, and printing of books was only sealing on a large scale." It may be even doubted that the Chinese invented gunpowder, or that they originated its

* Dr. Legge's Classics, vol. iii, pt. i, p. 100–1.

application to purposes of war, as the first maker of it is mentioned by themselves as having lived only about seven hundred years ago.* For a long time it was probably applied alone to fireworks, and various harmless and useful purposes. The catapult, a military engine for throwing stones, similar to what the ancient Romans had, is known to have been employed as late as the year 1273, or perhaps still more recently,—a circumstance which seems to prove that the Chinese at that period were as little acquainted with firearms as the people of Europe. To Jesuit missionaries must be given the credit of first having taught them how to manufacture the modern cannon, although such association of military pursuits with the priestly office may not be considered worthy of all praise. Brass, or copper, had long been known; but the Chinese were ignorant of the use of iron until about 700 B.C. This must have been one of the lost arts; for, more than three thousand years previously, Tubal-Cain was "an instructor of every artifice in brass and iron." The knowledge of this metal seems to have been imparted by a warlike race which invaded China from the West, bringing with them iron armor, war chariots, and round metal coins.† They may have invented the use of silk; but when we consider that the species of caterpillars which spin and prepare the fine glossy filament used in its manufacture were probably native to, and abounded in, that country as nowhere else, and that weaving is an art that has been practiced in all ages and in all countries, the merit of originality may not be conspicuously apparent. Moreover, the history of the silk manufacture is not a little

---

* Chalmers' "Origin of the Chinese." p. 34; also, see "A View of China," by Robert Morrison, D.D.

† Chalmers' "Origin of the Chinese," p. 33.

obscure, the tradition of the invention being carried back into mythological periods; while the usual European account affirms that Rome obtained it from Greece, and Greece from Persia, the last being indebted for it to China,—a chain sufficiently long to admit the possibility of a missing link somewhere. As the properties of the loadstone were very early known to the Chinese, it is probable that their claims to priority of discovery in this case are well founded; and yet, so far as history shows, the Arabs were but little behind them in the knowledge of the mariner's compass; while the art of communicating the magnetic virtue to steel, and suspending the needle on a pivot, is a European device.

From these examples, it may appear that the Chinese do not possess the remarkable inventive genius claimed by themselves, and usually attributed to them by the people of the West; although they are entitled to great credit for their industry and mechanical skill, which has rendered them so independent of foreign aid. No especial exaltation of the Anglo-Saxon is here intended or hinted at; for only a small proportion of our boasted modern civilization is strictly speaking our own. Much that we call ours belongs to the common stock of humanity. The philosophy of universal history, as yet unwritten, is destined to point out, in this direction, as in many others, the true and essential brotherhood of man.

It has been asserted, with some degree of probability, that the Shoo-King is for the most part simply a history of patriarchal men presented in Chinese garb. If this theory is correct, we have the interesting fact that the gods and ancestors of the Chinese lived in the kingdom of Nimrod, or, perhaps, at a time previous to the confusion of tongues, and may therefore be identical with prominent characters in our Bible history. Many of the truths and maxims of an earlier traditional faith, handed down through the teaching of Confucius, and others of the old masters, seem to point out a connection with the patriarchal dispensation. It is not altogether improbable that they possessed at one time a partial knowledge of the Hebrew Scriptures, and that these sacred records had a certain influence in giving tone to the writings of the early philosophers and teachers. Certain it is that there are philosophical and religious sentiments in these writings which are not unworthy of such a source.

Modern fame has charged the people of China with being inhospitable and bigoted, and with having erected about the empire on every side a wall of seclusion. It has not always been so, as we have begun to discover, and as we shall further see. In the second century before Christ, they made extraordinary efforts to open communication with the West. Enterprising travelers pushed their way beyond the nomadic tribes of Huns and Scythians to the very borders of Persia, where they procured a superior breed of horses, eagerly coveted by the Emperor; and brought back wine made from grapes, single-humped camels, ostrich-eggs, and, probably, other articles of commerce not definitely mentioned. At the same time, they became acquainted with the northern parts of India, called "Shindo" and "Dahara."

The position of the empire in the extreme limits of Eastern Asia rendered almost impracticable for many ages any attempt to reach it either by sea or by an overland route across the Himalaya mountains. Notwithstanding, embassies were sent from imperial Rome, and endeavors were made to reciprocate these high civilities. The first distinct account of China, and of its peculiar institutions and customs, has come to us from the Arabs. Their far-extended conquests brought them to the confines of that remote country; and many individuals, under the impulse of scientific and literary research which prevailed among their countrymen in no inconsiderable degree at that time, were led to explore the *terra incognita*. A translation by Renaudot from the itineraries of two Arabian travelers, gives us the result in part of their observations during the years 850 and 877. This curious and instructive work, although written over one thousand years ago, depicts the Chinese very much as we know them at the present day; which fact goes to prove both the fidelity of the writers and the antique and unchanging character of Chinese civilization.* They state that Arabian merchants, who came by sea, were permitted to trade at the port of Canfu, which was probably Canton; although describing them as suffering from the extortions of the mandarins of those days, until they forsook that emporium of foreign trade and returned in crowds to Siraf and Oman.

In the reign of Kublai Khan, the Mongol conqueror of China, who also dug the Grand Canal, Nicholas and Matthew Polo, two Venetian noblemen, visited his court. They were royally entertained, and, on their departure for Europe, invited to return. In 1274 they accordingly came back, bearing letters from Pope Gregory X, and accompanied by the youthful Marco, son of one of them. The lad soon became a favorite with the Khan, and devoted seventeen years to the service of his adopted prince. Having obtained, with great difficulty, permission to visit

* "China and the Chinese," by John Francis Davis, F.R.S., vol. i, pp. 20-1.

his native land, Marco and his aged father and uncle returned to Venice, after an absence of twenty-four years. They were so completely altered that their countrymen did not recognize them, and could hardly be persuaded of their identity. The accounts which they gave of the vast wealth and resources of the Chinese empire appeared incredible to Europeans in those days. The story is related that they determined, by a public display, to satisfy their friends as to the probable truth of their narrative. "All their kindred and acquaintances were invited to a magnificent feast. They then presented themselves in splendid dresses, first of crimson satin, next of damask, and lastly of velvet bearing the same colors, which they successively threw off and distributed among the company. Returning in their ordinary attire, Marco produced the rags in which they had all been disguised, ripped them open, and exhibited such a profusion of diamonds, rubies, sapphires, and precious jewels, as completely dazzled the spectators. On hearing of their wealth and adventures, persons of all ranks, ages and professions flocked to the house with congratulations and inquiries. Marco, whose society was courted by all the distinguished youths, stood forth as principal orator. Having often occasion, in his enumerations of people and treasure, to repeat the term *million*, then not common in Europe, the name Messer Marco Millione was applied to him, first in jest, but afterward in reality." Trying his fortunes in a war with the Genoese, he was taken prisoner, and employed the leisure of his captivity in writing a detailed account of his experience and observations abroad. His work was soon translated into the various languages of Europe; and the story of the teeming population, the flourishing cities, the boundless wealth, the curious customs, the refinement and civilization of a country hitherto unexplored, seemed more like a fiction of fairyland than sober and authentic narrative. The effect, however, was to stimulate the desire for a knowledge of the uttermost parts of the earth, and to start adventurous men in pursuit of the richest rewards of commerce.

Cristoval Colombo, a native of Genoa, by his familiarity with the writings of the famous traveler, became inflamed with a desire to share in the wealth of Cathay and the Indies, a part of which he piously proposed to devote to an attempt to rescue the Holy Sepulcher at Jerusalem from Infidel hands.* Dwelling in the town of Porto Santo, he watched the carved and worked driftwood which told him of inhabited lands to the West. By the aid of the works of Ptolemy, and other ancient geographers, he roughly computed that extent of the globe which he thought must stretch between Eastern Asia and the Azores, and was led to the conclusion that Japan, the "Sypangu" of Polo, must lie in about the locality now known to be occupied by Florida, beyond which he knew he must soon come to the realms of the Grand Khan ruling over China and Tartary. Picturing to Ferdinand the advantages of alliance and commerce with these countries, and to Isabella the merit of converting the millions of Cathay to the Catholic faith, he at length succeeded in interesting the royal pair in the fitting out of his peaceful Armada. Ignorant of the labors of those Arabian geographers who had measured a degree of the great circle of the earth, he had considerably underrated the circumference of the globe; and instead of the fair vision of a refined and luxu-

* "Messer Marco Millione," with commentary, by M. Pauthier, of Paris.

rious kingdom, the disappointed discoverer was greeted by the savagery of unknown islands, whose tropical beauty and natural wealth, nevertheless, suggested to him the name of Western Indies. The European impulse to discovery and conquest which had its origin in the marvelous book of Polo served to lead on the enterprise which culminated in the most sublime event of the age. To China is thus indirectly due the discovery of America. But for the faithfulness of that excellent amanuensis, Rusticien de Pisa, who wrought in the gloomy precincts of a dungeon, the free institutions and the material wealth of the United States might still have been undeveloped.

The history of modern intercourse between the West and the Far East properly begins with the year 1516, when Rafael Perestello sailed the first vessel that was ever conducted to China under a European flag. He was soon followed by another Portuguese trader, who, with a fleet of eight vessels, anchored near the port of Canton, and by his fair dealings gave great satisfaction to the authorities.

In 1596 Queen Elizabeth made an unsuccessful attempt to open up trade with China, by dispatching an envoy with a letter to the Emperor. The attempt was renewed in 1637 by an English fleet under the command of Weddell, who was very desirous of participating in the traffic at Canton; but, through causes hereafter to be explained, instead of peaceful commerce, warlike demonstrations resulted. Afterward, first at Ningpo, then in Formosa and at Amoy, and still later at Canton, a beginning was made of those commercial relations which within a century grew to such vast proportions.

The intercourse of the Russians with China was not

of a maritime character, and for many years was confined altogether to the northern extremity of the empire. We date the entrance of the Muscovite into this country as early as 1567, when the Czar John dispatched an expedition to explore the region beyond the great lake Baikal, which was so successful as to push on to Peking, but failed to obtain an interview of the Emperor on account of their having brought no presents. The first embassy proper from Russia was sent in 1653, with the view of establishing liberty of commerce, and was received with marks of honor; although it is asserted that the *katow*, or nine prostrations, was duly performed by the embassador Baikaff, which may have been interpreted as an act of inferiority or vassalage. The success of this formal attempt at reciprocity gives to Russia the distinction of being the first European power treating with the court of Peking. Peter the Great sent Lange, a Swede from Stockholm, to the eastern capital for the purpose of procuring Chinese decorations for his country seat at Peterhof, on the Gulf of Finland, to learn the oriental art of building, and with particular directions to study Chinese commerce. After a journey of fifteen months he arrived in Peking, and his advent excited much public curiosity. In the evening of the first day he was entertained at dinner by the governor-general of Western Tartary, by order of the Emperor, Kang-hi, and was soon after admitted into the imperial presence. He was permitted to share in the honors of the New Year festivities, when over ten thousand mandarins from the provinces came to pay their reverence to His Majesty, and when a display of fireworks was given in the Summer Palace, which for brilliancy and magnificent proportions has probably never been approached outside the Celestial Empire. The fifth embassy, commissioned by Catherine I, effected a treaty, concerning which a Russian historian remarked, one hundred years later, "that it opened to us the road to the capital of the Chinese empire, which is almost inaccessible to the other nations of Europe." The article relating to commerce runs thus: "Free trade shall exist between the two countries; the number of the Russian merchants which can come every three years to Peking shall not exceed two hundred, as has been formerly arranged. If merchants only are with the caravan, so shall they no longer be maintained as formerly. They must provide for themselves; but no difficulties will be put in the way of their commerce, and no duty shall be demanded. Besides these caravans, houses for trade shall be established for ordinary commerce at Kiachta and on the frontier at Nertchinsk."* Commercial relations have been maintained to the present day, with occasional disruption in the heat of diplomatic controversy or from the peril of warlike expeditions.

In addition to their political establishment, the Russians have long been allowed to maintain an ecclesiastical mission in Peking, the latter occupying the site of a Boodhist temple which was granted to them by Kang-hi. The design of the mission has been to maintain the Greek forms of worship among Christians of that faith, and to propagate the same among the heathen, a good degree of toleration having been extended by the government. There is a class of Russo-Chinese Christians, called Albazines, who are descended from captives taken in the Amoor wars. They were early admitted into one of the three most honorable "banners" of the Imperial Guard, and

---

* J. Dudgeon, M.D., in "Chinese Recorder," July 1871, p. 36.

still perform the usual duties and receive the customary privileges of regular bannermen, whose special duty is the defense of the capital.

The Mohammedans found their way into China within a century after the era of their Prophet, and have been permitted to hold their peculiar tenets and practice their singular rites and ceremonies. They are most numerous in the northern provinces, where, in some parts, they form a third of the population. Although having adopted the native costume and spoken language, they appear, nevertheless, to be a distinct race. They wish to be exclusive, and do not like to be regarded as one with the rest of the nation. The Koran is read in Arabic, and probably has never been translated into Chinese. They have their mosques, built after the Indian fashion, in which services are performed every Friday, and which are characterized by the entire absence of images. They are, in theory, strongly opposed to idolatry; and yet, conscientiousness in this regard can have no high value among them, as some of their race have held important official positions, and no resident officer in a city can omit the sacrifices to Confucius and the worship of the state gods. Circumcision is made indispensable to admission into the Mohammedan faith, and abstinence from swine's flesh is looked upon as a primary virtue, while in respect to general morals they are perhaps equally debased with their idolatrous neighbors. On the whole, they may be regarded as faithful followers of the Prophet, although not so attentive to daily prayers as many of their co-religionists, and few if any of them now make the pilgrimage to Mecca.

The introduction of Judaism was an event of the very early centuries, and it possibly occurred before the birth of Christ. A colony of Jews, consisting of seventy families, made their way through the empire to nearly the extreme limits of the East, where they settled at Kai-fung-foo, the capital of Honan province, on the banks of the Yellow river. That they should have been permitted to traverse the country in such numbers, occupying many months in the pilgrimage, and to maintain, as they doubtless did for a long time, the integrity of their religion, so distinct and divergent from the idol-worship carried on about them, and finally to effect a settlement in the center of a populous region, and to remain in undisturbed possession, speaks much for the tolerant spirit of Chinese institutions. This remnant of the posterity of Abraham have long suffered from the physical and moral decay which so often appear to be inseparable. They now number only about two hundred individuals, and retain almost none of their national characteristics, beyond a kind of reverence for the law and the seventh-day Sabbath. The last among them who could read Hebrew died nearly a century ago, and the final forfeiture of faith in the divine origin of their religion is sufficiently indicated by this one of their monumental inscriptions, expressed in purely Chinese forms of thought: "Although between us and the doctrine of Confucius there are differences of no great importance, yet the object of the establishment of our religion and theirs is the same. They are intended to inculcate reverence for heaven, veneration for ancestors, loyalty to the prince, and piety to parents, the five human relations, and the five constant virtues."*

* "The Religious Condition of the Chinese," by Rev. Joseph Edkins, D.D., pp. 257-8.

CHAPTER III.

TROUBLOUS TIMES.

PREVIOUS to the arrival of Europeans at Canton the government of China had given much encouragement to foreign commerce, and statistical records exist to the present day which show a perfect knowledge in that country of the advantages of trade with the nations of the West. Unhappily, a condition of things arose unfriendly to peace, and tending to a war of races.

In seeking for a cause of this change in the course of events, we are compelled to recognize, first of all, the arrogant pretensions to superiority on the part of the Chinese. They had never met with a people whom they considered at all comparable to themselves in point of civilization. Their traditions, and the culture of their schools, had deeply impressed the national mind that all but themselves were barbarians; while their long experience with the border tribes, and the conflict of ages with the aboriginal inhabitants, had shaped toward inferior and unfriendly states a policy of proud assumption, and of utter disregard of those just principles which they themselves confessed to be of great value in the home administration. Their fundamental maxim of intercourse with foreigners has been thus translated: "The barbarians are like beasts, and not to be governed on the same principles as citizens. Were any one to attempt controlling them by the great maxims of reason, it would tend to nothing but confusion. The ancient kings well understood this, and accordingly ruled barbarians by misrule. Therefore, to rule barbarians by misrule is the true and best way of ruling them." If the reader is tempted to interject here a severe and righteous criticism, let him remember the misrule of Holland in Java, of Great Britain in South Africa and in Hindoostan, and the treatment of the Indian by Americans, and discern, if he can, where to bestow the weightier censure. Although foreigners in their early advances were met, in a few instances, by haughty mandarins who interposed unnecessary vexations and subjected them to extortion and violence, we are compelled to go still further in our search for the origin of unfriendly differences which culminated at length in the strife of contending armies.

The good opinion entertained at Canton of Portuguese traders, on the occasion of their first visit, was entirely reversed by the outrageous conduct of those who came the following year; and the Chinese besieged them in port and drove them away. Others of their countrymen appeared on the coast, and succeeded in establishing trade at Amoy and Ningpo. The general character of their demeanor with the natives at the latter port may be inferred from the statement that on one occasion they went out in large parties into the neighboring villages and seized the women and maidens. This unmitigated outrage provoked the vengeance of the people, who rose upon them and "destroyed twelve thousand Christians, including eight hundred Portuguese, and burned thirty-five ships and two junks."*
Among the desperate adventurers from Portugal was one Ferdinand Mendes Pinto, who, having learned at Ningpo that to the northeast there was an island containing the

---

* Williams' "Middle Kingdom." vol. ii, p. 433.

tombs of seventeen native kings full of treasure, sailed thither with his lawless crew. He succeeded in finding the place, and did not hesitate to break open the monuments and invade the sacred and ancient dust of majesty; but, when about to secure his plunder, he was attacked and compelled to retreat with only a part of the booty. He afterward suffered shipwreck, and only fourteen of his followers escaped with their lives, who were taken prisoners and sentenced to be whipped and to lose each man a thumb. They were finally sent to Peking, where, instead of being consigned to torture and ignominious death, they were merely condemned to one year's hard labor.

The first Portuguese embassy, which was also the first by sea to Peking from any European power, in consequence of the unfavorable impression at court of the Portuguese character, came to an unfortunate end, in the humiliation, imprisonment and tragic death of the envoy, Thomas Pirez. In 1521, Alfonso de Melo, with six vessels under his command, arrived in China, ignorant of these events, and, attempting to open communication, met with a very unexpected reception. His men were "sent on shore for water, but returned with blood." He became immediately involved in conflicts with the authorities and the people, who put to death upward of twenty prisoners that fell into their hands; and the squadron shortly afterward sailed away from the coast.

About the middle of the sixteenth century a foreign settlement was commenced at Macao, on the extremity of an island near the southeastern boundary of the empire, under the pretext of erecting sheds for drying goods introduced under the appellation of tribute, and alleged to have been damaged in a storm. At length secure possession was obtained, and for a time Macao became the richest mart in all Eastern Asia. This splendid opportunity of illustrating western civilization was worse than lost. Portuguese vessels employed by the native government as convoy ships treacherously changed to freebooters on the high seas, and became infinitely greater scourges than the pirates they were paid to repel. The foreign city, moreover, became notorious as the seat of the coolie trade, which was largely kept up by the employment of kidnaping agents in various parts of the country. This settlement would have long since been taken and destroyed by the indignant Chinese, had they not dreaded the vengeance of European powers.

The trade between the Spaniards and the Chinese has been smaller, and their relations less important, than in the case of almost any other European nation; but justice to our subject will not permit us to pass over one suggestive fact. The Chinese long endeavored to carry on a trade with the Philippine islands, notwithstanding the Spanish masters of the soil treated them with peculiar severity, burdening them with taxes which the people of no other nation were subjected to. Their harsh treatment in Manila, although they were peaceful and industrious settlers, excited the attention and indignation of one of their countrymen, who, on his return to the continent, induced the officers of his own government to adopt the Spanish model in their treatment of all foreigners at Canton; and thus were perfected the principal features of the system of espionage and restriction of the "co-hong" which existed for nearly a century, until the treaty of 1842,—a striking example of pardonable retaliation.*

The Dutch first appeared off the coast in a fleet of war

---

* Williams' "Middle Kingdom," vol. ii, p. 437.

vessels, and made an attack upon Macao; but being repulsed, with the loss of their admiral and about three hundred men, they retired and established themselves on the Pescadores, some small islands between the mainland and Formosa. Their occupation of this position, so well calculated to menace the extensive commerce of those waters, was a source of annoyance to the authorities in Fuh-kien province. They proceeded, however, to erect fortifications, forcing the Chinese who had fallen into their hands to do their work, treating them with much cruelty. Liberty of trade being denied them, they annoyed the coast with their ships; and after repeated hostilities it was finally agreed that upon their removal to Formosa, with the promise of confining themselves to that locality, they should be allowed the privileges of commerce. Accordingly, the Dutch took possession of the proffered territory, called by the Portuguese, who discovered it, Ilha Formose, or the "Beautiful Island." In this new land they found the productions of nature in great opulence; and although few Chinese had settled there, it was still very populous with friendly tribes. At first much attention was paid to the moral interests of the islanders, among whom the Dutch enforced their own laws, and made, in nearly every village, the education of the children compulsory. Almost nothing was left of the ancient religion, laws, manners and customs of the nation, but the privilege of selecting from their own number a chief of each precinct, who should manage its affairs under the surveillance of a foreign military officer, with a force of twenty-five men at his command. The captains, or chiefs, were required to appear before the governor once every year; and those who had been found faithful were rewarded and promoted, but those against whom complaints were made were usually dismissed from office. Efforts were also put forth to introduce Christianity. The work was progressing favorably, and many thousands had been baptized, when the governors, fearful of offending the Japanese who were then persecuting and seeking to exterminate the Christians in their country, and apprehensive of losing the trade with the empire of the rising sun, opposed and restricted the benevolent labors of the missionary.

During the struggles consequent upon the overthrow of the Ming dynasty and the establishment of the present Tartar rule, many Chinese emigrated to Formosa, some of whom settled under the Dutch, while others formed separate colonies. Their industry soon changed the aspect of the island, and greatly increased its productiveness. The immigration began to assume such proportions as to alarm the Dutch, who took no measures to conciliate and instruct the colonists, but sought to repel them from their shores; consequently much irritation and jealousy prevailed on both sides, and the Chinese were ready to join in any likely attempt to expel the foreigner. The opportunity did not long delay. About the beginning of May, 1661, Koshinga, an independent Chinese chieftain, who had risen to fame and power amid the shifting fortunes of a struggle which ended in the triumph of the Tartars, appeared off fort Zelandia, having under his command a force of at least 25,000 men and a fleet of considerable strength. His appearance was so unexpected that few of the Dutch families could be taken into the fort, and a large number of men, women and children fell into the hands of the enemy. The unfortunate captives were cruelly treated, as a means of compelling the surrender of the fort. Failing in his object, and seeing that there was no way of capturing the garrison except by a tedious blockade and starving-out of the besieged, the chieftain resolved to obtain by threat what he could not readily gain by force. To this end he sent to fort Zelandia the Rev. Mr. Hambrock, a celebrated minister of the Dutch Reformed Church, who with a number of other clergymen had fallen into his hands, and whom he instructed to persuade the besieged to surrender their stronghold by offering them full pardon and permission to march out with all they had, and by threatening, in case of refusal, to torture the prisoners in the most horrible manner. Hambrock having received these orders, and having left his wife and two of his children as hostages with Koshinga, proceeded to the fort, where he faithfully executed his commission. But, Regulus-like, instead of persuading the besieged to surrender, he animated them with all imaginable reasons to a valiant defense, and encourged them to hold out, without so much as entering into negotiations respecting the surrender of the fort. He concluded his patriotic address with the statement that he knew very well that the sentence of death was pronounced over him, but that he had resolved to sacrifice all that he had, his life, wife, and children, rather than fall into despondency, treachery, and unfaithfulness toward God and his country; and he expressed hope that every one would take the same resolution, and follow his example, as he was convinced that Koshinga, seeing his cunning purpose defeated, would not fail to carry out his threat with direful vengeance, while any confidence that he would keep either faith or promise would probably be doomed to bitter disappointment. All those present were moved to tears by his generous and lofty motives, and urged him to remain with them, as he could do no good to the prisoners, but only throw away his valuable life. Two of his children, who were in the fort, filled the air with their heart-rending cries, and besought their venerated father to remain. His only reply was to ask whether they wished him to forsake their mother, brother and sister, leaving them to be tortured and cruelly murdered? They hushed their wailing, and one daughter fell prostrate to the ground, while the other clung to her father in the agony of despair. Seldom, if ever, has a generous soul been so tempted by conflicting passions as this noble man at the moment of his departure; and rarely has history presented a scene so tragical and sublime as that witnessed in the fort when, upon the point of leaving, Hambrock addressed its brave defenders in the following words: " Friends and brethren, I know that I am going to certain death; but I do so in the hope of doing a service to you and to my fellow men, the prisoners now in the hands of the enemy; that not at any time people may charge me with having caused the death of so many honest men and pious Christians. May God protect you, give you the desired help, and save you. Be of good cheer, and suffer the hardships of war with patience." *

Hereupon he departed, and returning to the enemy's camp, reported with a cheerful countenance to the merciless and enraged chief that the besieged had resolved not to surrender their trust, but to defend it against any assault; and so much the more because they were provided with all the necessaries for enduring a long siege. Orders were immediately given to kill the male prisoners,

---

*"The Political, Social and Religious Constitution of the Natives on the West Coast of Formosa," etc.; translated from an old Dutch work by Rev. W. Lobscheid, pp. 1-14.

and only twenty-three of the whole number, six hundred and thirteen, were spared. After having sprinkled the principal villages with the blood of the Dutch, the Chinese stripped the corpses of everything they had left and buried them in large holes. The women were distributed among the officers and soldiers, but were restored to their friends upon the capitulation of Zelandia. After a siege of nine months, with the loss of about sixteen hundred men, the Hollanders gave up the fort and abandoned Formosa, returning to their colony in Java.

The first English fleet, commanded by captain Weddell, having met a cold reception at Macao, was finally moved up to the mouth of the river, and a communication sent to the commander of the Bogue forts near Canton expressive of a desire to traffic. While waiting for a reply, the Portuguese employed the opportunity to misrepresent the English to the authorities,— furnishing another illustration of the contests of mercantile avarice frequently witnessed in the East, which has so unfavorably impressed the Chinese as to European character. The commanders resolved to end this disagreeable controversy by expelling the newly-arrived foreigners. The attack was begun by firing upon a watering-boat which was passing near the forts; whereupon Weddell's fleet displayed their ensigns, weighed anchor, and moved up with the flood to a position before the castle, each ship immediately opening a furious broadside. A force was dispatched to the shore, seeing which the inmates of the castle fled, and the boats' crews, entering the fortification, displayed the colors of Great Britain upon its walls. Not satisfied with this victorious result of the sudden and unexplained outbreak of hostilities, they proceeded to fire the council-house, to demolish what they could, to convey on board under cover of night all the ordnance they had found within the captured works, and ended by seizing two merchant junks. A third vessel was surprised, by whose boat Weddell sent a letter to the chief mandarins at Canton, expostulating with them for their breach of truce, excusing the assault upon the castle, and desiring the liberty of trade. This letter was not replied to in very gracious terms; but, after a little negotiation and the return of the captured guns and vessels, the ships were supplied with cargoes. Such was the unhappy introduction of Englishmen to the Chinese.

During the change of dynasty which took place soon after this event, attended by numerous conflicts and depredations of a piratical kind along the coast, the trade of all nations with China probably suffered more or less. Not until about 1684 did the English obtain a footing at Canton, and some years later they opened a precarious trade at Ningpo. The whole history of foreign commerce with China, up to 1840, is a melancholy and curious chapter in the course of international events. Instead of treaties and embassies, which usually constitute national dealings with a great people, there were negotiations with petty mandarins or provincial authorities; and not unfrequently, the vast concerns of commerce were reduced to the appearance of daily traffic or even to the lawless art of smuggling. Among the grievances complained of were the delay in loading ships, and the plunder of goods on their transit to Canton, the extortion of the underlings of office, the injurious proclamations posted over the country accusing foreigners of detestable crimes, and the difficulty of access to the high authorities. It was but natural that **English traders**, intent only on the gainful results of their long and perilous voyage, and without the protection of treaty stipulations, should forget that the ideas among the Chinese of their rights over those who visited their shores were not unlike those which once largely prevailed in Europe, especially before the Reformation; that the levying of export duties was really but a continuation of the internal excise or transit duties paid upon goods exported in native vessels as well as foreign; that, in the absence of light and knowledge, perverse ideas of maritime strangers from the West would inevitably obtain; and that the superstitious reverence for high official position excluded the subject as well as the foreigner from easy approach. The want of sympathy and union among Europeans themselves had the effect of frustrating their attempts at securing the friendly offices of the Chinese. For example, the British man-of-war, *Centurion*, captured a Spanish ship with a valuable freight of treasure near Macao, with which the commodore proceeded to the Canton river, being in want of provisions; but as the mandarins had their notions of "a ship which went about the world seeking other ships in order to take them," they caused numberless vexatious delays in furnishing the needed supplies, until at length the merchants suffered a purveyor to take provisions on board without the usual custom-house inspection. The animosities which prevailed between the English and the French were productive of much trouble to both. In a disgraceful encounter at Whampoa, one English sailor was shot and another taken prisoner; and, to settle the affair, an appeal was made to the Chinese government, which ultimately decided to allot to the English and French sailors separate and distinct islands for their recreation. In 1773 a case of sanguinary injustice occurred at Macao. A native had lost his life, and an Englishman, named Francis Scott, being accused of the murder, was tried and acquitted in the Portuguese court. The mandarin, however, obstinately claimed him, and threatened vengeance upon the town in case he was not delivered. Although it was urged in the Macao senate that it would be an unjustifiable proceeding to consent to the sacrifice of an innocent man, the vicar-general reached a different conclusion, and justified himself in the following singular manner: "Moralists decide that when a tyrant demands even an innocent person, with menaces of ruin to the community if refused, the whole number may call on any individual to deliver himself up for the public good, which is of more worth than the life of an individual. Should he refuse to obey, he is not innocent, he is criminal."

The doomed man was delivered into the hands of his enemies, making the unfortunate impression on the officials and the people at Canton that the foreigners could not command concert of action even when unanimous in the opinion of the justice of their cause, and confirming their own traditional belief that human life weighs little in comparison with public policy or material advantage.

A fruitful source of difficulty between the Chinese and English was the turbulent conduct of sailors. In the above-named city a party of seafaring men had been drinking in one of the native shops; a scuffle ensued; the crowd that assembled about the scene began to insult them, when the indignant and inebriated sailors put the populace to flight, killing one of their number in the on-

* Davis' "China and the Chinese," vol. i, pp. 61, 66.

set. Trade was immediately stopped, demands were made and rejected, old and bitter feuds were revived, life and property at the port and in every settlement on the coast put in jeopardy, and the days of peace and amity again postponed to the distant and uncertain future.

CHAPTER IV.

THE FORTUNES OF DIPLOMACY.

ALLUSION has been made to the unsuccessful attempt of Great Britain, in 1596, to open a friendly diplomatic correspondence with the court at Peking. The inability of the English envoy to reach the distant capital of China will sufficiently account for the failure of his mission. That the Russians were more fortunate in their enterprise we have also seen.

In consequence of an invitation from the provincial authorities at Canton, soon after the accession of the first Manchoo emperor, Shun-chi, and desirous of opening the way for their commerce in the great Eastern emporium, the Dutch resolved to send an embassy to the Chinese seat of government. Two eminent Batavian merchants, Goyer and Keyzer, headed the commission. On their arrival at Peking, they were provided with lodging and entertainment until the time appointed for the audience. The sovereigns of the East usually hold their levees at break of day, and in consequence of this custom the embassadors, to their great annoyance, were conducted to the palace and required to remain over night, sitting in their state dresses that they might be ready at the moment their attendance was required. The welcome dawn appeared at length, when, on a given signal, they, with a motley group of representatives of various tributary princes, followed an officer whose duty it was to usher them into the imperial presence. The hall of audience presented a scene of extraordinary pomp and splendor. The glittering dresses of the attendants, the gorgeous banners displayed on every side, the superb throne, around which were held on high golden figures of the sun and silver circles representing the moon, together with the crowd of mandarins in their state robes, produced a most imposing effect. " The Emperor had not yet made his appearance, but all the embassadors were directed to prostrate themselves three times before the empty throne, and at each time of kneeling to bow down their heads to the ground three times till their foreheads touched the marble flooring. The sound of bells soon announced the approach of Shun-chi, and all present fell on their knees as he ascended the steps, every eye being bent toward the earth, as if none were worthy to look upon him. He walked up the hall with a stately air, and seated himself on the throne, when the whole assembly arose, and the different envoys were led forward to do him homage by a repetition of the nine prostrations; but not a single word, nor even the slightest mark of notice, did the haughty Tartar vouchsafe to the disappointed Europeans, who withdrew with no very kindly feelings toward a prince before whom they had humbled themselves to so little purpose." *

Their presents, however, were received, and others given in return, and permission was granted to send an embassy once in eight years, at which time their countrymen might come in four ships to trade. The ill success of these diplomates has been ascribed to some adverse influence of the Jesuits, who were then powerful at court; but it may have been owing more to the contempt in which the Dutch people were held, both by the Tartars and Chinese, in con-

* "China and India," by Robert Sears. pp. 91-2.

sequence of the report brought to their ears that there was no emperor or king in Holland; for, being unable to comprehend the nature of a republic, they imagined that a nation must be very poor and mean which could not afford to maintain a king. The forcible seizure of the Pescadores by Dutch adventurers, some years before, and their occupation of Formosa, may also have contributed largely to this result.

The political status of foreigners in China had from the first been uncertain and unsatisfactory. The monopoly of English trade being in the hands of the East India Company, their Committee were empowered with large jurisdiction over British subjects, which could be exercised in trying emergencies; but the consuls of other nations had little or no authority over their countrymen. The "outside-kingdom men" constituted a community by themselves, subject chiefly to their own sense of honor in their mutual dealings. Their relations with the Chinese were reduced simply to a "state of nature." The arrival of a new governor-general, or collector of customs, or senior hong-merchant, involved a new course of policy, according to the personal character or individual prejudice of those functionaries. The want of a well-understood tariff encouraged smuggling, and this in turn provoked a spirit of bitterness and retaliation between the native and foreign merchants, which sometimes ended in a conflict with civil authority. There was no acknowledged medium of communication; and the consuls, not being credited by the Chinese government, could command neither respect nor recognition for their flags. To this state of things must be added the financial distress. The repeated failures of hong-merchants for very large sums due their European creditors, which there seemed no probability of recovering, appealed to the strongest instincts of fear and anxiety in the foreign breast. The British government was at length induced to turn its attention to the situation of the King's subjects in China, with the purpose of placing their relations on a more secure footing; and the Crown decided to send an embassy to Peking.

Colonel Cathcart was appointed envoy in 1788; but his death in the Straits of Sunda temporarily deferred the undertaking. In 1792 the Earl of Macartney received the royal commission, and accordingly proceeded from England in the *Lion*, a sixty-four gun ship, accompanied by Sir George Leonard Staunton as secretary of legation. His Lordship was instructed to obtain, if possible, the permission of the Emperor to trade at Ningpo, Chu-san, Tien-tsin, and other places besides Canton, and to secure such various advantages as might be obtained for the relief of British commerce in those parts.

That we may fully understand the difficult and delicate nature of the mission undertaken by the plenipotentiary, a slight digression may be allowed at this point, to show the Chinese estimate of certain questions necessarily involved in diplomatic intercourse with the outside world.

The reigning Emperor is regarded by his subjects as the chosen agent and representative on earth of the Ruler of the Universe. As such representative, his authority is unlimited, except by Divine principles. He is the only source of law and dispenser of mercy; the supreme criminal judge, legislator, executive, and commander of the forces. He is also *Pontifex Maximus*. Standing at the head of religion, he appears as the mediator between Heaven and his people, the only one qualified to adore the Supreme

Powers. He is Lord of the soil; all the forces and revenues of the empire are his, and he has a claim to the services of all males between the years of sixteen and sixty. No claim can be maintained against him; no right can be held in opposition to his pleasure; no privilege or immunity can serve as a protection against his wrath. As the "Son of Heaven," his sovereignty is absolute and universal, not alone over China, but extending by Divine right to "all between the four seas." This assumption is at least four thousand years old; it has survived many revolutions; it has gathered strength by the triumphs of many illustrious dynasties; and it is ardently supported by the most numerous official and the most powerful literary class in the world. Every device of state is used to give the impression of awe to all who approach the court of this oriental monarch. No person, of whatever rank, is allowed to pass before the outer gate of the palace in any vehicle, or on horseback. The vacant throne, or a screen of yellow silk, is equally worshiped with his actual presence. An imperial dispatch is received in the most distant provinces with offerings of incense and prostration, looking toward the capital. In all the chief temples of the land a tablet is erected with the imperial title *Wan Sui Yea*, " Sire of Ten Thousand Years," at whose shrine multitudes pay the same adoration as to the gods. In the principal audience hall of the palace there is an elevated and paved walk on which none can tread but the Emperor. When accessible to his adoring subjects, on state occasions, he occupies a high seat in the center of a vast and gloomy hall. Arrayed in double rows are the civil officers of the realm on the east side, and the military on the west. Nearest to the hall steps, and upon them, are the princes of the first and second degree, with the Manchoo lords, followed by the five orders of nobility, and these succeeded by the mandarins of nine grades. In the open space below, and distant from the throne, is performed the immemorial ceremony of the nine prostrations before the unseen Emperor, who, deep in the recesses of the hall, is concealed still more completely by a cloud of incense.

Lord Macartney, discarding the theory that the *kotow* was nothing but a ceremony, regarded it as a solemn rite by which the rulers of petty kingdoms had long been accustomed to do homage, through their emissaries, and was therefore to be construed as an act of vassalage if consented to on his part. He therefore refused to prostrate himself before the Emperor in the presence of his court, unless a Chinese of equal rank should pay the same reverence to a picture of the King of England. The effect at Peking was not simply an impression that Great Britain must not be registered among tributary nations. A purpose was formed that the proud embassador of England should take his departure with no one purpose of his mission fulfilled. But he was to be flattered with the appearance of success, in order to assure a diplomatic triumph. Enormous sums were expended by the Tartar government in the entertainment of Macartney and his suite, and the English historian has dwelt with much complacency upon the splendor of the reception which China gave her European guests,— the walks in the magnificent gardens of the Emperor, the picturesque and romantic navigation upon the imperial canal, and the many other evidences of regal hospitality and of high consideration at court. And yet all discussions on matters of business were politely and studiously evaded by the Chinese ministers and mandarins during the residence of the embassy at Peking; but, in his letter to the King of England, the Emperor did not omit to state distinctly that the British commerce must be strictly limited to the port of Canton. "You will not be able to complain," adds he haughtily, "that I had not clearly forewarned you. Let us therefore live in peace and friendship, and do not make light of my words." Ignorant as yet of what had actually transpired, and hoping that the embassy had been successful in conciliating the good-will of the Chinese government toward British trade, His Britannic Majesty followed it up by a letter to the Emperor, accompanied by presents. The Viceroy at Canton received the address with much satisfaction, and forwarded it, together with the presents, to Peking; and the record was duly entered in the provincial archives that *tribute* had been sent by the King of England to the "Son of Heaven."

English *hauteur* and Tartar *finesse* were unequal powers in this remarkable contest. But it may not be denied that certain substantial advantages resulted from the mission. It afforded the native government an opportunity of preparing for that future intercourse which could not be avoided, and of acquiring information concerning foreign nations which would in various ways be made available in every peaceful or warlike encounter. But the benefit was merely temporary and not very obvious. It is true that the trade went on without interruption for some years, and the mandarins improved in their conduct toward the merchants; yet the demands and duties were rather increased than diminished, and the personal liberty of foreigners gradually restricted within narrower limits. The dissolute and violent conduct of traders on shore, and of the merchant-marine, gave frequent occasion to the Chinese for aspersions and exactions, which treatment had the effect to irritate Europeans rather than to alter or modify their conduct, according to a principle of ethics well known and widely practiced in Eastern countries a century and more ago, i. e., that the heathen have no rights which a Christian people are bound to respect.

The ill success of Macartney's embassy induced the colonial Dutch government at Batavia to send a mission of salutation and respect to the Emperor Kien-lung, on the occasion of his reaching the sixtieth year of his reign. It was hoped, by conforming to Chinese ceremonies, to obtain concessions that would give their trade an advanced and superior position north of the Straits of Sunda. Isaac Titsingh, late chief commissioner to Japan, was duly accredited, and sent with a somewhat imposing cortége of clerks and interpreters. Van Braam, who accompanied the mission as second to his chief, gave to the world a most humiliating account of their adventures in the Chinese capital. They obsequiously yielded to every demand of court etiquette, although at times they must have been much embarrassed in making unfamiliar and extravagant genuflections and prostrations in their close-fitting dress. They were entertained with banquets and theatrical shows; they were even allowed to perform many skillful evolutions upon their skates, to the gratification of the Emperor, and to receive a present of broken victuals from his own table; but they were not permitted to speak about the all-important affairs that had induced them to take their long and perilous journey. They were graciously allowed to depart, but without having accomplished a single object, except saluting the Emperor.

The American flag was first hoisted at Canton in the year 1802. The consular agent for the United States was at that time, and for years subsequently, appointed from among the merchants resident in China, and called by the natives a *Tae-pan*, or "factory-chief," who had no salary whatever from his government, but was permitted to levy fees in business transactions with his countrymen, and to freely trade on his own account. A national representative, however, who was nothing more than a commercial officer, did not add much of importance or dignity to the American name, and could have little weight with the authorities in any great discussion or impending crisis. During our war of 1812 a British frigate cruised off the port of Canton to seize American vessels. Ignorant of the principles on which international intercourse is regulated among Western nations, and regarding every hostile demonstration between them in their waters as in a measure directed toward themselves, the provincial authorities ordered the Committee of the East India Company to send the war vessel away, saying that if the English and Americans had any petty squabbles they must settle them between themselves and not bring them to China. The Committee represented their inability to control the movements of men-of-war; whereupon the Chinese began a series of petty and vexatious annoyances against the merchants and shipping, such as prohibiting the employment of native servants, the sudden arrest of employés, delaying the loading of vessels, etc. A serious, and at one time very threatening, state of things succeeded; but the negotiations carried on by the Committee with the governor were apparently more successful than the work of the professional diplomates at Peking a few years before. Three important points were gained, viz., the right of corresponding with the government under seal in the Chinese language, the unmolested employment of native servants, and the assurance that the houses of foreigners should not be entered to make arrests without permission; nor were these stipulations ever retracted or violated.

The revenue accruing to the general government from duties and presents, and the employment given to millions of natives in different parts of the empire in the preparation and shipment of articles in demand for foreign countries, had caused Canton to become one of the greatest marts in the world. The continuation of the East India Company's charter depended largely upon their furnishing a regular and ample supply of tea for the English market. But notwithstanding this community of interest in a peaceful and growing commerce, partly through ignorance of the true principles of international comity and of trade, partly on account of other reasons already mentioned, the few half-imprisoned foreigners were constantly restricted, and the very existence of all commercial relations put in jeopardy. The British Foreign Office, nominally under George III, but really under the Prince Regent, being informed of the critical situation in China, and fully aware that upon a happy solution of this old and vexed question in the Far East certain important problems in India and other distant parts of the world depended, resolved to dispatch another embassy to China, in order, if possible, to agree upon some definite mode of conducting trade, and of communicating with the heads of government.

Lord Amherst, nephew of the nobleman by that name

who was once governor of Virginia, and later the commander-in-chief of the British army, was appointed embassador-extraordinary to Peking. Accompanied by Henry Ellis and Sir George T. Staunton, as second and third commissioners, with a suite of able men, and the illustrious missionary Dr. Morrison as principal interpreter, the mission reached its destination, August 28, 1816. The unseemly haste of courtiers to bring the dust-stained travelers at once before His Majesty, and the refusal of the embassy to conform to the prescribed etiquette of the court, were followed by summary dismissal without an audience. This abrupt termination of a distinguished and well-appointed mission naturally becomes to us a subject of speculation. It does not seem probable, as some have conjectured, that this *fiasco* was solely on account of the subject of ceremonial observance, important and significant as that may have been. Lord Macartney, who declined submitting to the prostration, was more honorably received than almost any other embassador that ever entered China; and we are not at liberty wholly to discredit the Emperor Kea-king's profession of ignorance as to the matter. There is every reason to believe that the failure of the mission should be attributed to the intrigues of the provincial government at Canton, whose emissaries, in connection with the high officers about the throne, doubtless predetermined the course of events. One object of the embassy was to complain of the Canton governor, who had inflicted so many vexations on the English; and that functionary, who was powerful at court, could not be expected to remain a quiet observer of transactions which might involve the loss of his fortune and his life. This theory is further confirmed by the fact that the journey of Lord Amherst through the interior to Canton was permitted without interruption, or any sign of unfriendliness from officials, and that his return to England was followed by a longer period of tranquillity, and of freedom from Chinese annoyances, than had ever been experienced before. It is plain that the Dragon Throne had suffered no indignity from the King's representative, because the imperial command to appear in audience had not been given; and it seems altogether probable that the Viceroy of Canton was content to rest with the present success of his scheme, without venturing upon any new provocation which might result disastrously to himself.

On his arrival at Canton, Lord Amherst was duly informed that a letter from the Emperor for the Prince Regent awaited him, which the governor was bound to deliver to him in person. Whereupon it was resolved by his lordship not to consent to any meeting with that dignitary, although he possessed the exalted rank of viceroy, unless the first place was yielded to himself and the commissioners. Accordingly, a yellow tent was erected, in which the governor, reverently lifting above his head with both hands the Emperor's message, which was wrapped in a roll of yellow silk, delivered it with much solemnity into the embassador's keeping. The whole party then repaired to an adjoining tent, where the superior rank and place of honor was assumed by Lord Amherst. The haughty mandarin betrayed his unfriendly feelings; but an attempt of his to be uncivil was met with such a sturdy British reception as made him shrink from further contact with his guests, and he closed the ceremonies of the day with a hurried leave-taking.

We have now reached an important epoch in the history

of foreign intercourse with China. Having seen how Spanish, Portuguese and other navigators carried their clumsy but wonderful craft into Chinese ports, and thereby laid the foundation of a commerce which must be reckoned among the greatest achievements of modern enterprise, while by their acts they sowed those first seeds of ill-will and distrust, the bitter fruits of which the generations following were destined to reap, we are brought at length to look upon the dark picture of the first representative Christian nation of the world in deadly conflict with a heathen people, whose natural instincts were for peace, and not for war.

CHAPTER V.

ORIGIN OF THE OPIUM WAR.

ON the 22d of April, 1834, the trade of the East India Company with China, after having continued just two hundred years, terminated according to the provisions of "the new act." Their transactions had been exclusively with the hong-merchants, who constituted a corporation for that purpose, under restrictive orders from Peking; and the two close-trading companies had from the first served as "international buffers." An experiment was now to be tried which alone could set at rest the question of the expediency of free trade against the Chinese monopoly. The English government, deeming the change about to be inaugurated one of great importance, concluded to place the control of affairs in the hands of a commission of experienced men. The King therefore appointed the Right Hon. Lord Napier chief superintendent of British trade, who arrived at Macao July 15, 1834. Associated with him in the commission were John F. Davis and Sir G. B. Robinson, formerly servants of the company, together with a number of secretaries, surgeons, interpreters, and a chaplain, whose united salaries amounted to £18,200. Being probably unaware of the long-standing rule which would require him to remain aloof from the provincial city until orders should be received from the capital giving directions to the Viceroy how to treat the English superintendent, and of the necessity of awaiting legal permission to proceed, he at once visited Canton. This unusual and hasty proceeding awakened the apprehensions of the Viceroy, who in delaying the formal reception had only acted in conformity with the duties of his official position. Knowing that he might be held responsible to his government for this infraction of order and etiquette, he issued an edict addressed to the hong-merchants setting forth the official view of the case, couched in language distasteful to the foreigner and at the same time calculated to inspire in the native mind a feeling of contempt for barbarian manners.

Lord Palmerston, in his letter of instructions to the superintendent, called his attention to the fact that he was expected to discover the best means of preparing the way for direct communications with Peking, but did not fail to add the wise and statesman-like suggestion, "bearing constantly in mind, however, that peculiar caution and circumspection will be indispensable on this point, lest you should awaken the fears or offend the prejudices of the Chinese government, and thus put to hazard even the existing opportunities of intercourse by a precipitate attempt to extend them." Careful adherence to these instructions would have produced a different impression from that which now unfortunately existed.

The Viceroy's estimate of the importance and dignity of the superintendent's office may be inferred from these words, which occurred in the before-mentioned edict: "As to his object in coming to Canton, it is for commercial business. The Celestial Empire appoints officers, civil ones to rule the people, military ones to intimidate the wicked. The petty affairs of commerce are to be directed by the merchants themselves; the officers have nothing to hear on the subject." Notwithstanding the evidence of his far-seeing wisdom in arranging some of the details of this commission, the great Palmerston committed a blunder in statecraft when he sent out Lord Napier to perform the most difficult task yet attempted by a representative Englishman in China, at the same time denying him the right to treat with the government at Peking, and withholding due notification of the appointment to the governor of Canton. The exact nature of the case is thus put by Dr. Williams: "The court of St. James chose to send out a superintendent of trade, an officer partaking of both ministerial and consular powers, and ordering him to act in a certain manner, involving a partial violation of the regulations of the country where he was going, without providing for the alternative of his rejection."* Having been instructed to *report himself* by letter at Canton, Lord Napier made an attempt to do so, but the officials declined to receive his communication. At the same time, this occurrence was reported at court, in a memorial from the Viceroy, who represented to His Imperial Majesty that the English superintendent had presented a letter, the face of the envelope bearing the forms and style of equality, although there was no means of thoroughly ascertaining whether the writer had or had not official rank, and also setting forth that orders had been issued to the hong-merchants to convey to him the regulations of the Chinese government, and that the dignity and sovereignty of the Emperor should be maintained, whose mandate and pleasure in the premises were humbly implored.

* "Middle Kingdom," vol. ii. p. 472.

The English commerce had hitherto been managed by the factory chiefs and the hong-merchants, and this new departure in the attempt to formally associate trade with the functions of the magistrate could not be at once approved and adopted in the absence of instructions from the supreme authority. Any variation from the usual and accepted order of things is a matter of suspicion to the Chinese, especially where dealings are to be had with foreigners whose integrity and uprightness have not been demonstrated by former experience. Moreover, to have granted official intercourse by letter, in the view of the native authorities, would have been to acknowledge the King of England as equal if not superior to the Emperor, and to permit foreign traders to come into their borders as equals, subject to no laws and customs, and to have opened the door for resistance to their authority, for armed opposition to their control, and so preparing the way for the final possession of their territory. That the latter idea was really entertained and feared, is proven by various circumstances, and is hinted at by the Viceroy in his edict stopping the trade, when, speaking of the necessity of restraining the movements of Lord Napier. he says, " With regard to territory, it would also have its consequences." The frequent displays of naval force, and the prompt and vigorous resort to superior armaments on almost every serious provocation, could but tend to confirm this fear.

The injudicious conduct of the English representative is further illustrated by the issuance of a proclamation to the people, in which he detailed the principal events which had transpired since his arrival, laying the whole blame upon the " ignorance and obstinacy " of the governor in refusing to receive his letter, and closing with these words: "The merchants of Great Britain wish to trade with all China on principles of mutual benefit; they will never relax in their exertions till they gain a point of equal importance to both countries, and the Viceroy will find it as easy to stop the current of Canton river as to carry into effect the insane determination of the Hong." The people were highly excited and divided in their opinions concerning this strange proceeding, and the governor was irritated beyond measure at the publicly-expressed contempt of his authority and character. The trade had already been interdicted, but the governor had evinced a desire, through his deputation, to make some amicable arrangement with the superintendent, when this occurrence dispelled almost the last hope of ever arriving at terms of accommodation.

Two frigates were ordered up to protect the shipping and persons of British subjects, and these being fired upon from the Bogue forts returned the fire, although little damage was done to either. Troops were stationed on both sides, but neither party seemed inclined to continue hostilities. Lord Napier finally announced his determination to retire to Macao, until reference could be made to England; and a fortnight after his arrival, and just three months from the time of landing, he died in the Portuguese settlement, his demise, no doubt, being hastened by the harassing nature of his position at Canton, which he had been compelled to endure in the trying season of a tropical climate, and the sufferings and annoyances he had experienced in the passage down.

In this whole transaction we may discern, on the one hand, the usual native ignorance of foreign customs and the misapprehension of the foreigner's real motive in his almost every act,—the inability, because of lack of opportunity, to discern between the Portuguese and English character,—the superstitious folly which more or less marks every private and public transaction of importance, and the pitiable notion of superiority to all outside people who come for traffic but come with tribute to "range themselves under the renovating influence of the glorious sun of the Celestial Empire"; and, on the other hand, we observe the Englishman's contempt of everything below the level of his own civilization, his religious regard for the rights of trade in defiance of all other rights, his impatience with idle ceremony and empty forms of official etiquette when they seem to hinder his grasp on the rich rewards of commerce, and his idea that the principles of equal justice and common brotherhood are to be regarded as of no binding force wherever dealings are had with the inferior races. This intimate contact of opinions and traditions wholly at variance, with no tie to conciliate or unite them except the selfish greed of gain, and the misunderstanding which would arise from mutual ignorance of the situation, to be adjusted through the medium of a strange language,—often ill-spoken and ill-written by incompetent linguists,—made necessary a war of words to be succeeded by deeds of blood.

That eminent statesman, ex-president Adams, was mistaken, however, when, in his public lecture upon the Anglo-Chinese question, he pronounced the rejection of Lord Napier's letter and mission a sufficient reason for war and the real cause of the subsequent contest. Undoubtedly those occurrences, and the bad blood engendered by them, had their far-reaching and unhappy influence;

but we are to look in another direction for the immediate occasion of active hostilities.

The exactions of the Portuguese at Macao drove from that place the opium trade, in 1822, to Lintin, a small island near the entrance of the Canton river. Here began a system of smuggling which soon extended along the coast, until nearly every small vessel outside the ports was engaged in it. The system of exclusion practiced by the general government was deemed sufficient justification of this form of traffic, and the local government had so far placed itself in a false position, with respect to the Emperor as well as to Europeans, by its long course of secret and corrupt practices in relation to the prohibited drug, that it was disabled from interfering to protect its own subjects at Lintin. Here lay armed smugglers in open defiance of all law and control, and natives were, on several occasions, shot from the decks of these ships. In one notorious case an English subject actually set fire to a mandarin's house.*

The new superintendent of trade remained at Lintin, on board a small cutter, during the season of 1835-6; and while here he sent a communication to his government, which must be regarded as a remarkable dispatch to be sent by the representative of a Christian nation writing from the midst of a fleet of smugglers on the shore of a pagan country. He recommends the purchase of a small ship for the permanent accommodation of the commission in its present position beyond the reach of Chinese officials, and, as there was little hope of establishing a proper understanding with the native government, except by a resort to force, suggests the occupation of an

* Davis' "China and the Chinese," vol. I, p. 122.

island off the mouth of the river. He refers to the illicit traffic, but thinks "smuggling carried on actively in the government boats can hardly be termed such," and proceeds to explain that "whenever His Majesty's government directs us to prevent British vessels engaging in the traffic we can enforce any order to that effect, but a more certain method would be to prohibit the growth of the poppy and the manufacture of opium in British India."

The Emperor had issued the first edict against opium in 1800, and there was not the least evidence to show that the court of Peking was not sincere in the attempt to suppress the growing evil. The cupidity and venality of certain provincial and marine officers on the coast could not be more justly quoted against the supreme government than could the successful bribery of customhouse officers in England be adduced as proof of the corruption of the treasury department. It would not be strange if the temptation of an increasing and lucrative trade should prove quite as powerful to the unenlightened native smuggler as to the English merchants and monopolists who placed the poisonous drug constantly within his reach. In consequence of a memorial from one of the court ministers to the Dragon Throne, favoring, for various political reasons, the legalization of the opium trade, the impression became general at Canton that this would be done, and increased preparations were accordingly made in India to extend the cultivation of the poppy. A counter-memorial, however, was presented to the Emperor, which urged that the laws be more strictly maintained; that the people would soon learn to despise all laws if those against opium-smoking were suspended;

that recreant officers should be superseded and punished; and urging, with great force of logic and eloquence, that the question did not so much concern property and customs duties as the welfare and vigor of the people, as its cultivation would occupy rich and fertile land now used for nutritive grains, and showing that "to draw off in this way the waters of the great fountain requisite for the production of food and raiment, and to lavish them upon the root whence calamity and disaster spring forth, is an error like that of the physician who, when treating a mere external disease, drives it inward to the heart and center of the body." Another memorial from one of the sub-censors mentioned the names of several foreigners, English, Parsees and Americans, residing at Canton, who were extensively engaged in smuggling; and in three edicts issued by the governor of Kwang-tung province the immediate departure of nine persons therein mentioned was required, but this command of the local government was totally disregarded.

In this posture of affairs, be it said to his credit, the superintendent, Captain Charles Elliot, manifested a strong, although vain, desire to see the many political and commercial evils growing out of smuggling done away. During the years 1837 and 1838 there was a constant struggle along the coast between the officers of government, the native smugglers, and the foreign dealers; although the latter generally avoided coming in collision with either of the other parties, while at the same time doing all they could to promote the sale. Captain Elliot, being now at Canton as the recognized head of British trade, received an order from the provincial authorities to drive away the receiving-ships from Lintin, and to send the

Emperor's command to his king that henceforth they be prohibited from coming. The rapid growth at the port of smuggling in small boats, and the numerous collisions occurring which seemed to hazard even legitimate commerce, induced him to transmit also to his sovereign a minute account of the condition of the opium trade. Lord Palmerston, in reply, stated that no protection could be afforded to "enable British subjects to violate the laws of the country with which they trade. Any loss, therefore, which such persons may suffer in consequence of the more effectual execution of the Chinese laws on this subject must be borne by the parties who have brought that loss on themselves by their own acts." And yet the English Foreign Office had been familiar for years with the inception and growth of the opium trade!

After much pains to take the sense of the empire, and having proceeded with the utmost deliberation, the Peking government indicated a determined purpose to suppress the contraband traffic. The number of foreign small craft under English and American flags plying up and down Canton river, in 1838, was over fifty, most of them engaged in smuggling. In some instances these were readily seized and destroyed; but when the foreign schooners, heavily armed and manned, sailed up the stream delivering the drug, the revenue cruisers declined to attack them. Collisions became more and more frequent between Chinese dealers and the authorities in consequence of the increased stringency of the orders from Peking, and the whole question was finally brought to an issue by the open transference of two boxes of opium by order of a British merchant from an American ship to the shore. The governor, resolved to show the foreigner what consequences befell natives who were condemned for smuggling, sent an officer with a party of fifteen to execute a convicted dealer in front of the factories. The officer was making preparations to carry his orders into effect, near the American flag-staff, when a body of foreigners sallied out, arrested the proceedings in the most violent manner, and in loud and angry tones ordered him not to execute the man there. A large number of natives soon gathered to witness the scene, whom the excited foreigners attempted to drive away; whereupon blows were exchanged, and the crowd of curious observers, now changed to a mob, put to flight the handful of their assailants and began to attack the foreign houses with stones and brickbats. The district magistrate appeared upon the scene with a small body of police and speedily quelled the storm. The Chamber of Commerce remonstrated to the governor against the square being used for any such public purpose as had been attempted; but that functionary announced his intention to execute all criminals convicted of smuggling opium in that very place, and asserted the same control over it as any other locality in the province. Captain Elliot, fully appreciating the fact that his countrymen stood before the empire as violators of the law, declared his intention of ordering all British-owned vessels to leave the river within three days. Little heed, however, was paid to his injunctions and entreaties; and, having failed in the attempt to secure the coöperation of the governor in driving out all obnoxious vessels, he had to content himself with issuing a public notice expressive of his purpose to shrink from no responsibility whenever the opportunity should occur of expelling a traffic which was rapidly staining the British character with deep disgrace and exposing the regular commerce to imminent jeopardy. Without proper support from home, and deprived of the sympathy and coöperation of the merchants, this honorable officer was wholly unable to put forth such action as would show the Chinese government that British power would not protect British subjects in violating the law of the land.

The imperial court was now fully resolved upon the policy to be pursued, having presented to the world the unprecedented example of a despotic pagan government taking the public sentiment of its own people before adopting a doubtful line of conduct. The minister who had proposed legalization was dismissed from office, three princes of the blood were degraded for using opium, and the arrests, fines, tortures, imprisonments, and executions for similar offenses in the various provinces, showed a determined purpose to abolish the traffic. The Chinese commissioner, Lin, who was invested with the largest powers ever conferred on a subject, arrived in Canton March 10, 1839. Nothing was publicly heard from him for some time, but it became known that he was busy making inquiries, and both natives and foreigners anxiously watched his movements. On the 18th the commissioner issued his first proclamation, which gave no uncertain sound. The hong-merchants were duly admonished and instructed, and the foreigners were required to deliver up every particle of opium in the store-ships, and to give bonds that they would bring no more, on penalty of death. Three days were allowed for compliance with these orders. A number of British, Parsee and American dealers, fully alive to the peril of the situation, subscribed 1,037 chests to be tendered to the commissioner, but the hong-merchants declared the amount to be insufficient. A request from Lin that Mr. Dent, one of the leading English merchants, should meet him at the city gate having been refused, two of the hong-merchants came to his house with chains upon their necks and bringing an express order for that gentleman to appear. Mr. Dent did not obey, fearing that the intention was to detain him as a hostage until the opium should be surrendered,— a fear apparently well-grounded because of his prominence as a merchant, and from the fact that he alone remained of the thirteen foreigners previously ordered out of the country. After some fruitless controversy between Captain Elliot and the native authorities, the servants were ordered to abandon their foreign masters, guards were stationed before the doors of each of the factories and on the roofs of the adjoining houses, and every precaution taken to place the whole community in duress. Every proposition on the part of the merchants or the superintendent looking to a compromise was promptly rejected or simply ignored by the commissioner, whose every movement exhibited the utmost vigor and determination. On the 27th of March, yielding to the pressure of events, Captain Elliot issued a circular in which, after representing himself, together with all the merchants of his own and the other foreign nations settled at the port, as forcibly detained by the provincial government, without supplies of food, deprived of their servants, and cut off from all intercourse with their respective countries, he put forth his order in the following terms: " Now, I, the said chief superintendent, thus constrained by paramount motives affecting the safety of the lives and liberty of all the foreigners here present in Canton, and by other very weighty causes, do hereby, in the name and on the behalf of Her Britannic Majesty's government, enjoin and require all Her Majesty's subjects now present in Canton, forthwith to make a surrender to me for the service of Her said Majesty's government, to be delivered over to the government of China, of all the opium under their respective control, and to hold the British ships and vessels engaged in the opium trade subject to my immediate direction, and to forward me without delay a sealed list of all the British-owned opium in their respective possession." Some guarantee being offered in this notice by the authorized agent of the Crown that all questions of ownership in the property thus surrendered would be considered and defined by Her Majesty's government, the requisition was promptly answered by the merchants, who, before night, surrendered into Captain Elliot's hands 20,283 chests of opium, which were duly tendered to the commissioner on the next day. The latter referred to Peking for orders concerning the disposition of the opium, and was commanded by the Emperor to destroy the whole in the presence of the civil and military officers, the inhabitants of the coast, and the foreigners, "that they may know and tremble thereat." The destruction was effected in the most thorough manner, by mixing it with lime and salt water in trenches, and then drawing off the mixture into an adjacent creek at low tide. Every precaution was taken to prevent any purloining of the precious drug, and one man was summarily executed for attempting to carry away a small quantity. Thus perished an amount of property rated at the cost price of nearly eleven million dollars.

A strange mixture of traffic and hostilities characterized the course of events during the remainder of the year 1839, until late in the season, when an engagement was precipitated near Macao between a Chinese fleet and two English ships of war, in which three junks were sunk, one blown up, and the remaining twelve put to flight. The commissioner finding it impossible to resume commercial relations without more or less complicity in the forbidden traffic, which was largely controlled from the Portuguese settlement and from the coasting vessels outside, declared the trade with Great Britain at an end after December 6, and forbade English goods to be imported in vessels under any other national flag.

The British government was bound to reimburse its own subjects for the loss they had sustained in the destruction of their property, but the only source of indemnity Captain Elliot could suggest was to make the Chinese pay for it. A demand of that nature and magnitude could not be enforced by the arts of diplomacy. An appeal to arms was inevitable. The formality of a declaration of war being dispensed with, Queen Victoria issued an order in council to the admiralty in which it was recited that "satisfaction and reparation for the late injurious proceedings of certain officers of the Emperor of China against certain of our officers and subjects shall be demanded from the Chinese government." The opening act of the drama, however, was not to occur until China had first extended to England the olive-branch, in the form of two official letters from Commissioner Lin desiring the Queen's assistance in putting down the opium trade, and in his sending to their countrymen, after kind and hospitable treatment, the surviving crew of the *Sunda*, an English vessel that had been wrecked on the Chinese coast.*

---

* See, for principal data, Williams' "Middle Kingdom," vol. ii, pp. 470, 472, 479, 493, 515, 516.

CHAPTER VI.

THE WAR AND ITS RESULTS.

IN the month of April, 1840, Captain Elliot received an official letter announcing the determination of the British government to appeal to arms in case the Emperor refused to settle existing difficulties without bloodshed. The Chinese apparently foresaw the coming struggle, and began to collect troops, repair their forts, and put in commission vessels to guard the coast. The advance of the English forces arrived off Macao early in the summer of the following year, under Commodore Sir Gordon Bremer, who soon published a notice of the blockade of the port of Canton. Moving northward with a fleet of twenty-nine ships, he anchored in the harbor of Ting-hai, and sent a summons to surrender the town and island. The Chinese officers in command of the place complained of the hardship of being made the victims of deadly attack by a strange foe whom they had never seen and had never wronged, confessed their inability to cope with such a force, but assured Sir Gordon of their determination to put forth a loyal defense. The peaceful dawn of the Sabbath, July 5, witnessed a portentous warcloud looming in the sky and over the devoted town, as all the vessels discharged their broadsides, hurling deadly missiles into the junks, into the tower, and through the lines of defense. Among the Chinese there was slaughter and dismay; with the English, an easy victory and no loss. The blockade of Ningpo, Amoy, and the mouths of the Min and Yang-tsz-Kiang rivers, having been secured, Admiral G. Elliot and Captain Elliot, joint plenipotentiaries, sailed for the Gulf of Pe-che-le, where they anchored near the mouth of the Pei-ho. Negotiations were had with Ki-shen, governor of Chih-li province, resulting in an agreement that His Excellency, by imperial permission, should meet the plenipotentiaries at Canton to treat definitely on all the points in dispute.

Meanwhile a few skirmishes had taken place elsewhere, and several prisoners had fallen into the hands of the Chinese. These unfortunate persons were not treated with unusual cruelty, and they suffered no peculiar hardship more than common prisoners, although one Englishman, a Mr. Stanton, who was held in captivity in Canton, came near meeting a horrible fate. The redoubtable Lin had it in mind at one time to immolate him to the god of war to insure the success of the imperial troops; but, learning that his prisoner had never been engaged in the opium trade, he relinquished that purpose.

The commissioner, although feared by foreigners and held in respect and awe among his countrymen, was made to realize the vanity of all trust in princes; for, in the midst of his active and important measures for the defense of the city and its approaches, he was suddenly ordered to return " with the speed of flames" to Peking, the Emperor signifying his great displeasure toward his servant for having failed to accomplish the object sought in investing him with extraordinary powers, i. e., the extermination of the odious traffic in opium among both foreign and native dealers.

Admiral Elliot, on account of ill health, resigned his

office soon after his return from the north, leaving the management of affairs to Captain Elliot. Ki-shen favored terms of accommodation, but found unexpected zeal for war among the natives, and a determination to resist rather than to grant full indemnity. All difficulties in the way of a peaceful adjustment were being overcome at Canton, when word arrived from Peking that the Emperor had determined to reject all demands. Hostilities being resumed, the Bogue forts were speedily taken by nine ships of war assisted by about five hundred troops and two steamers. The obstructions in the Canton river and the fortifications along the shore did not long detain the English fleet, and troops were stationed about the city prepared to coöperate with the ships in a general assault. But through the efforts of Captain Elliot a truce was obtained, and the authorities ransomed their city for the sum of six million dollars, besides agreeing to compensate for the destruction of certain foreign property to a very considerable amount. For some days mob violence prevailed inside the walls, and it is stated that more than a thousand persons were killed in the rancorous contest between lawless soldiers and the citizens. On the outskirts, the dispersed troops aroused the villagers to unite in driving off the invaders, until a tumultuous force of about fifteen thousand advanced upon the surprised English, but were easily put to flight. The next day they approached in still more menacing attitude, were again dispersed, and finally induced to retire under a threat to fire on the city, and also through the persuasions of one of the commissioners and the prefect. The British flag was hauled down from the forts, and the troops took their departure with considerable loss in killed and wounded and from sickness, but having inflicted far greater damage upon their enemies. A thoughtful American who has lived in Canton, and who made himself familiar with the incidents of this campaign, says that "in posting their forces, and placing their masked batteries, and equipping their troops and forts. the Chinese showed greater command of means and knowledge of war than it was supposed they possessed; but their lack of discipline and confidence rendered every defense unavailing."

Soon after these events a new plenipotentiary, Sir Henry Pottinger, with Admiral Sir William Parker, arrived direct from England to assume control of affairs. Under the joint command of the Admiral and Sir Hugh Gough, a strong expedition sailed northward. Amoy, Chin-hai, and Ningpo, in rapid succession, were taken and occupied. The Chinese, however, made a strong effort to recapture the last-named city, and opened the campaign by a well concerted night attack from a body of troops who during the day had entered the place in citizens' clothes; but their temporary success in capturing the western and southern gates suffered a most disastrous reverse under a resolute charge from the Europeans. Cha-pu, a strongly fortified city, was the next to fall; and here the Manchoo Tartars for the first time came in conflict with the English. Either through fear of indiscriminate slaughter, or else unable to survive the disgrace of defeat, these valiant defenders of the Dragon Throne perpetrated self-destruction in large numbers, first having immolated their wives and children. The expedition then proceeded to the mouth of the Yang-tsz-Kiang, where the fortifications were carried after a severe cannonading, the Chinese working their guns in reply to the English fire with more skill and effect than they had theretofore displayed. The governor-general, Niu-kien, who was posted in the rear of the batteries during the heat of the engagement, did not present a very inspiriting example to his troops, but quite made up for his lack of prowess in the field by the tenor of his dispatch in which he reported the defeat of the native forces, stating that he braved the hottest of the fight, " where cannon-balls innumerable, flying in awful confusion through the expanse of heaven, fell before, behind, and on either side, while in the distance he saw the ships of the rebels standing erect, lofty as mountains. The fierce daring of the rebels was inconceivable; officers and men fell at their posts. Every effort to resist and check the onset was in vain, and a retreat became inevitable." General Chin, who was in immediate command, displayed the greatest heroism, until, covered with wounds, he fell on the walls of the fort, bowing his head as he sank in death in the direction of the Emperor's palace. Shanghai was taken without further resistance and the city saved from pillage, although a ransom of three hundred thousand dollars was exacted.

The English were now fully resolved upon the capture of Nanking, the ancient capital of China. The expedition, having been reorganized and fully equipped, when sailing up the great river, struck the inhabitants along the shore with mingled astonishment and dread as they observed these leviathans from the western seas moving along indifferently with or against wind and tide, impelled by a mysterious and unseen force. Seventy-two steamers and transports of various kinds composed the fleet, and they were arranged in five divisions, with an advance squadron of five small steamers and tenders to survey the stream, each division having a frigate or seventy-four at its head. Although it would not have been considered a very formidable display in European waters, the magnitude of the ships as compared with the native river junks, their heavy armaments, the superiority of all the weapons of war, and the moral energy and thorough discipline of the troops, constituted an invading force which must be regarded as invincible against all possible resources of the semi-civilized empire whose pride and power it was now the purpose to humble.

In order to open a safe approach to Nanking, it was deemed necessary to occupy Chin-kiang-fu, or the "Mart-river city." To effect this, the general disembarked his little army and formed a land force of three divisions, the whole comprising seven thousand men, with an artillery brigade of five hundred and seventy rank and file. Captain Loch, who accompanied the general as an aid, tells us that while a party of volunteers were approaching the imperialist camp outside the city walls, and as they passed through a small hamlet on the hills, they observed "the village had not been deserted; some of the houses were closed, while the inhabitants of others were standing in the streets staring at us in stupid wonder; and although they were viewing a contest between foreigners and their fellow countrymen, and in danger themselves of being shot, were coolly eating their meals";—all of which is an illustration of the *sang-froid* sometimes exhibited by Chinamen in the midst of imminent peril, in striking contrast to their not infrequent display of opposite qualities, presenting a psychological problem which we do not venture to solve. The right center and left brigades made a successful assault upon the city. The walls to the north were escaladed, and the western gate was blown in; but seven boats carrying artillerymen, which had proceeded up the Grand Canal to the gate, were repulsed by a severe fire from the walls with a loss of three of their number; whereupon two hundred marines were landed, who, with three hundred Sepoys, succeeded in recovering the boats and carrying the wounded men on shipboard. The detachment then planted their ladders in the face of a spirited fire from the enemy, and carried the ramparts against all opposition. Although three gates had been captured, the place was far from being subdued. The Tartars, driven into the southern part of the city, bravely held out. A force sent along the ramparts to occupy the southern gate, soon encountered a body of eight hundred or a thousand men drawn up in an open space below, who commenced to fire with steadiness and regularity, but gave way as the party charged down the bank upon them. The dispersed Tartars kept up a scattering discharge of musketry along the streets and from the houses while the English army swept the city. Two regiments, as they marched into the southern quarter, met scenes of desolation and woe seldom equaled in modern warfare. Such was the feeling of terror and hatred toward the invaders that every Manchoo seemed to prefer resistance, death, suicide, or flight, to surrender. The doors of their houses were shut, and through the crevices men could be seen deliberately cutting the throats of their women and destroying their children by throwing them into wells. In one residence, no less than fourteen dead bodies, principally women, were discovered. It was estimated that out of a Manchoo Tartar population of four thousand not more than five hundred survived, the greater part having perished by their own hands. Captain Loch incidentally mentions the wanton destruction by fire of a large, well furnished, but deserted house, supposed to be the prefect's residence. The public offices were ransacked, all the arms and warlike stores destroyed, but only sixty thousand dollars in sycee were found in the treasury. When the populace began to pillage the city and suburbs, in one instance setting fire to the buildings at each end of a street in order to plunder a pawnbroker's shop without interference, the confusion became appalling. The Sepoys and camp-followers not only took their share of plunder, but parties were stationed at the gates to relieve the robbers of their rich booty as they attempted to pass out. Within twenty-four hours after the landing of the troops, the city and suburbs of Chin-kiang-fu were laid in complete ruins, and part of the eastern wall was subsequently blown up, and all the gates dismantled, in order to prevent any further resistance from that quarter on the part of the determined and courageous Tartars.

Some of the large ships were towed still further up the river toward Nanking, and the whole fleet in due time reached that city. In order to avoid a repetition of the dreadful scenes enacted at Chin-kiang-fu, the leaders of the expedition sent a communication to Niu-kien, the governor-general, stating that they were willing to ransom the city for three million dollars. Seeing that preparations had been made for a formidable assault, and that the distress ensuent upon the blockade was hourly becoming greater and greater, more than seven hundred vessels having been stopped at Chin-kiang coming from the south, besides a large fleet detained in the northern branch of the canal, the native authorities yielded to the demands of the situation and consented to enter into stipulations. A time and place was appointed to arrange preliminaries, and the delegates on the part of the imperial commissioners, and Major Malcom with Mr. Morrison for the plenipotentiary, met to settle the vexed question of credentials. The English suspicion was disarmed by the solemn manner in which the Emperor's commission was brought forth and presented, and their amusement excited at the dismay of the attendants at seeing the foreigners irreverently handle it and examine its authenticity with so little awe. The skeleton of a treaty was immediately drafted for the delegates to take to their superiors. After an exchange of ceremonial visits, the plenipotentiaries met in the college hall of the city to discuss and definitely arrange all questions at issue. The room was superbly fitted up, and a crowd of official attendants, dressed in elegant robes, graced the occasion. Sir Henry Pottinger was accorded the seat of honor, between Ki-ying and Ilipu, the commissioners. The formalities of reception and a sumptuous dinner in Chinese style being over, the business of the hour engaged the serious attention of those high functionaries. A treaty was at length agreed to, embracing the following articles of stipulation: 1. Lasting peace between the two empires; 2. The Chinese government to pay twenty-one million dollars,—twelve million being for the expenses of the war, three million for debts due the English merchants, and six million for the opium; 3. The ports of Canton, Amoy, Foo-chow, Ningpo, and Shanghai, to be thrown open to British trade and residence, and the trade to be conducted according to a well understood tariff; 4. The island of Hong-kong to be ceded to the Queen; 5.

All British prisoners to be unconditionally released; 6. All Chinese in the service of the English to be pardoned and held guiltless; 7. Correspondence hereafter to be conducted on terms of perfect equality; 8. When the treaty receives the Emperor's assent, and six million dollars are paid, the English forces shall withdraw from the river and the places now occupied, but Chu-san and Ku-lang-su to be occupied until all the provisions of the treaty are executed.

After these matters had been arranged, Sir Henry expressed a desire to say a few words upon "the great cause that produced the disturbances which led to the war, namely, the trade in opium." The mandarins at first declined entering upon the subject, but consented at once when assured that it should be treated in a strictly unofficial manner. Captain Loch states that "they then evinced much interest, and eagerly requested to know why we would not act fairly toward them by prohibiting the growth of the poppy in our dominions, and thus effectually stop a traffic so pernicious to the human race." The captain thus gives in substance Sir Henry's reply, which was really all that could be said in defense of his government: "This, in consistency with our constitutional laws, could not be done, and he added that even if England chose to exercise so arbitrary a power over her tillers of the soil, it would not check the evil so far as the Chinese were concerned, while the cancer remained uneradicated among themselves, but that it would merely throw the market into other hands." This method of reasoning on the part of His Excellency had the merit of being ingenious, and also enjoyed the advantage of being addressed to men who were perhaps incapable of making any very nice distinction in questions of casuistry, however otherwise it may appear to the enlightened statesman and philanthropist.

Four copies of the treaty were prepared in both languages; and, with impressive ceremonies, it received the necessary signatures on board Her Majesty's ship *Cornwallis*, the event being announced to the fleet and army by a salute of twenty-one guns and hoisting the union-jack and a yellow flag at the main and mizzen. The six millions were paid with but little delay; and upon reception of the Emperor's ratification, September 15, 1842, the secretary of legation, Major Malcom, immediately left to obtain the Queen's ratification, going by steam the entire distance from Nanking to London.

A large number of the officers in the army and navy received promotion, or honorary titles,—some during the progress of the war and others at its close. Sir Hugh was first created a baronet, and, after more service in India, elevated to the peerage with the title of Lord Gough, Baron of Chin-kiang-fu; while Sir Henry and the admiral obtained each the high distinction of Grand Cross of the Bath. The three interpreters, Messrs. Morrison, Thom, and Gutzlaff, whose services had been most important whenever communication was had with the enemy, and who were arduous and invaluable in arranging the final stipulations, received no distinctive mark of royal favor. The Emperor, so far from rewarding any of his servants who had been prominent in the struggle, expressed his displeasure at the conduct of those who had survived, but bestowed posthumous honors upon those who had died at the post of duty. Although many civil and military officers were condemned to death, but one of their number actually lost his life,—Governor Yu, of Chehkiang, who fled from Ningpo in 1841.

The ratifications of the treaty of Nanking were exchanged at Hong-Kong, ten months after it had been signed by the plenipotentiaries. The island was then formally taken possession of on behalf of the Queen, and the warrant read appointing Sir Henry governor of the new colony. The proclamation by the English and Chinese authorities, which soon followed, giving effect to certain tariff and commercial regulations, has been justly characterized as one of the most important documents ever issued by the Chinese government, as by it China fully opened her ports and people to foreign intercourse. Commissioner Ki-ying thus expressed himself in this remarkable state paper: "Henceforth, then, the weapons of war shall forever be laid aside, and joy and profit shall be the perpetual lot of all; neither slight nor few will be the advantages reaped by the merchants, alike of China and of foreign countries. From this time forward all must free themselves from prejudice and suspicions, pursuing each his proper avocation, and careful always to retain no inimical feelings from the recollection of the hostilities that have before taken place; for such feelings and recollections can have no other effect than to hinder the growth of a good understanding between the two peoples." As further evidence of the conciliatory attitude and pacific intentions of the imperial government, it may be stated that all the natives engaged in the service of the English during the war were liberated, and of the many hundreds who had served on ship and ashore against their country, none were molested in any way for so doing.

A supplementary treaty was also concluded, which made

provision for the settlement of debts, for treatment of criminals, for the restraint of British subjects, for the registry of Chinese vessels at Hong-Kong, etc. By special request of Ki-ying, an article was admitted extending to all foreigners who had previously traded at Canton the same privileges English subjects were to enjoy at the various open ports.

The publication to the world of the treaty of Nanking caused a sensation in Europe and America. Prussia, Belgium, the Netherlands, and Spain, all sent out their representatives to seek some advantage in the new adjustment of commercial relations. The gentlemen so commissioned arrived in China during the latter part of the year 1843, and most of them had interviews or communication with Ki-ying before his return to Peking in December. The government of the United States appointed the Honorable Caleb Cushing embassador to the Chinese court. He having arrived in China in the frigate *Brandywine*, Commodore Parker, February 24, 1844, took up his temporary residence at Macao, where he organized the American legation, consisting of himself as sole commissioner and envoy extraordinary, Fletcher Webster, Esq., as secretary to the special Mission, with the Rev. E. C. Bridgman, D.D., and the Rev. Peter Parker, M.D., for joint Chinese secretaries, and Dr. Bridgman to serve as chaplain, five other gentlemen being retained in subordinate positions. When Mr. Cushing announced to the lieutenant-governor of the province his desire to convey to Peking a letter from President Tyler to His Majesty, the information of his arrival was immediately sent to court, whereupon the Emperor reappointed Ki-ying commissioner, with higher powers than before, indicating a favorable disposition toward Americans. After the usual visits of ceremony, negotiations were entered upon and favorably concluded at Wang-hia, July 3, 1844, when the two plenipotentiaries signed a treaty "between the youngest and oldest empires in the world," which was in due time ratified by the Emperor and the President and Senate. All the important advantages accorded to the English were included in this treaty, which also provided for the erection of hospitals, chapels and cemeteries at the five ports, and for the visits of ships-of-war to any part of the coast. Having accomplished the main object of his mission, and being content to deliver the presidential letter into the hands of an officer of rank, Mr. Cushing embarked for the United States without seeing the other ports, making only a transient visit at Canton and Hong-Kong. In 1845 the French embassador, H. E. Th. de Lagrené, was able to conclude a commercial treaty on the basis of the American stipulations, including as an additional item a qualified permission for the reception and exercise of Christianity among the people of the empire.

The cities and provinces swept by the storm of war had suffered much. In some instances the authority of the officers was materially weakened, and for a time anarchy threatened the disruption of the whole civil power within those limits. The destruction of property was enormous, considering the extent of territory actually traversed; and the sums exacted as ransom money, with the amount finally paid in obedience to the demands of the treaty, greatly added to the embarrassment of the provincial authorities, upon whom this burden principally rested. At Canton the anti-foreign sentiment became intense, and the hostility of the citizens proceeded to such a length that the local government became utterly powerless to secure to foreigners a larger space for residences and freedom to enter the city; and as a result, there having been failure to carry out the stipulations in these respects, several vessels of the British navy made warlike demonstrations at the Bogue and up the river, thereby restraining the mob spirit and reinforcing the authorities. Notwithstanding these unfavorable conditions, the external and internal relations of the Chinese empire at the close of the year 1844 were exceedingly hopeful. The magistrates had largely resumed their functions, the bands of lawless desperadoes were gradually dispersing, and the people seemed to be entering upon a new career of peaceful industry. No popular ill-will was manifested at Amoy on account of the heavy losses its citizens had sustained, nor at Ningpo or Shanghai for their occupation by English troops, and the British consuls at the five ports had all been received, while trade was commencing under favorable auspices. The one dark and ominous feature of commerce with China, however, still remained,— the unlicensed and rapidly extending opium traffic, carried on in schooners plying up and down the coast, and lying outside the limits of every port to deliver the drug.

One important result of the war was a breaking down of the intolerable assumptions of the Peking court, and the partial demolition of those ancient barriers of ignorance and superstition which, in every age and among every semi-civilized people, have stood in the way of international comity and universal progress. We may not stay our regrets that the effect of kindness, honorable dealing and peaceful missions, had not been fairly tried, and so the opportunity of exemplifying to a great heathen nation the lofty principles of justice and humanity was forever lost; but we will gratefully accept the issue which, under Divine Providence, inaugurated a new era in our relations with this empire of the Orient.

Members of the British Parliament expressed their gratification at being at last out of a bad business; but, as Dr. Williams has observed, "their desire, frequently uttered, that the light of the Gospel and the blessings of Christian civilization might now be introduced among the millions of China, seemed very like a kind of peace offering of good wishes, somewhat in the manner of the Hebrews offering a kid when they had committed trespass."

CHAPTER VII

RENEWAL OF HOSTILITIES—THE NORTH CHINA CAMPAIGN.

THE right of entrance into the walled cities at the ports opened to commerce not having been clearly expressed in any of the treaties, the local rulers at Canton were eventually disposed to resist every demand looking to a consummation so much desired by foreign residents, who were rigidly confined to the suburbs. The rulers were strongly supported by the people, whose spirit of opposition and prejudice seldom omitted an occasion to manifest itself. In 1847 the governor of Hong-Kong, Sir John F. Davis, under directions from the English Foreign Office, made a demand upon the governor-general to open his provincial city to the ingress of British subjects, as was the case at all the other open ports, and sought to enforce his demand by the occupation of several forts along Canton river. But the popular excitement became so intense that Sir John abandoned his purpose for a stipulated period of two years, at the end of which time the English authorities indefinitely adjourned the whole question.

In October, 1856, a native vessel making use of the British flag, without, as the Chinese asserted, any right to do so, was called to account and summarily dealt with. The English demanded an apology for Chinese soldiers having boarded the lorcha off Canton, but Commissioner

Yeh refused to give it, at the same time making so much concession as to send the crew to the English consulate to be examined. In consequence of this refusal, hostilities were commenced. The British bombarded the city wall opposite the governor-general's palace, into which they forced an entrance, and afterward attacked and destroyed the Barrier Forts. In retaliation, the Chinese burned the foreign residences, and gradually compelled all foreigners to withdraw from the city and river. These events were discussed in open Parliament, and excited much public attention in England. The ministry proposed war with China; and, on an adverse vote of the Commons, appealed to the country and were sustained by the new House. Her Majesty's government thereupon resolved to demand a revision of the first treaty, with an apology for the grievances that had occurred in the south, and also that further privileges should be enjoyed, more especially that the English minister should be permitted to reside at the capital and come into direct communication with the Chinese supreme authority.

A Roman Catholic missionary, the Rev. M. Chapdelaine, had been murdered in the province of Kwang-si, and the circumstances of this tragic event had excited the indignation of the French people. There were various other causes of complaint on the part of France; and the courts of Paris and London readily agreed on an armed remonstrance with the Peking government. The United States and Russia declined an invitation to enter the alliance, but consented to coöperate in all purely diplomatic advances.

The first important and decisive movement resulted in the total destruction of the Chinese fleet and the capture of Canton. Commissioner Yeh, who is said to have ordered the beheading of one hundred thousand rebels in the course of his official career, was taken prisoner and sent to Calcutta, where he soon afterward died. A London *Times* correspondent accompanied the distinguished captive in his voyage, and regaled the British public with a minute account of his personal appearance, habits, conversation, etc., in a series of well-written letters. The campaign having opened auspiciously for the allies, Lord Elgin and Baron Gross demanded that imperial commissioners should be sent with authority to conclude a new treaty, Shanghai being designated as the place of meeting. The Chinese, in accordance with their traditional policy to keep foreigners as far away from the capital as possible, insisted that the interview should be held in Canton. The English and French representatives determined not to submit to this requisition, and proceeded to the mouth of the Pei-ho, the port of Peking, where they were joined by Mr. Reed and Admiral Count Putiatine, the American and Russian ministers, the united squadrons numbering nearly forty vessels. The governor-general of Chih-li came down to open negotiations, and the plenipotentiaries of the United States and Russia had nearly completed the revision of the treaties, when a rupture occurred with the English and French, who regarded the governor-general's powers as inadequate, and who sent word to the Emperor that unless an officer with higher authority was sent from the capital they would bombard and take the Ta-koo forts. This threat was carried into execution, and several steamers proceeded up the river opposite Tien-tsin. The unexpected arrival of the foreign embassadors in that city, accompanied by an armed force, occasioned great excitement among the native population, and thoroughly alarmed the government. Two commissioners of high rank and enlarged powers were dispatched to treat with Lord Elgin and his associates.

The negotiations of Tien-tsin may justly be regarded as the second or third epochal event in the modern history of China. The four leading Western powers stood face to face with this great heathen nation, in the persons of their able representatives. It was the beginning of a new order of influences destined to extend over Eastern Asia, and to affect in many ways the most venerable of human institutions. An article allowing the profession of Christianity by the natives of China was introduced into each treaty, although the code of the empire had for many years made the acceptance of a new and strange religion a capital offense. Various points were discussed and adopted by which new and important advantages were secured to traders, including the opening up for foreign residence and purposes of commerce two new ports on the island of Formosa, with the cities of Swa-tau, Che-foo, Tien-tsin, one city in Manchooria, and three on the Yang-tsz-Kiang, although the Chinese with all their subtle art sought to avoid concessions. Lord Elgin exerted a leading influence in the various conferences, and preserved a very determined and authoritative bearing. It was said that "a mere hint of proceeding to Peking was sufficient to take the most doubtful clauses through the perils of diplomacy." The Chinese were ill-prepared to defend their capital, while the English were armed, aggressive, and confident.

The two imperial commissioners repaired to Shanghai by the overland route, where they met the foreign ministers, the result being a thorough revision of the tariff and commercial relations. All that now remained to be done in perfecting a formal peace was to send the treaties to Europe and America to be duly sanctioned, after which they were to be ratified by the Emperor at Peking. In the month of June, 1859, the representatives of "the four treaty powers" appeared at the mouth of the Pei-ho, pursuant to the understood plan for the exchange of the ratifications. The passage to Tien-tsin was found to be filled with obstructions to prevent the entrance of the gun-boats, and it was discovered that extensive warlike preparations had been made to resist and exclude the foreign embassadors. It is believed that the Chinese did not at first contemplate breaking faith with foreign nations. The terms of the treaty, which were really the result of a *coup de main*, and which had been exacted with a dictatorial air and haughty assumption of superiority, involved not only much larger concessions than had ever been given to any "outside kingdom," but was a practical surrender of that preëminence which from time immemorial had been claimed and exercised over the surrounding nations. In order to maintain the prestige and authority of the government at home, it probably became necessary to submit with at least apparent good grace to the foreign demand; but it was simply impossible to do this with a formidable fleet of gun-boats in the Pei-ho, anchored not more than eighty miles from the Emperor's palace, with evident intention of using force and intimidation, as in the previous instance, should the arts of diplomacy fail of complete success. These considerations should be esteemed sufficient justification of the course adopted by the Chinese on this occasion. The embassies were not rejected nor in any manner treated with indignity. The commissioners informed them that they were expected at Peking, but that the channel of the Pei-ho was effectually closed, and that they must proceed by another route. At the same time assurances were given that they would be treated with all due consideration and respect if they would but leave their gun-boats at the mouth of the river, and, with a limited escort, put themselves under the care and guidance of the servants of the Emperor. That these professions were sincere, we may conclude from the fact that the American minister, the Hon. J. E. Ward, accepting them in good faith, visited Peking; and, although refusing obeisance before the throne, and therefore unable to secure an audience, was nevertheless so successful as to effect the exchange of ratifications. The English and French, who could see in this proposition of the Chinese only a persistent determination to treat them as inferiors and to subject them to petty annoyances, with a probable sinister intention of some kind the nature of which could only be surmised, expressed their determination to go to Peking by the usual and direct route, and to take with them as large a company of foreign soldiers as they wished. But the Chinese were prepared for the emergency. Several gun-boats were disabled by the fire from the forts, a storming party was repelled, and the allied forces were obliged with great loss to withdraw and give up the attack as a complete failure. While the English and French were thus compelled to retire discomfited, the ministers of the United States and Russia, who had taken no part in this encounter, gained all the advantages sought or expected by them.

The repulse of the allied forces at Ta-koo, however humiliating and disastrous for the time being, could have but one result. It was now determined to carry the war to the very gates of Peking, and make the Chinese acknowledge the supremacy of Western nations. Talienwan, a fine bay in the most southern peninsula of Leautung, situated directly east from the embouchure of the Pei-ho, across the Gulf of Pe-che-le, about three hundred miles distant, was chosen for the rendezvous of the British expedition, and a large marine and land force was soon collected at that point. On the 9th of July, 1860, Lord Elgin arrived at the bay, "the breath of Mars issuing from his nostrils, much to the delight of the whole army." The French were located at Che-foo, where, at a conference between the two commanders-in-chief, Sir Hope Grant and General Montauban, a plan for the joint expedition was arranged. Soon after, the ships were all formed into line according to their divisions, and proceeded slowly across the gulf to within five miles of land. Anchored near the fleet was the United States ship *Hartford*, with the American minister, Mr. Ward, on board, and also a few Russian ships of war. After a short reconnoitering expedition up the river, under protection of the American flag, an offensive movement was begun by the landing of a small detachment of the allied force on a mud-bank. The soldiers were compelled to flounder and struggle for fully three-quarters of a mile before reaching anything like a firm footing. Most of the men were disembarrassed of their lower integuments, and one gallant brigadier pursued his line of march at the head of the column with no other garment than his shirt. Other troops followed in larger numbers, and, without a single shot having been fired by the enemy, the outer and comparatively unimportant forts were occupied. The secret of the desertion and abandonment of these fortifications was partly revealed when the sappers dug out four mines, which were intended to operate as infernal machines on a somewhat extended scale. The neighboring village of Peh-tang fell into the joint possession of the English and French. Sir Hope Grant had given strong injunctions against looting; but, notwithstanding every attempt to enforce his orders, the provost-sergeants first connived at and then became active participants in the plundering, which soon spread on all sides. The French officers made no effort to prevent a sack, and their men rushed into the houses, ruthlessly destroying what they could not appropriate. Many of the villagers had escaped, numbers of both men and women had committed suicide, and the few natives that still lingered by their domiciles watched with the eye of despair the destruction of all the property they possessed in the world.

An advance northward was met in great force by Tartar horsemen, who stood in unbroken line some two thousand yards before the invading columns, their appearance, as described by a spectator, being "magnified by the mirage into giant warriors on giant steeds." The Armstrong guns in front were ordered to advance and open fire at a range of fifteen hundred yards. Shell after shell burst over the devoted heads of the enemy, but the line remained unflinching for some time, closing up instantaneously the gaps that were made in their order by the murderous missiles. An attempt to charge and surround the English was persisted in despite a galling fire from rifles, cannons and racket batteries that "would have tried any troops in the world," as General Napier declared in his dispatches. After more severe fighting, the First Division and the French gained possession of the entrenched camp that commanded the road from Peh-tang to Sin-ho, while the retiring Tartars streamed away in the direction of the Ta-koo forts. In this first battle of the campaign, as the English commandant justly observed, the enemy behaved "with courageous endurance." But what could their force of six or seven thousand cavalry, armed with bows and arrows and spears, and their wretched gingals, do against ten thousand well armed and disciplined British troops supported by five thousand French?

Sin-ho and Tang-koo were next captured; and in the different mandarin residences of those towns, Chinese letters and other documents were discovered which possessed a curious interest as revealing the train of Chinese ideas on their relations to the hostile foreigners. One of these was a decree from the "Great Council of Peking" to San-ko-lin-sin, generalissimo of the Forces, and to Hong-fuh, governor of Chih-li, inclosing the ultimatum sent to the government by Mr. Bruce at Shanghai, with some extracts from the newspapers. It comments on the rebellious language of the "barbarians," mentions the fact that their ships were surveying the coast in the neighborhood of Ta-koo to find a landing-place, quotes the newspaper statement as given in a letter from Commissioner Hao that an invasion of thirty thousand men is projected, and alludes to a debate in the House of Commons on the subject of the war. In the reply of San-ko-lin-sin and Hong-fuh to the above, it was stated that the "barbarians" would not venture again to attack the forts in front; that they would in all probability land at Peh-tang, which was indeed unprotected, but in their attempts to cross the plains toward Sin-ho the invincible Tartar cavalry would find no difficulty in cutting up thirty thousand such troops as the enemy possessed; and that if by any extraordinary good luck they should succeed in passing Sin-ho, then they would certainly run their heads against the forts as they did the year before. From this it is quite apparent that the Tartar general made the fatal mistake of supposing that the English and French had been laboring under cowardly fear ever since the defeat of 1859, and that their announcement of preparations on a large scale was only a mask to cover their apprehension and discomfiture. But one naturally wonders how a people so indifferent to foreign politics as were the Chinese should have managed to acquaint themselves with the speeches relating to their affairs delivered in the House of Commons.

An advance force was pushed forward to a position near the Ta-koo forts, when, after fatigue parties under the direction of the Royal Engineers had worked all one night, and other necessary preparations had been completed, two officers were sent with a flag of truce to the north fort to hold an interview with the commandant. That worthy showed his head through an embrasure and demanded their business. They replied that they had come to offer terms of capitulation: whereat the mandarin became indignant and declared he would accept no terms, and that if the allied forces wanted the forts they had better come and take them. The attack was finally commenced early one morning, and as soon as daylight ad-

5*

mitted of the enemy's observing the advance of the storming column they opened fire from all the different forts. The attack had not proceeded long before a magazine in the upper north fort blew up with a terrific roar and explosion, shaking the ground for miles around as by an earthquake. Some few minutes afterward a similar explosion in the lower north fort occurred, effected by a shell from the gun-boats lying at the mouth of the river. The field guns were then advanced to within five hundred yards of the inner south fort, and under their heavy fire a breach was soon made. A party of French and English infantry approached to within thirty yards, intending to storm the apparently disabled fortifications; but the enemy emerged from their cover and opened a sharp fire of musketry. A gallant attempt of the French to escalade the walls was rendered ineffectual from the vigorous resistance of the Chinese. The efforts of the sappers to lay a pontoon bridge over the wet ditch were unavailing, no less than fifteen of the men carrying it being knocked over in an instant and one of the pontoons destroyed. A reinforcement both of artillery and infantry was brought forward and the attack pressed with greater vigor than ever, when the breach was mounted and carried, the garrison being driven step by step and hurled pell-mell through the embrasures on the opposite side. Consequent upon this decisive action, the south and lower north forts hauled down their flags of defiance and substituted the flags of truce, and this was followed by an unconditional surrender of the whole country on the banks of the Pei-ho as far as Tien-tsin. The victory was dearly bought, as a large number of the casualties were among the English officers, twenty-two of whom were wounded, besides seventeen men killed and one hundred and sixty-one wounded, the French sustaining a loss of about one hundred and thirty, and some of their officers killed. The loss of the enemy was far greater; for their dead lay everywhere, both inside and outside the forts, and their list of casualties was thought to have been not less than two thousand. Among the slain was the general in command of the forts, who fell by the revolver of a captain of the Royal Marines.

Robert Swinhoe, staff interpreter to Sir Hope Grant, in his "Narrative of the North China Campaign," volunteers the statement that "The Tartars undoubtedly fought like brave men, hurling down all kinds of uncouth missiles at the storming party, and when our troops had effected an entrance every inch of the ground inside the fort was disputed." But he is inclined to think that the bravery of the enemy was very much the result of despair, as by blocking the assailants out they had pretty effectually blocked themselves in. He further says, "The fearless conduct, however, of the Cantonese coolies in our lines excited considerable admiration. They seemed to enjoy the fun, and shouted with glee at every good shot that carried a murderous mission, no matter whether it committed havoc among the enemy or bowled over our unfortunate fellows; and those in French employ were conspicuous in the front assisting the troops and standing up to their necks in the ditches holding ladders over their heads to enable the men to cross. All this, it will be argued, shows no lack of pluck in the Chinese character when opportunity is given for its demonstration; but we must not forget that the people from whom these corps were taken were mostly thieves or pirates hardened to deeds of blood, and depending largely upon such acts for their maintenance." "Many of the officers," he says, "maintained that if the Chinese were drilled and led they would make excellent soldiers. This I do not attempt to gainsay, knowing, as all must know, how many of the Asiatics and instinctively cowardly races, as the Bengalees and Turks, have turned out under such treatment."

The approach to Tien-tsin from the river was defended by a small fort on each bank of the Pei-ho, situated about two miles below the city. Inland from these forts on either hand extended long crenelated walls, which, taking a semi-circular sweep, girded the town and its suburbs, with an estimated length of fifteen miles. This fortification did not seriously impede the march of the allies, although, had it been defended by sharpshooters, it might have given considerable annoyance to the advance force. The wall, which has been appropriately termed "San-ko-lin-sin's folly," was constructed of mud, and had been recently thrown up under the directions of the generalissimo, evidently as a bugbear to frighten at a distance. It bore no marks of mounted guns, and had, in all probability, been raised with the intention of beating back light-armed troops, an idea having prevailed among the Chinese that the English were a peculiarly maritime race, who, while they could manœuver large guns on shipboard, were quite unpracticed in field artillery.

San-ko-lin-sin had proved himself a good engineer by the masterly manner in which he had constructed the forts and made them impregnable from the sea. Having made every preparation for the encounter with a naval power, the indignant mandarin deemed it an unpardonable breach of military etiquette, known only among "barbarians," to approach the Ta-koo fortifications in the rear! As a general, he had wholly miscalculated his enemy, and now nothing could be done but to allow the victorious allies to advance in force, and then to call in the assistance of diplomacy to delay their further progress in numbers. To inveigle them forward in small parties, under the blinding title of guards to the foreign ministers, while he might have time to complete his last and formidable preparations for the defense of Peking, doubtless became his policy at this critical juncture. This plan, which well nigh succeeded at one time, soon came to naught, and the line of march was resumed.

Frequent fighting, much of it mere skirmishing, with now and then a serious encounter, marked the slow progress of the invading army. The usual plunder and wanton destruction of property in the captured villages was alike participated in by the English, French, Seikhs, and Cantonese coolies, the efforts of British officers to prevent it proving of little avail. The approach of the foreign soldiers produced general alarm and trepidation among the population, the appearance of the black and turbaned Punjaubee troops exciting a peculiar terror, and many cases of self-destruction transpired.

Some time after one of the engagements, in a cemetery where the carcasses of horses and their lifeless riders were mingled in promiscuous and deadly confusion, a British officer discovered a solitary native who presented a fitting type of the horrors and desolations of war. The unfortunate man, emaciated and quite bereft of sense, no doubt through wounds and starvation, was plucking up the grass by handfuls and eating it. The officer spoke to him, and tried to get him off the place; but in reply he returned a vacant stare and shrieked menacingly, and the narrator left him sitting like a specter among the dead.

CHAPTER VIII.

THE BELEAGUERED CAPITAL.

ALTHOUGH the early history of Peking is involved in obscurity, we are able to go back as far as the thirteenth century in our quest of positive information concerning this ancient city. Without doubt, it was besieged and taken by the Mongols under Zingis Khan; but we are inclined to regard as apocryphal the statement of the Chinese historian that the inhabitants, for want of ammunition, discharged ingots of gold and silver upon their assailants during that notable siege. Kublai Khan rebuilt it, and made it his capital in 1260. The Mongol dynasty continued to occupy this seat of empire till it was expelled from China, in 1367. In 1421 the third emperor of the native Ming dynasty transferred his residence thither from Nanking. When the Manchoos, in 1644, assumed the government, they found a magnificent city ready for them.

Peking, or *Pae-ching* in the court dialect, i. e., "Northern Capital," is built on a gently sloping plain, surrounded on three sides by a semicircle of mountains; which fact, together with the happy distribution of the neighboring rivers among the astrological divinities that are supposed to dominate the earth's surface, constitute peculiar advantages in a geomantic point of view. To the west, northwest and south are the imperial parks. In various directions are numerous temples: some of them venerable with the dust and decay of centuries, others extensive, elaborate, populous with deities, and resplendent with barbaric art. Frequently near at hand, but not in every instance, are to be seen the cities of the dead,—marked by the grave, the monument, and the ancestral tablet. The Ming Tombs, situated in a beautiful valley thirty miles northward, are entered by a gateway cut in solid marble seventy feet long by fifty feet high. The curious traveler may at any time be admitted through these lofty portals, when, advancing between six rows of pine and cypress trees on either side, entering the Dragon and Phœnix Gate, then emerging among various works of nature and art, until, having traversed the long avenue lined with colossal elephants, lions, unicorns, camels and horses, and the figures of military and civil mandarins, each statue wrought out of a single stone, he may at length stand before those windowless palaces where the high and mighty rulers of China repose in the dread sleep of ages. Not very distant to the northwest is the Yuen-ming-yuen, or Summer Seat of the Emperor, and nearer yet, in village-like clusters on every side, are the extensive suburbs.

As the environments are of peculiar interest, so the imperial city is notable in itself on many accounts. It consists of two continuous cities, each separately surrounded by walls, the entire circumference being twenty-five miles. The North City, which is nearly a perfect square, consists of three inclosures, the outer one having formerly been occupied exclusively by the Tartar garrison, but now is used for purposes of trade and residence by a mixed population of Chinese and Manchoos. The second inclosure is inhabited mainly by the latter race, and is intended to contain certain distinctively national institutions. The inner inclosure, or "Purple Forbidden City," constitutes the palace, and covers half a square mile of ground. The main wall, which has nine gates with a semicircular *enceinte* outside of each gate, is about forty feet high, is broader than it is high, and is defended by massive buttresses, and approached at intervals on the inside by inclined planes of substantial masonry. The top of the wall affords a vast open space, greatly increased by the broad buttresses, which is of sufficient extent to afford perfect ease in deploying an army. There is a tower over each of the gates, besides one at each corner, and they are built of brick, in some instances more than a hundred feet high, having a large number of embrasures for cannon. The walls of the Southern City are twenty-two feet in height, and inclose a parallelogram nearly five miles long and two miles wide. The whole population is reckoned by native tables at two and a half millions, but a careful foreign estimate would not place it much above one million. Although not among the most populous, it must be regarded as one of the most remarkable, cities of the world. Not only is it the seat of an empire far more extensive than Rome possessed in its palmiest days, surrounded by walls and towers acknowledged to be built on a scale truly magnificent, but it has other characteristics not unworthy of renown. Its great bell, which Virbiest says is 120,000 pounds in weight, or 94,600 pounds heavier than the weight of the bell of Erfurt, "the queen of bells"; its Yung-ho-kung, a Lama monastic institution containing from thirteen to fifteen hundred devotees, and a colossal image of Maitreya, the coming Boodha, seventy feet high, with a prayer-wheel reaching upward through successive stories to an equal height with the image; its Temple of Heaven, where once a year is displayed the most pompous religious ceremonial perhaps ever witnessed in the whole pagan world, when the Emperor himself officiates as the High Priest of three hundred and fifty million people; its provincial college, within whose walls ten thousand students periodically gather in eager contest for the honors of superior scholarship, with the yet more august Hall of Precious Harmony, where the Son of Heaven presides in person and awards to successful competitors the highest literary degree; its extensive rice granaries and other depositories of imperial revenue; its immense yamuns provided for the several departments of state and presided over by the chiefs of government; and, above all, the palace, where, surrounded by a triple wall and guarded by a host of bannermen, His Supreme Majesty dwells amid scenes which can alone be adequately pictured and admired by the oriental imagination,— together with the inferior princely palaces, the innumerable lesser temples, and the many objects of art and monuments of antiquity,— contribute to make the Chinese metropolis at least the most unique and famous of Asiatic cities.*

On the 5th of October the whole force of the allies approached, when a halt was sounded near some grass-grown brick-kilns, from the tops of which the officers obtained their first view of the long-secluded capital of the Celestial Empire. The city lay at a distance of some six miles, almost hidden by its long line of wall, but the towers looming conspicuously through the clear at-

---

* Rev. J. Edkins. D.D., in Williamson's "Journeys in North China." vol. ii, pp. 313-392.

mosphere. The English general and staff officers assembled on the top of a mound to deliberate on the plan of attack; but in consequence of a request from the French commander-in-chief, proceedings were delayed till the morrow, and the troops bivouacked and pitched their tents where they were.

Next morning betimes the march was resumed. The French general advanced at once on the Summer Palace, accompanied by an English brigade. The latter met at one point a procession of Chinese travelers, the chief personage being a pale young man seated in a large sedan, who was much alarmed at the unexpected appearance of foreign soldiers, and who, knocking his head against the bottom of the chair, prayed the privilege of being allowed to pass, as he was only a civilian engaged in escorting the coffin of his father to his native village. The brigadier, through his interpreter, assured him that none of his people would harm him. This, doubtless, the gallant officer really believed; but his men, without the knowledge of their commander, afterward seized the coffin for the sake of the mules that carried it, and these latter being properly secured, the former was thrown into a ditch.

It was ascertained from a servant of the Emperor, captured the next day, that His Majesty, who was suffering much from ill health, had left some fifteen days before for Gehol, his northern hunting and pleasure grounds in the borders of Tartary, carrying with him his thirteen wives and a large retinue. The retreat had been made in great haste, but Prince Kung had stayed behind till the evening previous, when the intelligence was brought that the allies were actually marching on the place.

The prince had finally taken a precipitate leave of the premises, giving directions to the eunuchs, some three hundred in number, to make a valiant defense. The French assaulted the palace, and, on bursting open the doors, the eunuchs opposed their entrance to the holy precincts of the Dragon Hall; but two of their number being killed and others wounded, and seeing no hope of making a successful resistance, the remainder ignominiously retreated. Meanwhile, Sir Hope Grant, after a slight skirmish with a picket of Tartars at the Tih-shing suburb, had driven them into the city gate, and was awaiting the auspicious moment when a combined attack could be arranged.

The French were encamped in front of the grand entrance to the Yuen-ming-yuen, under the trees between two artificial lakes. After the capture of the entrance, a guard had been posted at the gate, and for a brief time the soldiers were restrained in their fierce instinct for plunder. But soon General Montauban himself led the way into the palace, solemnly protesting all the while that he had strictly prohibited his troops from entering within its walls, as he had determined that no looting should take place before the British came up, that all might have an equal share. On the center of a wide pavement, and facing the gate, stood the grand reception hall, into which the eager foreigners pressed their way. Here they found themselves on a smooth marble floor in front of the Emperor's throne, and in a spacious apartment where everything was calculated to inspire with awe the chosen few who were privileged to draw near on ceremonial days and render obeisance before the much-dreaded Brother of the Sun and Moon.

"Imagine such a scene," says Swinhoe. "The Emperor is seated on his ebony throne, attired in a yellow robe wrought over with dragons in gold thread, his head surmounted with a spherical crown of gold and precious stones, with pearl drops suspended round on light gold chains. His eunuchs and ministers, in court costume, ranged on either side on their knees, and his guard of honor and musicians drawn up in two lines in the courtyard without. The name of the distinguished personage to be introduced is called out, and as he approaches the band strikes up. He draws near the awful throne, and, looking meekly on the ground, drops on his knees before the central steps. He removes his hat from his head, and places it on the throne floor, with its peacock's feather toward the imperial donor. The Emperor moves his hand, and down goes the humble head, and the forehead strikes on the step three times three. The head is then raised, but the eyes are still meekly lowered, as the imperial voice in thrilling accents pronounces the behest of the great master. The voice hushed, down goes the head again and acknowledges the sovereign right, and the privileged individual is allowed to withdraw. The scene described is not imaginary, but warranted by the accounts of natives. How different the scene now! The hall filled with crowds of a foreign soldiery, and the throne floor covered with the Celestial Emperor's choicest curios, but destined as gifts for two far more worthy monarchs. 'See here,' said General Montauban, pointing to them, 'I have had a few of the most brilliant things selected to be divided between the Queen of Great Britain and the Emperor of the French.'"

Various compartments of the palace were visited, among

them the Emperor's bedroom. Here was seen the imperial couch, curtained over and covered with silk mattresses. A small silk handkerchief, with sundry writings in the vermilion pencil about the "barbarians," was under the pillow, and pipes and other Chinese luxuries were on a table close by. The English treaty of 1858, with its envelope, also lay on a table, besides a large quantity of pencilings in the Emperor's own hand, most of which had reference to the allies. The English narrator states that he and his companions were proceeding to examine the objects of interest as we would the curiosities of a museum, when to their astonishment the French officers commenced to appropriate everything they took a fancy to. "Gold watches and small valuables were whipped up by these gentlemen with amazing velocity, and as speedily disappeared into their capacious pockets." After allowing this sort of proceeding to continue for awhile, the general insisted upon the crowd following him out, repeating the statement that looting was strictly prohibited! Presently an officer accosted him and imparted the information that they had caught a Chinese stealing an old pair of shoes out of the imperial grounds. "Bring him here," said the indignant general. "Have we not said that looting is strictly forbidden?" The trembling prisoner came forward, when the general exhausted his wrath in plying with his cane about the shoulders of the luckless scapegoat.

By this time the French camp was revelling in silks and *bijou* articles of rare curiosity or of great value. Watches, pencil-cases set with diamonds, jeweled vases, and many other curios were shown by their exultant possessors, one officer exhibiting a string of splendid pearls, each pearl being of the size of a marble and the whole representing almost a fabulous sum. Sir Hope Grant and staff having arrived at length, General Montauban welcomed him, and positively assured him that nothing had as yet been taken from the palace; but as the latter walked through the camp his own eyes must have undeceived him. Lord Elgin next came up, and, filled with indignation at what he saw, uttered his protest, saying in plain terms, "I would like a great many things that the palace contains, but I am not a thief." On Sunday morning, the 7th of October, all restraint to looting was withdrawn, and officers and men, English and French, were rushing about the place in a most unbecoming and excited manner. In the eagerness for the acquisition of valuables, respect for position was completely lost sight of, and the most perfect disorder prevailed. Officers and men of all ranks might have been seen with their heads and hands brushing and knocking together in the same box, as they sought to secure its contents, or in the scramble going on over some collection of rich and costly robes. Not only was licensed theft everywhere busy and everywhere successful, but a spirit of wanton destruction seemed to inspire nearly every one. Some would play pitch-and-toss against the large mirrors; others would amuse themselves by taking "cock" shots at the chandeliers; while some of the Frenchmen were armed with clubs, and what they could not carry away they smashed to atoms, crowning their work of destruction in the interior of the palace by setting fire to the Emperor's private residence.

A commission of prize agents was formed by Sir Hope Grant for the purpose of collecting together curiosities to dispose of for the benefit of the army, and the officers composing it were busy all day in making their selections. As numbers of the officers and most of the men had by their duties been deprived of participating in the spoil, and fearing the dissatisfaction that seemed inevitable and that might have very serious results, orders were issued by the English commander-in-chief to call in all the loot acquired by the officers. The British share of the plunder was put on exhibition in the hall of a large Lama temple, and the whole was disposed of during a sale continuing over three whole days, and was largely attended both by officers and men. The proceeds amounted to thirty-two thousand dollars, many articles, of course, having been disposed of at a figure far below the real value. Besides this sum, the amount of treasure secured was ascertained to be about sixty-one thousand dollars. For weeks, in either camp, little was talked of but curiosities purloined from the Summer Palace. Numbers of the French officers had acquired considerable fortunes, and their men were scarcely less favored. For several days the soldiers were constantly to be met with in a state of intoxication, while much disorder and serious disturbances occurred in their camp, the acquired disposition to plunder constantly breaking out in the direction of neighboring villages.

The work of spoliation and the sale of an emperor's effects beneath the walls of his own capital having been completed, the great achievement which the allies had set before themselves was now to be attempted. The Chinese were given to the 12th for the surrender of the Anting gate. The plan of attack contemplated a breach in the wall some fifteen feet from the ground, and the troops entering by the breach, reaching the summit of the wall to the right, were to proceed to the gate and at once occupy that commanding position. A trench had been pushed within one hundred yards of the point of attack, and the batteries were all prepared as the hour named for the surrender drew near. The gunners stood by their pieces; a storming party was being paraded; Mr. Parkes, interpreter, and Colonel Stephenson, deputy adjutant-general, had repaired to a position near the wall to receive any overtures the Chinese might make, while General Napier stood by the guns with a watch in his hand. Five minutes to twelve! The artillerymen could scarcely restrain their eager excitement, and the order to fire was almost on the lips of the general, when Colonel Stephenson came galloping to the spot and announced that the gate had been surrendered. A party of British and Punjaubees immediately entered the city, driving the populace before them, and then took possession of the gate, quartering themselves on the right side. The French also marched in, with drums beating and colors flying, and pushing some distance farther along the broad street, returned and established themselves on the left side of the An-ting.

In the afternoon of the day of the surrender, several prisoners were restored to the allies in a fearfully emaciated condition. The bodies of a number of other captives who had died in the hands of their enemies were also surrendered, among them being the remains of Mr. Bowlby, the ill-fated correspondent of the London *Times*. The sad fate of their countrymen, who had doubtless perished from the cruelty and neglect that too often mark the conduct of the Chinese toward their prisoners of war, aroused great indignation in the British camp. Had it not been for the fact that Sir Hope Grant had given his word that Peking would be spared if the gate was immediately surrendered, the consequences of this state of feeling, which was shared alike by the men and the chief officers of the army, might have been terrible to that city. Lord Elgin determined, as the most that could be accomplished under the circumstances, to level His Majesty's rural retreat to the ground, and to insist on compensation for the bereaved friends of the deceased to the amount of 300,000 taels, or about $500,000. The French refused to coöperate in the destruction of the palace, and condemned the measure as a piece of barbarism, forgetting that they had already committed the chief offense in purloining and demolishing the works of art it contained, besides having tarnished the character of their army by the unjustifiable act of burning a valuable library found in the Emperor's private residence. The First Division, under General Michel, soon accomplished the task assigned it. The long column of smoke rising to the sky, and, as the day waned, increasing in magnitude and growing denser and denser until wafted, like a vast storm-cloud, over Peking, told the distant observer the devastating work of the fire-fiend. Before sunset of the 19th every building in the imperial grounds had been fired, and many of the peasants' houses adjoining had been caught by the flames, and were fast being reduced to ashes.

Lord Elgin followed the act of retribution by this formal notice to Prince Kung: "Unless before 10 A.M. on the 20th the Prince informs the undersigned in writing that the sum demanded as compensation for the British subjects who have been maltreated or murdered will be ready for payment on the 22d, and that he will be prepared to sign the convention and to exchange ratifications of the Treaty of Tien-tsin on the 23d, the undersigned will again call on the commander-in-chief to seize the Imperial Palace in Peking, and to take such other measures to compel the Chinese Government to accede to the demands of that of Great Britain as may seem to him to be fitting." Every preparation was made to carry out the threat on the palace inside the city, and troops were already detailed for the attack, when a communication was received from Prince Kung conceding everything demanded.

It was thought that the Russian embassador residing in the capital had tendered his friendly services in bringing about the concession, by pointing out to the Chinese the folly of holding out any longer against such powerful enemies. The news was also received at this time that an army of Shen-si insurrectionists were pushing for Peking, with a view to avail themselves of the present crisis to extend their depredations. The proximity of these rebels had, no doubt, incited the Chinese to precipitate the settlement of their difficulties with the foreign foe.

The whole of the indemnity was paid by Prince Kung at the stipulated time. On the 24th Lord Elgin entered the An-ting gate in his green sedan-chair, carried by sixteen coolies in scarlet livery, his staff on horseback on either side, and proceeded to the Hall of Ceremonies, attended by a procession of infantry and cavalry, forming altogether a force of eight thousand men. The line of march lay through one of the principal streets of the city, and the Chinese had mustered in large numbers on either side to witness this display of the British army. After marching about one mile the long column halted before a gate over which was written, in conspicuous letters, "Board of Ceremonies." Passing through this gate into a large court-yard, Lord Elgin found Prince Kung and numberless mandarins already in waiting in the open hall, standing at the farther end. As his lordship advanced up the avenue inside the gate, between the opened ranks of his troops, they presented arms, and the band saluted him with the national air. Advancing to the seat of honor, he motioned the prince to take the lower seat on the right, while Sir Hope Grant assumed his position on the left. From the chair of the commander-in-chief, and ranging behind a row of tables down the hall, sat and stood the inferior English officers, and behind similar tables on the right were ranged native princes and mandarins of every button. The attachés and interpreters of the embassy stood behind his lordship and Sir Hope Grant, at a central table whereon were placed dispatch-boxes, paper, and other necessary official apparatus; and the prince had standing by him three mandarins of rank.

The preliminaries having been arranged, the High Commissioners proceeded to exhibit their respective full powers. Two articles which had not been proposed in the previous convention were admitted,— legalizing coolie emigration and ceding to Her Majesty's government the peninsula of Kow-loon, opposite Hong-Kong. Following the signature of the convention came the exchange of the ratifications of the Treaty of Tien-tsin. A minute, recording the proceedings which had taken place in connection with the exchange of ratifications, was then drawn up in duplicate, and, receiving the signature and seal of each of the plenipotentiaries, one copy was given to Lord Elgin and the other to Prince Kung. The business having been concluded, the prince tendered a banquet, which was declined through fear that the treachery of the Chinese might have poisoned the food; and Lord Elgin immediately took leave, accompanied by the procession as before. Soon after, the guns on the An-ting gate announced to the world that peace had been concluded between Great Britain and China. The French exchanged ratifications on the following day; and, being less suspicious than their Anglican friends, readily accepted the proffered banquet, which passed off with much ceremony, and in entire good faith on the part of the princely host.

The Roman Catholic cathedral of the Jesuits in the Northern or Tartar City had long been deserted, as the celebration of Catholic services within its sanctuary was forbidden, and the cross had disappeared off its summit. Two priests residing in the capital disguised in Chinese garb, having gained the influence of the French in reinstating the establishment and erecting a new cross, had now renovated the place and put the sacred edifice into thorough repair. The officers of the allied army were invited to attend the reopening service, when once more the *Te Deum* was chanted within its long-neglected walls, in grateful homage to the Almighty Maker.*

* "Narrative of the North China Campaign," by Robert Swinhoe, pp. 271-361.

CHAPTER IX.

ROMAN CATHOLIC MISSIONS.

THE tradition that Christianity was introduced into China by the Apostle Thomas seems not to be well founded. Among the three thousand Hindoos in the country helping to propagate the Boodhist faith, frequent mention was made of a celebrated ascetic named Tamo (the full name in Sanscrit being Bodhidharma) as having come from India by sea, early in the sixth century. The first Romish missionaries, having very insufficient information on the history and religions of China, caught at the name Tamo as a Chinese form of the word Thomas; and the conceit was strengthened in their minds by the description of his character as a severe ascetic and a worker of miracles.

It is possible that the light of truth spread to China in the early ages of Christianity, as Arnobius speaks of the effects of the Gospel among the Seres, or Chinese, as also among the Persians and Medes, in the year A.D. 300. And as several monks returned from that country, about the middle of the sixth century, with the eggs of the silk-worm, it is probable that these teachers of religion had resided there for some time.

Chinese history mentions the arrival of certain priests from Ta-tsin, or Judea, who appeared at court and were approved by the Emperor, which event is placed in A.D. 639. These were doubtless Nestorian Christians. The principal record of the success of their mission is a celebrated monument in Shen-si province, discovered early in the seventeenth century by Romanists, and recently visited by Protestant missionary travelers who have given to the world a trustworthy account of the same. An inscription upon it in Chinese and Syriac contains a short history of the sect from the year 630 to 781; and also gives a summary of Christian truth.* The Churches planted by them flourished for several generations, and acquired considerable influence at court and among the people. Bishops and archbishops were appointed from Persia, their ecclesiastical headquarters. But this oriental Church by degrees lost its ardent faith, its evangelistic enthusiasm, and departed from the truth and simplicity of the Gospel; and its dependent societies in China, no longer visited by spiritual teachers from abroad, gradually declined, until the last of their converts were incorporated in Catholic missions. It has been affirmed, however, that "there is reason for supposing that in certain mountain districts whole villages and tribes of Nestorian Christians are still found, and that they have preserved to this day the Scriptures among them." Through the instrumentality of some of these early missionaries, the art of writing was introduced among the Mongols; and a monument of their enterprise and skill is seen in the present Mongolian alphabet, which is also that used by the Manchoos, or ruling Tartars, it being a modification of the Syrian character.†

Rome began her first formal efforts for the conversion of China under Pope Innocent IV, more than six hundred years ago; but it was not until she sought to recover in

---

* "Christianity in China," by Abbé Huc; Williamson's "Journeys in North China " vol. i, pp. 380-383.

† Edkin's "Religious Condition of the Chinese," p. 19.

the East her losses by the Reformation in the West, that she seriously set about the work of evangelization. In passing along the coast of China, on his way to and from Japan, Francis Xavier felt his soul fired with a strong desire to proclaim the tidings of salvation to the multitudes dwelling in this vast empire. His amazing courage and perseverance brought him at length to the island of San-shan, about thirty miles southwest of Macao, where death closed his illustrious career. Xavier fell at the threshold of China, his great enterprise seemingly brought to an end; but his zeal in this direction led others to undertake the mission. Various attempts were made by the Dominican, Augustine and Franciscan orders to enter the country, but they all proved unsuccessful. Valignano, the superior of Romish missions, residing in Macao, as he walked over the hills in the neighborhood of that city, would often cast his eyes across the bay to the coast of China and exclaim, "Oh, Rock, Rock, when wilt thou open!" He finally selected three Jesuits, Paccio, Roger, and Ricci, to carry out, if possible, the undertaking he had so much at heart.*

The second period in the history of Romish missions in this country properly begins with the time when Matteo Ricci established himself at Canton, in the year 1581. This remarkable man, after a residence of seventeen years in various provincial cities, at length passed through the interior of the country to Peking, where he made the most artful use of his scientific attainments in carrying forward his important enterprise. A number of European scholars of the Jesuit class soon joined him, who

* "Modern Christian Missions," by Rev. M. J. Knowlton, in "North China Herald"; republished in "The Chinese Recorder," April 1870.

added greatly to the celebrity of the mission. While they were engaged in the capital, other propagandists were less conspicuously but effectively employed in the provinces.

Ricci became very influential at court, and succeeded in converting to the Catholic faith several high officials. Of these, Paul Siu, a native of Shanghai, was chief; his daughter, also, who took at her baptism the name Candida, became a zealous adherent. This lady, married at the age of sixteen and left a widow with eight children at thirty, after reserving a sufficient portion of her income for the support of her family, devoted the rest of her ample fortune and the remaining forty-three years of her life to benevolent Christian work. She erected, at her own expense, thirty-nine churches with as many priestly residences, in various parts of the empire. She also printed one hundred and thirty books prepared by the missionaries, established a hospital for abandoned infants, "and seeing many blind people telling stories for a livelihood, she caused a number of them to be instructed, and sent them forth to relate the events of the Gospel and sacred history." After reaching a venerable age, and having spent more than a generation in deeds of charity and in various efforts to promote the religion she professed, the Emperor conferred on her the title of *Shojin*, or "virtuous woman,"—a most distinguished mark of His Majesty's favor, the fame of which was spread abroad in the provinces.*

Her worthy example was emulated by another lady of rank, who bore the Christian name of Agatha.

The success of Ricci, who had been appointed superior

* "The Chinese Recorder," April 1870. p. 313.

of all the missions by the general of the order, awakened the jealousy and bitter opposition of the *literati*. A persecution arose, which continued four or five years, and an imperial edict was obtained commanding the missionaries to depart from Peking to Canton, there to embark for Europe; but, taking the opportunity of a critical state in the affairs of the government, Paul Siu memorialized the throne in behalf of the missionaries and secured their recall. This persecution was preceded by the death of Ricci, and for some time there was no one of sufficient ability to take his place. Paul Siu, however, continued to exert his great influence in their favor, and the missions flourished under his patronage. In the year 1628, John Adam Schaal, a German Jesuit, arrived at Peking, and was favorably received by the Emperor. His talents and learning soon placed him in advance of all his brethren, and gave him extensive influence among the chiefs of government.

A change of dynasty occurred about this time. The Manchoos having been called in to aid in putting down two rebel chiefs, not only performed that service but proceeded to take possession of the capital and establish their own prince on the throne of the Celestial Empire. In the North, Schaal and the other missionaries prudently gave in their adhesion to the Tartar rule, while in the South the Christians joined the Ming standard. A pseudo-emperor, under the title of Tung-li, established his seat of government in one of the cities of Kwang-tung province, his cause having been valiantly and successfully championed by two Christian Chinese generals, Thomas Kiu and Luke Chin. Tung-li's mother, wife and son were baptized with the names Helen, Maria and Constantine. Pope Alexander VII was induced to give some sort of recognition to this movement, and the southern missionaries were permitted for a time to indulge the hope of witnessing a procession of occurrences in the Far East which would find their parallel alone in the great events of early Latin Christianity. But this expectation of having a Chinese "Constantine the Great" was soon cut off by the untimely death of their emperor and the establishment of the Manchoo, or Ta-ching, dynasty. During these troublous times, extending over a period of thirty years (1630–1660), the missions suffered much, as the priests retired to places of safety from the molestations of soldiers and banditti, and the converts were left without spiritual instruction.

The first Manchoo emperor, Shun-chi, conceived a friendship for Schaal and his coadjutors. The able and artful Jesuit was commissioned to reform the calendar, and he accomplished the task with honor to himself and prestige to the cause he really had at heart. He subsequently received the appointment of President of the Astronomical Board, with the title and authority of an officer of the highest grade. It is said that the youthful Emperor condescended to terms of familiar intercourse with him, and often visited him at his own residence. During the reign of this monarch the missions enjoyed a marked degree of prosperity, their greatest success being in Shensi, where in former times the Nestorians were very numerous.

When Kang-hi came to the throne he was but eight years old, and Schaal became his tutor. The foreign teacher, however, was not long allowed to enjoy his eminence. A distinguished literary man published a book full of false accusations against the Romish priests. Influenced by the statements thus made public, the four regents pronounced the sentence of death on the missionaries, and condemned Schaal "to be cut into ten thousand pieces." But these servants of the Pope were not permitted to receive the crown of martyrdom, as the execution was delayed, and they were finally set at liberty, although Schaal sank under his reverses and died at the age of seventy-eight. Missionaries in all parts of the country were arrested, and three Dominicans, one Franciscan and twenty-one Jesuits were banished to Canton, four priests only being allowed in Peking.

At fifteen years of age Kang-hi assumed the reins of government. Ferdinand Verbiest, who was recognized as the natural successor of Schaal, and had been reinstated in his office in the Astronomical Board, presented a memorial for the recall of his banished brethren. The petition was favorably received, and the priests were put in possession of their churches, but were forbidden to make converts. The imperial order being secretly disregarded, no less than twenty thousand neophytes were baptized during the first year of the restoration, and the Emperor's maternal uncle was soon after added to the number. An Arabian astronomer, who, in constructing the Imperial Almanac, had committed the egregious blunder of inserting an intercalary month in the current lunar year which should have consisted of only twelve lunations, afforded Père Verbiest an occasion for proving the superiority of his own science. He also added to his renown by publishing a book, entitled "The Perpetual Astronomy of the Emperor Kang-hi"; and His

Majesty was so well pleased with the work that he made the author an officer of the first rank, conferred on him the title of *Ta-jin*, or "Magnate," and ennobled all his kindred. Kang-hi, in a famous visit to the provinces, on several occasions showed more favor to the Jesuit missionaries than to his own officers; and this example of the court was followed by the mandarins in all parts of the empire. The smothered feeling of hatred on the part of some of the officials would occasionally burst out in a flame of persecution; but even this critical state of affairs had a happy result, as it gave occasion for the Emperor's proclamation in favor of Christianity.

These were "the palmy days of Roman Catholicism in China." Several propagandists are said to have baptized one thousand or one thousand five hundred persons annually, and in the single province of Kiang-nan they are believed to have numbered at one time one hundred churches and one hundred thousand converts. Jesuits, Dominicans and Franciscans, from Italy, France and Spain, flocked to the land. Louis XIV became greatly interested in this distant province of the Pope's empire, and appointed the sum of nine thousand two hundred livres as a pension to twenty of the self-denying missionaries. The Jesuits were fortunate enough to cure the Emperor of a dangerous fever, who, in token of his gratitude, devoted a portion of ground within the Imperial City near the palace to sacred purposes, and contributed largely toward the erection of a church. Between the years 1708 and 1718, a geographical survey of the empire was accomplished by order of Kang-hi, under the direction of nine Jesuits employed for the express purpose; and all reliable maps of China are founded on the results of this remarkable survey.

The great success of the Romanists, in the reign of one of the most celebrated of the rulers of China, might have resulted in a triumph for Catholicism unsurpassed by any other achievement of the Propaganda, but for their own dissensions, which led the Pope to interfere, and so precipitated a conflict between His Holiness and the Dragon Throne. These disputes related mainly to ancestral worship and the Chinese term for God, subjecting to the perils of debate some of the most ancient and honored institutions of the land, besides involving incidentally questions of spiritual and temporal supremacy. The case, according to competent authority, stood as follows : "Decree of Innocent X, in 1655, condemning ancestral worship as idolatrous and sinful; decree of Alexander VII, 1656, approving such worship as being but a mere civil institution; decree of Clement XI, in 1704, condemning ancestral worship; answer to the petitions of Jesuits, in 1700, from Kang-hi, in which he declared *T'een* meant the true God, and that the customs of China were merely political; decree of the Emperor, 1706, declaring that he would countenance only those missionaries who allowed ancestral worship, and that he would persecute those who followed the opposite practice."* The Pope's first legate to Peking, Tournon, sent out in 1703, after studying the situation a few years, issued two decrees in opposition to the Emperor, which so incensed His Majesty that he expelled the ecclesiastic from his capital. About this time he also banished several priests

---

"The Chinese Recorder," May 1870 p. 342.

from the country, and allowed a severe persecution to rage in several of the provinces.

With the alienation of their powerful friend, the Emperor, passed away the glory and prosperity of the Jesuits in China. When Yung-ching ascended the throne, in 1723, remonstrances and petitions from the officials and literati were sent in great numbers to Peking, "complaining that Kang-hi had shown the foreign teachers too much favor, and that they were a dangerous class, because their converts acknowledged no other authority than the priests." The subject was referred to the Board of Rites, by whose advice the Emperor issued a decree the following year, retaining those priests already near the throne for the service of the state, but banishing all others to Canton and Macao. Those in Peking were permitted to celebrate divine worship, but were restrained from proselyting. The sentence against the other missionaries was rigorously executed; and many of their churches were either destroyed, changed to Boodhist temples, or converted to other uses,— leaving more than three hundred thousand converts without adequate pastoral supervision or the rites of the Church. The government, however, did not fully accomplish the object sought in this persecution, as many of the priests revisited by stealth their scattered and suffering flocks, and not a few of the native pastors proved themselves worthy of the trust committed to their hands.

In the reign of Kien-lung a fresh search was made for foreign priests, when churches were plundered and property confiscated; and Peter Seng, with five of his Dominican brethren, in Fooh-kien province, were put to death, besides other agents of the Church being seized and tortured. In 1784, four missionaries, detected on their way to Shen-si, were sent in chains to Peking. This circumstance arousing the native suspicion and hatred, another fierce persecution arose. An imperial edict was issued against the Roman Catholics, every effort being made to apprehend the foreigners wherever concealed in any part of the empire; and their native adherents were severely dealt with. Of the priests sent as captives to Peking, one died of hardship on the way, five succumbed under ill treatment after arriving at their destination, and twelve were allowed to languish in prison. A number of native priests and assistants who had accompanied them were branded on the face and banished to Tartary as slaves for life. Amid the fiery trials through which they were called to pass, many of the missionaries exhibited a high type of courage and devotion, as in the instance of three of their number who generously delivered themselves up in order to save their flocks from peril and distress on their account; while multitudes of native Christians throughout the empire remained steadfast amid the gathering storm. In subsequent periods of persecution, a number of priests suffered martyrdom, eminent among whom was Dufresse, Bishop of Sze-chuen, who was beheaded. The above-named province, considered after Peking itself, as the principal theater of Romish influence, witnessed the varying fortunes of missions until 1824, when the Sze-chuen college was recommenced; since which time the work of propagandism has been quietly carried on, with occasionally some interference from the enemies of the faith. In 1833 there was but one foreign priest in the capital, and after his death there were none to take his place for several years.

A candid observer of Catholicism in China will not only admit that many of its agents displayed a zeal and heroism deserving of the highest praise, and worthy of being imitated by their Protestant brethren in the foreign field, but must confess that without doubt multitudes have been brought to a saving knowledge of Christianity through their labors. Still, the truth of history requires the statement that it has been too much the policy of the spiritual delegates of Rome to accommodate themselves to Chinese idolatrous practices. It is said that Ricci, who must be regarded as the real founder of Romish missions in China, lived for seven years with the Boodhist priests, adopting their peculiar dress, imitating their manners, and humoring their prejudices. According to one author, he and Roger sought "to conceal their real intention, recurring unblushingly to a falsehood, affirming that their only wishes were to make themselves masters of the Chinese language, and to become acquainted with the arts and sciences of the country."* He is charged with going so far as to disfigure the religion of Christ "by a faithful mixture of pagan superstitions, adopting the sacrifices offered to Confucius and ancestors, and teaching the Christians to assist and coöperate in the worship of idols, provided they only addressed their devotions to a cross covered with flowers, or secretly attached to one of the candles which were lighted in the temples of the false gods." It is but just to say, however, that he so far compromised the truth of Christianity as to call forth protests and opposition in his own Church. As evidence of the fact that this eminent Jesuit continued his doubtful practices to the end, it may be mentioned that the symbols of Boodhist idolatry are found before his tomb in the cemetery near Peking.

---

* Sir Andrew Ljungstedt's "Macao," quoted in "Chinese Repository," vol. i, p. 136.

The incense urns, candlesticks, and flower-jars, cut in marble and arranged in the order followed in all Boodhist temples, show a willingness up to the time of his death to use idolatrous customs.

We are told that the first monk who visited the Mongal Tartar court " was rather pleased than scandalized by the near resemblance of the rites of the Chinese Boodhists to the forms of Catholic worship," although another distinguished Romanist did not so look upon the striking similarity, and declared that the Boodhist religion had been invented by the Devil for the express purpose of bringing a reproach upon the Mother Church!

It is true that the successors of these men have been in the habit of calling pagan images idols and styling Romish idols images: but the heathen are not quick to recognize such nice distinctions; nor even the converts themselves, we may suppose, as the commandment against idol worship has been thrust out of the decalogue by their foreign teachers. Messrs. Gabet and Huc, two French priests of the order of Lazarists, while on a journey to Thibet, had a molten image made for their own adoration, from a European model, which was not only the work of men's but pagan hands, and was made at a place where a huge image of Boodha had just been cast and forwarded to Lhassa. In parts of the country, at stated times in the year, Roman Catholics have processions in honor of the Holy Mother, which do not differ from the heathen processions in any respect except that an image of the Virgin is paraded in the place of the usual Chinese idol. As may be inferred, a high standard of morality and religious instruction is not generally maintained among the native Christians. The word of

God does not have free circulation among them, and they do not keep inviolate the Sabbath day.

The knowledge of the sciences was at first successfully employed, as we have seen, in securing influence among the ruling classes. The Jesuits amused the court with a variety of philosophical experiments of an ingenious nature; such as producing artificial rainbows from the transmission of the rays of light through prisms, with their subsequent reflection. They also exhibited the uses of the telescope and the microscope, and employed with great effect a *camera obscura*, by means of which every object passing outside was made visible on a table within the apartments of the palace. They presented to Kang-hi the first clocks and watches seen in China. Pumps, syphons and fountains, constructed by them according to the most recently discovered principles of hydrostatics and hydraulics, were applied to purposes of use and ornament in the imperial grounds.*

After Schaal, who obtained such distinguished honors at the court of the first Manchoo emperor, succeeding missionaries were officially employed for two hundred years to assist or direct in observing the motions of the heavenly bodies, and in constructing the calendar. Two of their number pleased the emperors by their skill in casting cannon. Verbiest at one time cast three hundred and twenty pieces, and then blessed his work in a solemn manner, giving the name of a saint to every piece. A set of very fine instruments of gray bronze made by him while president of the Board of Works, consisting of a celestial globe, a sextant, a quadrant, a sun dial, etc., are to be seen to this day in the Astronomical Observatory

* Davis' " China and the Chinese," vol. ii. 276; Sears' " China and India," p. 98.

at Peking, and among them may be noticed, also, a large azimuth instrument, sent as a present to Kang-hi by the King of France. All the distinguished Jesuits were best known either as geographers, mathematicians, astronomers, inspectors of cannon, political negotiators, or artful diplomatists.

Few missions in pagan lands have been favored with the sympathy of the rich and noble so much as the early papal missions to China, or have enjoyed to a greater degree the patronage of the ruling power. Their nominal success was no doubt at one time very great, although so soon followed by a period of dearth and persecution. The perpetual strife among the priests themselves first invited the active hostility of their foes. But when they began to assume the honors and the functions of political power, and the papal assumption proceeded to the length of a public invasion of imperial sovereignty, it was but natural that the Emperors should denounce them as disturbers of the peace and take measures to drive them out of the country. Sir Rutherford Alcock, late British minister at Peking, in a work on Japan, remarks: "The determining cause of the downfall and the destruction of the Roman Church in Japan, is to be sought in the pretensions to a spiritual supremacy, which is but another name for the monopoly of power, since all that is political or secular must bow to God's vicegerent on earth, who claims the right to bind and to loosen, to absolve subjects of their oath and fealty, and dethrone kings by his edict." A similar cause in China produced a like effect, only less destructive in its havoc among the Catholic societies and establishments.

Although the Romanists have not recovered their

ancient power, it must not be thought that they are now either inactive or unsuccessful. According to recent statistics,—which are presumed to be reasonably accurate,—they have in the Celestial Empire forty bishops, four hundred and fifty foreign and five hundred native priests, forty sisters of charity who have in charge thousands of orphans, sixty colleges with learned professors and many students, and five hundred thousand communicants. They have two great churches in Peking, one of which, the French cathedral, is an imposing structure of white marble, and adjoining are the palatial residence of the bishop and homes of the priests. At Canton a cathedral has been for many years in process of erection that will, when completed, exceed in magnificence any sacred structure on this continent, excepting, perhaps, the grand cathedral on Fifth Avenue, New York. At Kiu-kiang, the holy fathers engage in the tea trade, with native converts to do the outside business, where they have been known to reap a profit in one year of ten thousand dollars. In Shanghai, the Jesuit fathers annually receive one hundred thousand dollars through the Agra Bank for church purposes; and one of their number controls two million dollars for the Church. Under French protection they have regained their confiscated estates, have erected cathedrals and multiplied churches. Their bishops and priests assume the habits and authority of civil mandarins. They give great attention to schools and orphan asylums, and by this means obtain almost absolute control over vast numbers of children.

The government of France affords every protection to the foreign priests in their work, and to native converts in the exercise of their religious rights. It has been said that the power of all the Protestant missionaries combined would have failed in the attempt to erect a church surmounted by a cross overlooking the Emperor's palace; and yet the Romish missionaries, backed by French influence, lately succeeded in doing this. A French consul recently went to the length of calling Protestants to account for distributing "Pilgrim's Progress," in which he considered his religion was spoken of disrespectfully.

Certain European representatives of the Pope have thought it necessary to protest against Protestantism in China, and accordingly have sought to impress their converts with such statements as that the faith taught by themselves is not the same as the "American religion"; that the religion of the English is only three hundred years old, and had its origin in the fact that King Henry VIII was not allowed by the papal Father to divorce his wife; that their own is the true and ancient form of Christianity; and that salvation is only to be found within the pale of the Catholic Church.

The old antagonisms existing in this country and in Europe are destined to be renewed in the Far East. Protestantism must speedily occupy that field with a well equipped army of heroic missionary workers, or she will soon have to contend at a great disadvantage with the vast forces of paganism on the one side, and a legionary foe of kindred blood but hostile faith, powerfully entrenched, on the other.

CHAPTER X.

PROTESTANT MISSIONS.

THE conversion of Robert Morrison, and his call to be a laborer in distant and destitute parts of the world, were simultaneous events. The spirit of God found him an apprentice in the humble capacity of last and boot-tree maker, at about the age of sixteen. Yielding to divine impressions, he consecrated himself unto the Lord, and his prayer was "that God would station him in that part of the missionary field where the difficulties were the greatest, and, to all human appearance, the most insurmountable." Although remaining in his father's workshop, he at once began his studies and his Christian labors for the conversion of others. He toiled with his hands twelve hours a day, often with the Bible open before him. The very next day after his apprenticeship was completed he entered at Hoxton Academy, and thence, in due course, went to the Theological School at Gosport. In February 1807, just after completing his twenty-fifth year, he was appointed to China by the London Missionary Society. As the East India Company refused all missionaries passage in their ships either to China or to India, he proceeded by way of New York, arriving at Macao in September, but soon took up his residence in Canton. For some time he observed a quiet and unobtrusive manner of life, occupying a room in one of the American factories, and applying himself to the language with such diligence as seriously to affect his health. His better judgment impelling him to a more public and social habit, he was much encouraged by restored vigor and newly-awakened sympathy among the foreign residents.

At first he had to encounter much opposition from his own countrymen. The well-known policy of the East India Company, the gigantic immoralities perpetrated in the name of commerce and under the plea of necessity, the public, private and social vices which seem to have spontaneous and natural growth in every isolated European community where the restraints of home and religion are unknown, were influences unfriendly to the work of a Christian missionary, and even more to be dreaded than the ignorance and superstition of paganism. The interdict laid upon foreigners going into the interior, and the prejudice and hostility existing on all sides among the people, arising from unhappy conflicts between the local mandarins and foreign merchants, as also between the imperial government and the Jesuits, rendered impolitic, if not impossible, any direct public attempt to propagate Christianity.

But this first and lone representative of Protestant evangelism in the Chinese empire fortunately won the friendship of Sir George T. Staunton, and of Mr. Roberts, the chief of the British factory at Canton. The latter advised him to undertake as his great missionary work the translation of the sacred Scriptures into the Chinese language. His linguistic talents were soon in demand, and in 1809 he accepted the appointment of translator under the East India Company. This position secured him official connection, immunity from petty persecutions, and a salary sufficient to provide for his family and enable him to carry on his studies without much expense to the Society. The entire New Testament was published in 1814, about half of it having been translated by Morrison, the remainder being a revision of a manuscript which he had found in the British Museum. He also undertook the compilation of an Anglo-Chinese dictionary, and in this important enterprise received the generous support of the wealthy corporation whose servant he was. The work was completed in six large volumes in 1823, at a total expense of about sixty thousand dollars, and it has been an invaluable aid to students of Chinese literature, alike indispensable in mercantile, diplomatic and missionary circles.

During all this time Mr. Morrison did not lose sight of his mission as a preacher of the Gospel. When he had acquired a moderate command of the spoken language he commenced a private Sabbath service, which was attended by his domestics and a few other natives. Notwithstanding his great labors in translation and on the dictionary, he found leisure for the writing of tracts, as also for teaching and preaching, although the little band of hearers accustomed to assemble in his apartments never expanded into a regular public congregation during his lifetime. His first convert, Tsai Ako, was baptized in 1814, and maintained a consistent Christian character until his death four years subsequently. He rendered a valuable service to his country by accompanying Lord Amherst to Peking, in 1816, as interpreter to the embassy. Eight years later he visited England, whither his fame as a missionary and a scholar had preceded him, and was honorably received by the great and good in that Christian land. Before he had taken his departure from China he had the pleasure of ordaining a native convert, Liang A-fah, to the office and work of an evangelist, who continued faithful in his religious profession and in his love for preaching even after suffering persecution and long banishment from his native land.

During the time which elapsed between his return to China and his death Dr. Morrison was abundant in labors, giving his usual attention to the Sabbath services, and making material additions to his already long list of published works. He died in 1834, having spent almost twenty-seven years in China, and most of that time alone in the missionary work.*

Dr. Milne, a co-laborer and intimate friend, observes, with reference to his peculiar traits of character, "the patience that refuses to be conquered, the diligence that never tires, the caution that always trembles, and the studious habit that spontaneously seeks retirement, were best adapted for the first Protestant missionary to China." Realizing that the work of elevating and evangelizing the Chinese empire must be done through the language of that people, he set himself to the task of providing adequate text-books, chief of all the Holy Scriptures, being stimulated by the reflection that the results of his labors would be preserved in the living speech of a third part of the human race. Any attempt to imitate the method of Ricci would have proven futile, as China was a sealed country when Morrison landed on its shores, and the reaction against Romanism had closed the door of opportunity against all public efforts to promulgate a religion which had been placed under the social and po-

---

* Williams' "Middle Kingdom," vol. ii, pp. 325-330; "China and the Gospel," by Rev. William Muirhead, pp. 131-2.

litical ban. It is even improbable that he could have lived in the country at all without the powerful protection of the East India Company, who could not well dispense with his services. His last letter breathes the spirit of one who had well nigh accomplished a mission to which he felt divinely called, although the desire of his heart was as yet unrealized. "I wait patiently," said he, "the events to be developed in the course of Divine Providence. The Lord reigneth. If the kingdom of God our Savior prosper in China, all will be well; other matters are comparatively of small importance." But he was permitted to see the coming day of China's redemption only in promise and prophecy. Scarcely did the first twilight of its early dawn greet his eager gaze; for, after all his toil and faith and prayer, but three or four converts from the masses of heathenism around him could be gathered to receive his dying benediction.

Six years after Dr. Morrison's arrival in China he was joined by the Rev. William Milne, who was compelled by the Romish clergy to quit Macao immediately, but found refuge for a time in Canton. Soon after, Mr. Milne took his departure for the Indian Archipelago, where he labored principally among the Chinese settlements. Returning thence he attempted to resume his work at Canton and vicinity, but found it very difficult to carry out his purpose, as the Company's Committee refused to countenance him in any way, and he finally embarked for Malacca, where he spent the remainder of his life.

In 1829 the American Churches first entered this field by sending to Canton the Revs. E. C. Bridgman and David Abeel. To D. W. C. Olyphant, a devout and wealthy merchant of New York, must be ascribed the honor of being the father of the mission. The American Board of Commissioners for Foreign Missions came to a determination to commence their labors in China in consequence of his offer of a passage and a home in that country for a year to one who would undertake the work. And not only did he assume responsibility in the beginning of the enterprise, but remained its faithful and munificent friend to the end of his life. He died on his way home from his fourth visit to China, and was buried in the English cemetery at Cairo. After being told that he could not recover, he said, "I do not wish to live for the sake of worldly riches and comforts, but for the sake of missions I could have desired to remain a little longer." Such was his principle for thirty years, and he added to it the force of consistent practice.*

The first missionary efforts north of Canton, of a permanent nature, were made in 1840 by Dr. Lockhart in the establishment of a hospital at Ting-hai. But the great impetus to Protestant evangelism was given by the treaty of 1842, when the five ports were opened to foreign trade, and Hong-Kong was ceded to the Queen as British territory. Canton, Amoy, Foo-chow, Ning-po, and Shanghai were chosen in view of their adaptation for commercial purposes, but they also proved to be of special interest and importance in a missionary point of view. These centers of population and avenues to the interior were speedily occupied by the leading societies of England, Germany, and America.

The list of missionary workers sent out prior to the year 1842 numbered not less than sixty, including, besides those already mentioned, such illustrious names as Walter

* "The Life of Bridgman," edited by Eliza J. Gillett Bridgman, pp. 37, 189.

H. Medhurst, Charles Gutzlaff, S. Wells Williams, Stephen Johnson, Peter Parker, William Dean, W. J. Boone, John Stronach, James Legge, James C. Hepburn, and others. Soon after his return to this country from China, that distinguished diplomate, the Hon. Caleb Cushing, gave to the public, through the Rev. Septimus Tustin, chaplain to the United States Senate, the following testimony in favor of these self-denying laborers in the foreign field and the cause so worthily represented by them: "I have great pleasure in communicating the information desired in your favor of the 15th inst. It is true that in the late negotiations with China, the most important, not to say indispensable, service was derived from American missionaries, and more especially from Dr. Bridgman and Dr. Parker. They possessed the rare qualification of understanding the Chinese language, which enabled them to act as interpreters to the legation; their intimate knowledge of China and the Chinese made them invaluable as advisers, and their high character contributed to give weight and moral strength to the mission; and while their coöperation with me was thus of eminent utility to the United States, it will prove, I trust, not less useful to the general cause of humanity and of religion in the East. But the particular service rendered by the American missionaries in this case, is but one of a great class of facts appertaining to the whole body of Christian missionaries in China. In the first place, other legations to China have been equally dependent on the Christian missionaries for the means of intercourse with the Chinese government, of which well-known examples occur in the history of the successive British embassies of Lord Macartney, Lord Amherst, and Sir Henry

Pottinger. In the second place, the great bulk of the *general* information we possess in regard to China, and nearly the whole of the primary *philological* information concerning the two great languages of the Chinese empire, namely the Chinese and the Manchu, are derived through the missionaries, both Catholic and Protestant." Here follows a long list of philological works prepared by different missionaries, which we omit, and proceed to the concluding paragraph of Mr. Cushing's letter. "In thus briefly answering your inquiry on a single point in the history of Christian missions, namely, their *incidental* usefulness, permit me to add that, eminently great as this their incidental utility has been, it is but a small point, comparatively, among the great and good deeds of the religious missionaries in the East. There is not a nobler nor a more deeply interesting chapter than this in the history of human courage, intellect, self-sacrifice, greatness, and virtue; and it remains yet to be written in a manner worthy of the dignity of the subject, and of its relations to civilization and government as well as to the Christian Church."*

Although but few of the missionaries were able to secure permanent and safe residences within the limits of the empire during a period of thirty-five years after the arrival of Dr. Morrison, they neither abandoned their enterprise nor allowed themselves to remain idly waiting. A number of these workers had lived for years on the borders outside, at Macao, Malacca, and Batavia, bestowing their labors principally among emigrant Chinese in the countries and islands about the Straits of Sunda. When China was thrown open they were prepared to enter it with the

* "Life of Bridgman," pp. 131-134.

advantage of a previous acquaintance with the language and the character of the people.

In 1844, Dr. Medhurst, of the London Society, reached Shanghai, bringing from the mission at Georgetown in the island of Penang a well-equipped printing office for the manufacture of books and tracts. This was an important reinforcement to the work undertaken at Macao and Canton, a number of years previously, by the Rev. E. C. Bridgman and S. Wells Williams, of the American Board. The "Bruen Press" issued the first number of the *Chinese Repository* in 1832, published by Mr. Bridgman, who continued to conduct it until the year 1851, after which Dr. Williams was sole editor of the work to its twentieth volume. The magazine was issued at irregular intervals, as the necessary manuscript could be furnished, the object being to "impart information concerning China, and so to arouse an interest in the spiritual and social welfare of her millions." This publication having proven of great value, both as to direct missionary intelligence and in the field of Oriental scholarship, similar attempts have since been made, first from the Foo-chow Methodist Episcopal Mission Press and later at Shanghai.

No translation of the Scriptures has ever been published in China by the Romanists;* but Protestant missionaries have from the first regarded the giving of the Bible to the millions of that country as a matter of high importance. The first attempt of this kind, in which Morrison was aided toward the last by Milne, was attended by circumstances of peculiar difficulty and embarrassment. The East India Company did but little, as a body, for the encouragement of Chinese literature, beyond a small annual grant to the

* Edkins' "Religious Condition of the Chinese," p. 235.

Anglo-Chinese College at Malacca, and the printing of Morrison's dictionary; and, although that learned missionary was their official translator for twenty-five years, the Directors not only never contributed one penny for carrying on his work of translating and printing the Bible, but set themselves against all such efforts.* The difficulties thus encountered, together with the imperfect understanding of certain philological questions, had conspired to produce an edition of the Scriptures which, though deserving of very great commendation, was still open to much improvement. As the missionaries increased in numbers and efficiency, it was deemed needful that a revision or new translation of the New Testament should be made. A Committee of Delegates was appointed for this purpose, representing the principal English and American Societies, consisting of the Rev. Drs. Medhurst, Bridgman and Boone, with Messrs. John Stronach and Walter Lowrie. The last named lost his life soon after at the hands of pirates while on his way to Ningpo, and Bishop Boone was prevented by infirm health from engaging in the work to any great extent. The Committee began its labors at Shanghai in the summer of 1847, and the result was a scholarly production, clear and idiomatic in its style, and deemed by many a true and faithful translation into the Chinese language. As the Delegates were thought to possess peculiar qualifications for the work, it was resolved to commit to them the task of translating the Old Testament, the Rev. William C. Milne being added to their number. The year 1854 witnessed the completion of their undertaking, in the presentation to the native Churches of China of a complete standard Bible in the classic lan-

* Williams' "Middle Kingdom," vol. ii, p. 465.

guage of their own country, which was followed, however, some two or three years later, by a revision of the whole at the hands of Dr. Bridgman and the Rev. M. Simpson Culbertson.* A committee was engaged for six years on a version of the New Testament in the Mandarin colloquial language, completing their task in 1872. The Old Testament, in the same dialect, was translated by the Rev. Joseph Schereschewsky, now missionary bishop of the American Episcopal Church, and published in 1874. This last complete version of the Bible into the Chinese language, in style, idiom, and diffusiveness of expression, approaches the spoken language of North and Central China more nearly than the Delegates' Version, and is, therefore, more readily understood and approved by the common people. Numerous editions have been issued, in whole or in part, adapted to the various Southern dialects.

Missionaries generally have given much attention to the distribution of the Word of Life, but the British and Foreign Bible Society early resolved to make every attempt to circulate it far and wide through the empire. Accordingly, in 1863, the services of Mr. Alexander Wylie, for some time in charge of the printing establishment at Shanghai, were engaged for the special work of superintending the circulation of the Scriptures. Since then that gentleman has traveled more or less in fourteen of the provinces, having two Europeans associated with him as colporteurs. The National Bible Society of Scotland has accomplished much in the same direction; its agent, the Rev. Alexander Williamson, having distinguished himself by his extensive journeys in Manchooria, Mongolia, and

---

* Muirhead's "China and the Gospel," pp. 140-144; "The Bible, in China," by A. Wylie, Esq., pp. 10-12.

several northern provinces. The work of the American Bible Society in China, under the general superintendence of the Rev. L. H. Gulick, M.D., has been carried on from the three principal centers,— Peking, Shanghai and Foochow,— where the Scriptures are printed and kept in store by the mission presses. The Sacred Volume has thus been scattered in the most thorough and systematic manner, chiefly by sale at small prices, and must have been placed in the hands of a vast number of people.

A practical method in the art of printing, combining both rapid and neat execution, was a *desideratum* at an early day in the history of missions. A set of more than a hundred thousand Chinese types had been cut in wood at Paris, but they were so large and cumbrous as to be of little service in ordinary presswork. Specimens of movable type were executed by private firms in England from time to time, and Mr. Watts completed a font quite in advance of anything of the kind before attempted. But the honor of completely overcoming the initial difficulties in this important enterprise was reserved for Protestant missionaries actually in the field. The zeal and devotedness of the Rev. Samuel Dyer, for some time stationed at Penang, achieved the first real success. By a combination of native labor with European art, he succeeded in bringing out a font of unsurpassed elegance, and at a practicable cost. Since then, William Gamble,— who in 1858 became superintendent of the Presbyterian Mission Press in China,— after numerous experiments at Shanghai, succeeded in applying electric science to the perfection of the art, and printing by movable types is now as much a matter of course in Chinese as in any European language, not only in the mission presses at Hong-Kong,

Foo-chow, Shanghai and Peking, but to some extent in native establishments, where the advantage of this method is coming to be understood and appreciated, especially when small or fine print is desired.*

The first agents of the Propaganda gave much attention to literature; and while some of their books contain the purest Christian truth, others teach frivolous superstitions,— illustrating and enforcing celibacy, the celebration of the mass, the making of pilgrimages to holy places, and relating miraculous incidents in the lives of Chinese saints. From data within our reach, we are compelled to the conclusion that the modern Romish missionaries write but few new works on secular or religious subjects. They content themselves with the use of the old ones, although the scientific treatises are based on obsolete theories, such as the Ptolemaic system of the universe instead of the Copernican, and the "four elements" — fire, air, earth, and water — hypothesis in natural philosophy, no change being made in any of their text-books on the basis of recent improvements in the mathematical sciences.†

Their Protestant brethren, however, largely devote their learning and enthusiasm to the production of works in almost every department of research, from the tract and school-primer up to portly volumes for the library of the student and scholar. A large proportion of this literature will compare favorably with the works of our best authors in the West, no inconsiderable part consisting of simple translations of standard English, German and American

---

* "Notes on Chinese Literature," by A. Wylie, in the preface. "Publications of Protestant Missionaries," by same author, in preface.

† Edkins' "Religious Condition of the Chinese," pp. 247-8.

books, competent native talent generally being employed to assist in giving the requisite idiom and classic finish.

A volume issued from the press at Shanghai, in 1867, entitled "Memorials of Protestant Missionaries," etc., gives a list of their publications in Chinese to the number of seven hundred and forty-six, including one hundred and eighty-nine in the various dialects, forty-eight of the latter being Roman and eight Phonetic. A great majority of these works are placed under the general head of Theology, but the remainder are classified as Sacred Biography, Catechism, Prayers, Hymns, Miscellaneous, Educational and Linguistic, History, Government, Geography, Mathematics, Astronomy, Medicine, Botany, Physics, Almanacs, Serials, etc. To these might have been added a catalogue of works for the German and English speaking public, embracing a wide range of topics, and containing invaluable contributions to the fund of human knowledge. Not least to be esteemed are some of the translations from the multitudinous native literature,—conspicuously Dr. Legge's "Chinese Classics," with Prolegomena and Commentary. A celebrated American divine thus eloquently expressed his appreciation of what is attempted and may yet be accomplished in China by missionary authorship: "When once you have mastered the written language you command a common medium of thought for the empire; for although, from the diversity of the local dialects, the people of different provinces cannot understand each other's language, they can each other's writing. In this respect China has the advantage of India, where twenty-nine languages are spoken. No other language puts a man in communication with so large a portion of the human race. Alexander conquered the world, but he could not communicate with it. Rome laid her belt of a thousand miles around the Mediterranean, but her empire was a Babel. England puts her arms around the globe, but her tongue cannot reach a hundred million souls; nor can the French, or the German, or the Sclavic. The Arabic possibly may, but the Chinese may reach hundreds of millions. Indeed, the human race may not very unequally be divided into two portions: 1. The Chinese; 2. All other nations. To reach the latter you need three thousand and sixty-three languages; to reach the first, only one. Happy the genius who shall write parables for the heart of this mass! thrice happy he who shall write songs of Zion for this choir of three or four hundred millions of human tongues!"*

In a country where learning is so highly esteemed that the ambitious and intelligent of all classes aspire to a knowledge of letters, the missionary is compelled to give early attention to schools. This has been done with eminent success at the treaty ports and in many of the interior stations. Thousands of children and youth have thus been placed under Christian instruction, and several theological seminaries are serving well the purpose of their founders.

It has been asserted that "no argument from miracles or any other is so impressive to the heathen mind as the conduct, the life, of a missionary or a convert, resulting from the power of the Gospel Spirit." One leading element in the mysterious influence of a good life is disinterested benevolence. Modern medical science, as applied by the missionary physician, is to the heathen not only well-nigh miraculous, but it is a new and striking reve-

* Bishop Thomson, before the A. M. E. M. Society, in 1864.

lation of beneficent interest in their welfare. Dr. Morrison took the lead in this form of Christian work when, in 1820, with Dr. Livingstone, of the East India Company's factory, he opened a dispensary at Macao, in which medical relief was afforded to many persons. A few years later Dr. Colledge, also connected with the Company, who was supported to a limited extent by contributions from the foreign community, undertook with great success a similar enterprise. The benevolent doctor received letters from many of his patients expressing grateful appreciation of the aid rendered them. From among these, one poetical effusion has been preserved, in which the writer, who had been healed of a painful disease of the eyes, returned thanks in true Chinese style, as follows:

> "He lavishes his blessings, but seeks for no return;
> Such medicine, such physician, since Tsin, were never known;
> The medicine — how many kinds most excellent has he!
> The surgeon's knife — it pierced the eye, and Spring once more
>   I see.
> If Tung has not been born again, to bless the present age
> Then sure, 'tis Su reanimate again upon the stage.
> Whenever called away from far, to see your native land,
> A living monument I'll wait upon the ocean's strand."

In 1835 Dr. Parker opened, in Canton, a hospital for the gratuitous relief and cure of diseases among the Chinese, since which time the best professional skill has been applied in this form of missionary work at nearly all the centers of foreign influence, conspicuously at Shanghai, Peking, Han-kow, and Tien-tsin. The recent opening of the London Mission hospital in the last-named city must be regarded as an epochal event. Viceroy Li Hung-chang, who had contributed four thousand taels, about six thousand dollars, toward the erection and equipment of the building, presided on the occasion, attended by forty high officials. His Excellency was escorted to a raised seat in the waiting room, where he sat regarding with evident complacency the assembled native and foreign guests. An address was read, in elegant Chinese style, by Dr. Mackenzie's teacher, to which the Viceroy replied in complimentary terms. He was then led about the premises, showing by his quick, ready glance and questions how deep and genuine was his interest in the work he had so fully inaugurated in China. Returning to his seat of state, he listened to addresses from the Russian and British consuls, making appropriate replies to them; and when the British consul expressed the wish and hope of all present that this noble benevolence might add greater fame to the Viceroy's name than had ever come to him through the glory and the consequent suffering of war, he said he had done what he had done as a matter of personal duty to the multitudes of Tien-tsin and Chih-li. On the following Sunday, a religious meeting of prayer and praise fitly ended the consecration of the hospital, from whose dispensary two thousand patients had already received substantial tokens of the foreigner's healing art.

Foreign lady physicians, although but recently beginning their work, have found a field of usefulness rapidly opening before them. They have been called in repeated instances to attend the wives of Mandarins and to go long distances into the country to visit poor women. Miss Leonora Howard, M.D., located at Tien-tsin, has been especially fortunate in reaching both the upper and lower classes through her female patients. The wife of Viceroy Li is chief among her patrons, and she has free access to and great influence over many ladies of high rank.

The various medical missions in China have achieved gratifying results, and are permitted constantly to repeat in a measure the "miracles of healing" with which Christianity was inaugurated. In the language of Dr. Williams, who has had abundant opportunity to observe their workings, "the experience of past years in China has conclusively shown that where a physician and a preacher join their labors in a missionary hospital, both of them speaking the language, few plans are better adapted for removing prejudice, relieving disease and pain, otherwise irremediable, collecting audiences well fitted for patiently hearing the Gospel, and imparting a knowledge of its great truths to people rendered somewhat ready to lend a willing ear by a sense of suffering and experience of the unbought kindness bestowed upon them."

But the chief reliance in the work of evangelism is the oral proclamation of the Gospel,— first, by the foreign missionary, directly to the people without the aid of interpreters; and, secondly, by native preachers, who have been providentially raised up and duly qualified for their sacred office. Under the profound conviction that the darkness of heathenism has no power of its own to turn itself into day, and that it can only be dispelled by the light,— finding much assurance, not only in the promise which accompanies the Great Commission, but in the fact that the Gospel, as proclaimed by humble and obscure men, achieved its first victories in the high places of Greek and Roman civilization, a civilization conspicuous for the wealth of its culture as also for the wonders of its corruption,— the Protestant missionary goes forth to preach the glad tidings which shall be to all people. He does not always confine himself to stated places and times of worship; but in populous thoroughfares, in public tea-gardens, in the area of some frequented temple, or in the open market-place, he takes his stand, and by earnest speech attracts and holds the attention of the multitude. He also makes extended tours into the unknown regions beyond, seeking every opportunity in the cities and villages to herald his message of salvation.

In the more advanced stages of this work much use is made of public chapels. Many of these are open daily; and in some instances, a staff of preachers maintain the services for three or four hours at a time. It was once estimated that, in the seven stations in China of the London Society, together with their chief outposts, the number of separate services carried on amounted to not less than one hundred and forty a week, or more than seven thousand a year; while the sermons, addresses, conversations, and discussions, amounted to thrice that number.* The regular Sabbath services for native members of the Church are attended by orderly and attentive congregations; and the foreign missionary, notwithstanding all defects of manner, idiom, accent, and tone, is usually the favorite preacher.

Otherwise than heretofore in India, the congregations in China contain people of all classes. It is no disgrace for a literary gentleman, or a man of wealth or official title, to be seen listening to a Christian teacher. As to the method of discourse to heathen audiences, the more experienced missionaries seek some adaptation to the circumstances and capacity of their hearers. The address of St. Paul to the Athenians furnishes them an excellent model, which, intentionally or not, they often imitate with much

---

* Dr. Mullen's Report for 1866.

effect,—dwelling upon the first principles of natural religion in opposition to their atheism and idolatry, and finding sometimes a decided advantage in quotations from the native classics. But attacks upon idolatry and superstition are usually received with good humor and careless assent. The hearer may even enjoy the destruction of popular fallacies, as he has never had any hearty faith in them. Custom is mightier with him than logic, and he does not recognize so much the sinfulness as the absurdity of prevalent notions. It is necessary to put forth moral appeals; to speak of duty, and purity, and love; to proclaim more distinctly the supreme Lord of the universe, the true object of worship, who is not only the Father and the Benefactor of all, but who, in his wise and holy sovereignty, has appointed a day in the which he will judge the world in righteousness. This may be received by the listener with uneasy attention and in doubtful mood, but still without any inclination to dispute. But when the preacher begins to proclaim the more peculiar doctrines of Christianity, he does not always carry along with him the audience as before. The offense of the cross has not ceased. Some will hold both the messenger and his message in contempt; others will treat the subject with indifference and unconcern; while there are those who have had their interest awakened, and their attention directed savingly to eternal things.

CHAPTER XI.

HINDRANCES TO EVANGELISM.

THE difficulties attending missionary work in China are numerous and extraordinary. We shall not attempt to enumerate them all, as the scope of this volume will admit only a brief mention of such as may be most readily understood by the reader.

I. One of the most serious lies in the nature of the language. The foreign teacher and preacher are confronted on their arrival in that country with the fact that there are practically two languages to be acquired, and that each of these is probably more difficult of acquisition than any other form of speech on earth.

The written or classic language is not a representation on paper of the sounds uttered in the dialect, but is entirely distinct from it. In order to read and understand books on common topics, it is necessary to be acquainted with a large number of arbitrary characters,—certainly not less than four thousand, while any just claim to scholarship must imply familiarity with eight or ten thousand. The standard native dictionary defines about forty thousand. The labor of committing to memory even the smallest number mentioned is very great. Nothing in the character itself fixes its pronunciation, and the sound must therefore be learned from the living teacher. Many different characters are pronounced alike; and this singular difficulty is increased by the fact that, while each symbol has its peculiar tone when by itself, the several tones often modify and revert in combination. The spoken language, although essentially monosyllabic, is so characterized by tones and inflections, with aspirated and guttural modulations, that the average adult foreigner finds close application and great industry indispensable to correct and idiomatic speech. The numerous dialects of the empire, moreover, serve more or less as lines of limitation to the itinerant preacher.

The missionary frequently experiences much embarrassment in the effort to communicate evangelical and spiritual truths in a tongue somewhat barren of words and phrases adapted to convey such sentiments. Some forms of thought possessing peculiar attraction and beauty to the cultivated Christian mind will lose all their significance when put in Chinese dress; although it must be acknowledged that the Scriptures are susceptible of more accurate translation than any other book has been found to be, and that the surprised student will discover, now and then, a new and happy meaning attaching itself to some familiar passage as he reads it in these pagan symbols. A peculiar bias of culture, or differing theological views, doubtless, has had something to do with the diversity of theory and practice found among Protestant missionaries in regard to the Chinese terms to denote God and Holy Spirit. Although little is said by way of controversy on this subject, and the *odium theologicum* is a thing unknown in the Protestantism of China, it cannot be reasonably doubted that the different words, in the literature and the preaching, used to signify the first and third Persons in the Trinity, have done much to confuse the native mind.

II. Another obstacle to the spread of Christianity among the Chinese is their national vanity. The term by which they most frequently designate their country is *Chung Kwo*, or "Middle Kingdom." It is used from a popular idea that China is situated in the center of the globe; and accordingly, in native maps, the empire is pictured as a great continent, while the various other countries are made to occupy insignificant positions on the sides of the earth. They suppose that they possess the highest type of enlightenment and civilization,— that they are the imperial race among the tribes of men. Their Emperor is called "the Son of Heaven," because he is sent by the Great Supreme to rule over all nations: their capital is designated as the "Seat of Universal Goodness," for the reason that the most refined and purifying influences are supposed to proceed from it in the form of laws, maxims, customs, and ceremonies. They imagine that their soil produces the richest and the greatest variety of grains, fruits, and vegetables; that the sun shines upon their favored land with a peculiar glory, and the moon beams forth with bright and benignant rays unknown in any other clime; and that Heaven has bestowed upon them the wisest of sages and philosophers, as well as the most illustrious of kings and emperors. They also believe that their gods are the most powerful of all the deities, and that their religion is the most ancient,— therefore, being nearest the source of all things, is the purest and the best. Taught these ideas by all that is sacred in religion and by all that is venerable in classic lore, they are not prepared to accept at once the instructions of a foreign teacher, since that would imply that they were inferior to the hitherto almost unknown nations of the West.

The probable influence of our modern civilization on China has been greatly overrated. A distinguished British consul, commenting on the character of the ruling and influential classes, gives it as his opinion that "returning emigrants fall back instinctively into their native notions and conceits, looking back upon their foreign sojourn as an ordeal happily over." The same writer submits the following interesting leaf from the volume of his experience.

"Even men of some pretense to social position, who have of late years visited the West in a quasi-diplomatic capacity, have shown no sign of having been impressed by what they have observed, or moved to introduce like innovations and advantages into their own country. Chung How, the only really high-class mandarin who has visited Europe, disappointed me keenly when I was conversing with him last August, by exhibiting the most listless indifference to my suggestions as to the vast collection of novel and interesting sights which it would be well for him to see whilst in this country. I happened to attend him at Shanghai when he embarked for the first time on board of one of the finest vessels of the French Messageries fleet, and took possession of his cabin for the voyage. The next time when I met him was in his handsome room at the Grosvenor Hotel a day or two after his arrival. Yet on both occasions he took as little heed of his novel surroundings as he would have done when stepping on board of one of his own wretched Chinese junks, or walking into one of his still more primitive native hotels. To my mind there must be something more in this than an affected indifference arising out of simple conceit. It must be the result of an inborn incapacity in the untutored Chinese mind to entertain any subject save by the particular process of thought, or in connection with the particular association to which it has been schooled by custom and tradition."*

Whatever may be the correct theory as to Chinese immobility when brought in contact with our most brilliant inventions, it is a noteworthy fact that native passengers and shippers in foreign vessels seldom betray a single emotion of admiration or wonder on account of science, labor, or means expended in the construction of the vessels in which they or their goods are being conveyed, although most of these now plying on the Yang-tsz-Kiang are among the largest and finest river steamers that Americans can build. It is clearly not the case that the Chinese are destined to accept our Gospel because they admire our Science.

III. Another great impediment to the rapid evangelization of this peculiar people is the universal ignorance. Skillful advantage is taken of this by the literary and official classes to create popular prejudice against the new religion.

Some few years ago a Chinese pamphlet, entitled "A Death-blow to Corrupt Doctrines," came to light, which proved to be a subtle and most powerful attack on foreigners and the Christianity which is inseparable from them. The book opens with an extract from the "Sacred Edict" suppressing strange religions, thus artfully giving the whole work the stamp of official authority. Following this is what purports to be a collection of facts respecting Roman Catholicism, which contains some grains of truth but intermingled with the vilest falsehoods and almost unspeakable blasphemies. The indulgence of the

* "The Foreigner in Far Cathay," by W. H. Medhurst, H.B.M. Consul, pp. 177-179.

basest passions is described as the chief characteristic of all connected with the Christian religion. An accusation currently reported and believed among the people is stated as follows: "At death both eyes are secretly taken out and the orifices sealed up with a plaster. The reason for extracting the eyes is this: From one hundred pounds of Chinese lead can be extracted eight pounds of silver, and the remaining ninety-two pounds of lead can be sold at the original cost; but the only way to obtain this silver is by compounding the eyes of Chinamen. The eyes of foreigners are of no use for this purpose; hence they do not take out those of their own people, but only those of the Chinese." The second part consists of miscellaneous quotations selected from Chinese books of history, travel, etc. From the "Mirror of the West" an extract is thus quoted: "In England they have the art of cutting out paper men and horses, and, by burning charms and repeating incantations, transforming them into real men and horses. These they use to terrify their enemies. They may, however, be dissolved by beating a gong, or by spouting water over them." Another work, "Records by the Far-travelled Sight-Seer," furnishes this item: "The people of France, without exception, follow the false and corrupt T'een-choo religion. They have also devilish arts by which they transform men into beasts, so that those who see them cannot discern the difference. They continually go to the various seaports, and other places, and kidnap the people of the Flowery Land, and carry them to their own country for slaves." After an ingenious and able misrepresentation of the Roman Catholic religion, comes an eloquent petition from Ho-nan province for the "Expulsion of the

Non-Human Species." Notwithstanding its great length, we venture to transcribe this paper as a graphic picture, not only of the ignorance and prejudice respecting foreigners widely entertained in China, but also of the native method of reasoning on the claims of Christianity, omitting only a few sentences, which, if inserted, would by their vulgarity soil our pages.

"Alas! depraved discourses are daily gaining ground, and right principles are gradually on the wane; strange doctrines are perversely advancing, and the minds of men are all in agitation.

"As to these insubordinate English who live on a contemptible mud-bank in the ocean, and are ruled sometimes by a female and sometimes by a male, their specific character is half human, half beast, described in the Silurian records as the 'naked reptile,' and termed in China *te-jin*.* Under the Ming government they made little progress. In the period Seuen-tih, Matthew Ricci, Jules Aleni, and others, first introduced their national religion of 'Jesus the Lord of Heaven,' misleading the people. At that time there were some men of intelligence who secretly connived at their proceedings, till the Emperor being memorialized to expel the intruders, they were forced to return to their own countries.

"Our dynasty, carrying to the extreme its benevolence toward men from afar, permitted them to open a trade at Canton in 1775. Now, our sacred sovereign entertained no thoughts beyond that, nor did he look for any advantage from them. Who could have imagined the unfathomable character of their wolfish hearts? The chasm of their covetous nature is difficult to fill; they pay no

* A kind of *Ichthyantrophos*, a monstrosity of the Silurian tribe.

regard to superabounding, all-enduring, favors, but on the contrary give free course to their wild and insane imaginations.

"Those who have come to propagate religion, enticing and deluding the ignorant masses, print and circulate depraved compositions; daring by their deceptive extravagancies to set loose the established bonds of society, utterly regardless of all modesty. At first, when they feared that people would attack them, they disseminated their principles in private; but now in every place they are holding forth their inducements, deliberately practicing their perversions in open day; trouble and disturbance pervade all quarters, and the feelings of the people are in incessant commotion. When the conflagration has commenced, where will the calamity end? If the young serpent is not crushed, what can be done with the full-grown reptile? Why hesitate or delay in crushing it to death? We here point out some of the reprobate principles of these people.

"*First.*—Heaven is one and undivided, ruled over by *Shang-te*, a name which they have changed to *T'een-choo* (Lord of Heaven), of whom they make Jesus the impersonation. If we examine into the history of Jesus, we find he was born in the second year of Yuen-show, during the reign of Emperor Gae, of the Han dynasty. But previous to Yuen-show was heaven really a vacant throne awaiting an occupant, or was it ruled over by some other person, like the successive generation of the Six Dynasties?

"*Second.*— Since Jesus is the Lord of heaven, his inscrutable holiness ought to surpass the conceptions of men; but if we examine what is said of him, we find he had merely the power of healing disease. Now, if the power of healing disease constitutes a holy man (or sage), then

Peen-tsco, Hwa-tow, and others who could restore the dead to life, were all holy men. Furthermore, this world is very large; but how many can Jesus, an individual man, save?

"*Third.*—Those who are produced by Heaven will certainly be protected by Heaven. But Jesus was little more than thirty years in the world when he was crucified by the king Pa-tow. He was unable to preserve his body; and to say that his spirit can impart happiness, it does not require much intelligence to see the absurdity.

"*Fourth.*—What is still more ridiculous, he was betrayed to death by his disciple Kwan Yin-paou, a deed surpassing in atrocity that of Fung-ming, who shot (his teacher) E; for Kwan Yin-paou killed his master simply because he coveted the king's seventy odd pieces of silver. Jesus did not know his own disciple; and who will believe that he can know whether other people are good or bad?

"*Fifth.*—Although the adherents of the religion only worship Jesus, yet being divided into the two sections of Roman Catholics and Protestants, these are continually railing at each other, so that we have no means of determining which is right and which is wrong.

"*Sixth.*—According to that religion, all kinds of sin are pardoned by the Lord of Heaven, and all who join their communion enter heaven's hall. To say nothing about whether any one has seen a hall in the expanse of the azure heavens, admitted that there is such a place, and that the good and the vicious alike enter there, is it likely that God (*Shang-te*) is thus excessively impartial in the bestowment of his favor?

"*Seventh.*—In Japan they have cast an image of Jesus which is placed between the landing-place and the public thoroughfare, to be kicked and defiled by those who pass by. As he affirmed that he had angels at his command, how does he voluntarily submit to these insults in silence without some miraculous utterance? His divine efficacy is not equal even to that of the most insignificant plants; where then is the propriety of calling him the Lord of Heaven?

"But the injurious character of their pernicious principles cannot be thoroughly exhausted. They do not dress the tombs, nor worship the parental tablet, thus ignoring their ancestors. Their father they address as 'venerable elder brother,' and their mother as 'venerable elder sister,' thus ignoring the parental relation. Daughters in a family are not given in marriage, but retained for the disposition of the Bishop, thus ignoring the matrimonial relation. They have no distinction of rich and poor; but those who join their communion give up their money, indicating an utter absence of modesty. They do not observe the distinction of male and female, but all bathe in common, thus betraying an utter want of shame.

"They cut out the heart and scoop out the eyes (of the dead), using the remainder of the carcass as medicine for cattle. . . . They administer the stupefying decoction of anæsthetic juice to stultify the mind and confuse the thoughts. The chief in authority are white demons; those who officiate are black gentlemen; and whatever they do is of the most binding obligation. On the other hand, the great Yu, Prince T'ang, Wan-Wang, and Woo-Wang, they characterize as devils. Hence, formerly when this religion was introduced into Africa, they put the Africans to death; when it was introduced into India they annexed India to their empire; when it was introduced into Japan they were the cause of rebellion in Japan.

"The wealth of our central flowery land is a hundred thousand times that of the barbarians, and their hearts have long been yearning after it, so that their present attitude resembles the aim of Sze Ma-shaou,* as the mere traveler may understand. If a speedy precaution is not taken to drive them out, we shall find some day our ancient civilization of several thousand years' standing, supplanted by the semi-canine customs of the savage regions,— a consummation much to be deprecated.

"When men acquire a little spirit, and while with head oppressed and grieved at heart they feel the time to be insufficient, how can they talk of still deferring? In such a case, if no one ventures to expose the falsehood, ignorant people are misled by them. These say that by acquiring wealth and securing happiness they may avert an age of calamities, not knowing that they are mere dupes, and what flows in at one end runs out at the other. We have not seen all the adherents of that religion become wealthy, but there are those of them who perish from poverty and hunger, their miseries springing from a perennial root. Their words are of a class with catching the wind and grasping a shadow, unconscious that they are simply ranking themselves with the brute creation. When intelligent people become the objects of their vain declamation, these fear to stir up strife and raise a quarrel.

"Now, since the 22d year of Taou-kwang [1842], these perverse barbarians have put forth their rebellious views with effrontery. At the time of their piratical raid on

---
*A traitor in the time of the Three Kingdoms.

Canton, who was there to come to the rescue? When they pillaged in succession Fooh-kien and Chih-kiang, who was there to come to the rescue? They have overrun Kiang-soo, they have thrown Shan-tung into confusion, they have extended their depredations to the Celestial Capital and other places, and yet who has come to the rescue? Now having insolently invaded the metropolis, and inflicted a deep wound on our national existence, while no one comes to the rescue, is it likely that they will fold their hands and go away? Why do we still fear their empty talk, and refrain from deliberating on a plan for their slaughter? Their country is fifty thousand *li* from China, beyond a triple ocean; how can the life or death of men be overruled at a distance of fifty thousand *li* across the ocean? At first, when they clandestinely entered the interior, they bribed our lawless seaboard people. The real barbarians are few in number, and we southern men, hitherto loyal and patriotic, will certainly not be made their tools. Furthermore, the water of the lakes is exceedingly shallow, so that a barbarian steamer would find it difficult to enter; but should they come, with our various military strategies we are more than a match for them. Why should we, in apprehension of the difficulties, refrain from cordially combining for a deadly onslaught?

"But as to those who are the victims of their deception, who have long been getting more and more polluted, till their very vitals are afflicted by the venom, it were insufferable to kill them without first giving them warning. Thence this premonishment is issued that they may renew their course. If they still cleave to their delusion, then let the heads of families and the village elders combine the population and arm the neighborhoods, to seize the offenders, that they may be placed in some solitary region, or hurled beyond the seas, to take their place among the strange things of creation; for they must by no means be allowed to disgrace the Central Land with their various abandoned and corrupt practices.

"The above suggestions being acted on, the solicitude of the Prince will be merely like postponing an evening meal; the misery of the people will be that of eradicating poison from the system; the hearts of the multitude will be more correct, and the national manners will be long preserved. Let us all with united force exert ourselves in combination. Oppose not this notification."

Doubtless the above work, written by a man of much ability, receiving official endorsement in many places, and being widely circulated among the *literati* and by them communicated to the ignorant class, had much to do with the spirit of unrest and suspicion that prevailed so extensively through several of the provinces a few years since, culminating in the massacre of Tien-tsin. Incredible as it may seem, stories of the vilest practices, and of the most absurd and wicked customs, among all adherents of Christianity, are commonly reported and generally credited,—a condition of things inseparable from the profound ignorance of everything foreign which prevails through a greater part of the country. Precisely of this nature were some of the evils against which primitive Christians in the Roman empire had to contend, calling forth the noble defense of Tertullian and a large part of the apologetic literature of the Fathers.

IV. Not the least among the hindrances to evangelism must be accounted the superstition of the people. With the views they entertain of the power of disembodied spirits, and of their ghostly influence on the affairs of this world, such belief having its flower and fruit in the ancestral worship, the Chinese must necessarily have constantly before them the fear of demons and hobgoblins.

Several events occurring at Ningpo, in the year 1846, strikingly illustrate this fact. During the summer a long-continued drought threatened to destroy the rice crop, and the people were much excited and alarmed in consequence. Processions in honor of the Dragon, and other religious ceremonials, were vainly resorted to in the hope of inducing the gods to send rain. The rumor was circulated that unknown enemies of the public good were putting out poisoned cakes, dropping them in the streets or surreptitiously placing them among those in the bakers' shops, and that in consequence many persons had died in a neighboring town. It was stated that when the bereaved friends went to their graves to weep they found the coffins open, and discovered that the eyes of the deceased had been cut out and their brains abstracted, for the purpose, it was supposed, of making medicine. Then came the report that on a certain night all the fowls in the neighborhood lost some of their principal feathers,—a fact to be accounted for on the supposition that they had been plucked by ghosts, who would transform them into swords to be employed in killing men and women.

At this stage the public mind became somewhat quieted; but, as the drought continued and the terrors of famine threatened the people, the excitement was renewed and became more intense than ever. Placards were posted about the city stating that some of the neighboring districts were beginning to be annoyed by the presence of evil spirits, and that these nocturnal visitants might soon be expected at Ningpo. The general alarm was increased by the story that some persons living near the east gate had been aroused from their sleep in the night by strange noises, as though a large body of men were marching through the street with loud outcries. Similar sounds were afterward heard above the houses; and many were convinced that the ghosts of the Chinese and English soldiers who had fallen in the late war were fighting their battles over again. While all were expecting some great inroad from the spirit-world, at about four o'clock on the morning of the 4th of August, the whole population were suddenly aroused from their slumbers by a terrible commotion. The houses seemed to be rocking on their foundations, and a mysterious and awful sound, like muttering thunder, rolled along the affrighted air. The very tiles on the roofs of each building were heard rattling and crashing as if beneath the tread of advancing legions. A cry of horror and dismay arose from every part of the city, and the echoing shout was heard from house to house, "The ghosts have come! the ghosts have come!" Instantly the most frantic efforts were made to drive away the Prince of Darkness and his demon host. Gongs were made to boom, tables and chairs, pots and kettles, were lustily pounded, while those who could do nothing else were leaping up and down, throwing their arms about and clapping their hands and screaming with all their might. Rarely has the world witnessed such a horrid din and such a scene of utter confusion and dismay as broke over this Chinese city on that eventful morning.

8*

The shock of an earthquake was the immediate occasion of the alarm, albeit a respectable literary gentleman argued against the possibility of such an event, from the fact that it had not been predicted in the Imperial Almanac! Whatever might be said, the popular excitement for some time would not down; and ghosts of lions and tigers, as well as of men, were made to throng the air. It was a generally accepted theory that the foreigners residing in the city were in some way connected with these ghostly visits; although some differed from the common belief in the supposition that it might be exclusively the work of Roman Catholics, and others laid this grave allegation at the door of Boodhist priests. The Rev. Mr. Culbertson, who resided at the time in Ningpo, was accustomed to take evening walks with his family on the city wall; and the report became current that he kept multitudes of demons shut up in a bottle, and that he had been seen, on one of these occasions, to draw the cork, and with a blast from his mouth and a movement of his arms to send the whole troop flying over the city to do their work of death.*

The principal characteristics of Chinese superstition are: ancestral worship, consisting of divine honors to the dead; necromancy, attended with table-turning and other spiritualistic manifestations; astrology, making use of lucky and unlucky days in every important event in private, social and public life; geomancy, always in request in selecting sites for burial and in the construction of dwellings; charms and amulets, regarded as absolutely necessary in cases of danger, sickness, and demoniac influence. These all are deeply founded in national history and national character, and all are in direct antagonism to the precepts

* Culbertson's "Religions and Superstitions of China," pp. 173-179.

and the practice of Christianity. The missionary, as the exponent of a new doctrine and a new life, finds, at first, that both are constantly misinterpreted by the people with whom he has cast his lot. His most heroic and self-denying acts, conceived in prayer and executed in holy purpose, may strike the heathen around him as the clearest evidence of wild adventure or satanic impulse. He cannot even erect a chapel without some peril of awakening the gravest apprehension among his neighbors, particularly if the structure has an unusual elevation; and a steeple or cupola is especially an object of dread, as it is supposed to interfere with the atmospheric currents, which, under the direction of the gods, have to do with the showers that water the earth.

V. Another difficulty attending missionary labor in the Far East, repeatedly mentioned or alluded to in these pages, is implied in this statement: In respect to morality and religion, the Chinese nation has not yet discovered our superiority. Nor is this to be wondered at. The West is still imperfectly known; and where there has been actual contact the happiest results have not always been realized. The political intrigues of the Jesuits had much to do with the overthrow of Catholicism in that country. The foreign name is deservedly associated with the opium trade. Also the coolie traffic, which has been attended with all the horrors of the old African slave-trade, is thus inseparably connected. The whole bloody train of war, unjustified by any adequate cause, including spoliation and dire vengeance on the innocent, has come in swift ships from West to East. Under the auspices of lawful commerce, pictures are imported from Europe, among which are found large quantities of stereoscopic views of the vilest and most obscene character, displaying before the eye vices and crimes of our race which we would blush to name. The author himself has more than once been filled with hot indignation at seeing these views publicly exhibited on the streets of Peking. They are scattered far and wide through the country; and it is believed that in many of the interior cities Chinamen might be found who are making large incomes by showing them to hundreds of natives daily.

Drunken sailors on shore, or desperate adventurers in command of piratical fleets on the coast, or foreign thieves and robbers infesting the rivers and canals of the country, have been taken, by those who have had but limited opportunity of observation, as our fit and worthy representatives abroad. The favored sons of fortune in mercantile houses, or the *attaché* of some consulate, under the plea "that there is something peculiar about the tropics which excites certain passions in a higher degree than in temperate regions,"— that "the brilliancy of the skies and the beauty of the atmosphere conspire to influence the nerves against philosophy and her rigid tenets, and forbid their practice among the children of the sun,"— throw off the restraints of virtue and abandon themselves to social crime, consorting with the pagan ministers of their shameful pleasure. In business transactions with strangers from Western lands, the natives have also found that duplicity and dishonest dealing are not confined to their own countrymen. Such facts as these, thrust upon the attention of a people who, in their vanity and ignorance, are accustomed to regard all but themselves as barbarians, have doubtless created among them, at least outside the range of direct missionary influence, the general conviction that the European races are ambitious, unscrupulous, violent, covetous, and licentious; and that they are below their own level in respect of morals and religion.

Some of the peculiar embarrassments under which the work of publicly preaching the Gospel is carried on in China cannot, perhaps, be more fittingly illustrated than by the experience on one occasion of a missionary, thus narrated by himself in *The Chinese Recorder* for June 1871.

"My duties led me on a certain evening not very long ago to the missionary chapel, which it is my custom to open on the week-days for the benefit of those who may be desirous of hearing the Gospel. I had scarcely entered and taken my seat before a Chinaman came in, and with a cool and business-like air at once occupied one of the empty benches. Usually before the preaching has well commenced, those who do stroll in do so in a lounging, easy, indifferent kind of way, as though curiosity were the only possible motive that could have brought them in. This man, however, seemed as though he had come by special appointment, and it were a matter of supreme importance that the subject in hand should be finished off as quickly as possible. It would have been difficult to say from the man's appearance to what position in life he belonged. His dress bordered on the shabby, and the style of the man seemed to indicate that he was more familiar with the artisan class than with any other. His face, however, had a peculiar look of sharpness and intelligence, such as one is accustomed to meet with among the more educated. His conversation, too, was so interlarded with book phrases, and his general knowledge of his own literature was so very extensive, that it was evident his dress gave no proper clue to his status in society. The more I looked at the man, the more was I struck with his general appearance. There was intelligence, but there was combined with it a certain look of dissatisfaction. He seemed like a man whose ambition had soared high, but whose projects had all failed, and consequently the disappointment that failure had produced had become stamped upon his expression.

"After a few commonplace remarks, in which he had said that this was the first time he had ever been in a missionary chapel,— which statement, however, I mentally declared to be untrue,— we turned to the subject of religion. At first he began to defend idolatry as a thing introduced and organized by the sages in older times, and that therefore the ceremonies in connection with it were binding upon the whole Chinese nation. He referred to the classics in confirmation of what he said; but, upon a closer investigation of the texts quoted, he had to acknowledge that his interpretation of them differed very materially from those of the recognized commentators. Indeed, he finally agreed that it was not till so late as the Han dynasty, which was very considerably later than Confucius, that idolatry began to be the fairly recognized medium of worship in China.

"Turning from this point, he said: 'Very good; I grant you there is nothing very strong that can be said in defense of idolatry. But,' he continued, 'we have our sages with all the writings they have transmitted to us. They contain doctrines of the highest and purest character, and it is these that after all are the real powers in our nation's morals. It seems to come to this: you have the doctrines of your sages and we have ours. Why not rest content with what we mutually possess, instead of your striving to induce us to lay aside ours and believe in yours?' I agreed with him that if it were simply a question of differing sages there was no use in our coming to China to interfere with the systems they possessed. The case, however, was very different from that. The real question at issue was one between the doctrines of the Bible and those propounded by man,—whether, in fact, God was to be the teacher or man. I, however, demurred to his statement that the doctrines of the sages, in their highest and purest aspect, had any appreciable influence at the present time in leading the nation to do what is right. I challenged him to produce me one instance, either from among the *literati* or the mandarin class, who are the most thoroughly imbued of any of the Chinese in these doctrines, who were in any degree striving to carry out the principles they contain. He somewhat hesitatingly agreed that the instances were certainly very rare.

"Whilst in the very act of admitting this, the easy manner he had hitherto assumed in his conversation with me seemed to slide from the man, and like a flash of lightning a look of suppressed hatred and bitterness spread instead. 'Oh, then,' he said, 'your object in coming here is to teach us charity and benevolence and truth and uprightness, is it?' I said, 'Yes.' 'If this be your object, why is it that you yourselves act in a spirit so directly the reverse of these, and force upon us instead your abominable opium? If your nation believes in these doctrines as divine, why has it imported this poisonous stuff to bring poverty and distress and ruin throughout our land?' And as he went on he became excited, and his eye flashed, and his eloquence grew. Chinaman-like, he rolled his head from side to side, whilst the congregation (which in the meantime had grown largely) looked on with approving sympathy. I was so utterly taken aback that I could do nothing but quietly sit still until he had given full expression to his feelings. My surprise arose not so much from the matter as the manner of his accusation. It was given forth in the most offensive language, and with a force such as I had never met with on any previous occasion.

"After he had finished what he had to say, the congregation that was scattered about,—some sitting on the forms, others leaning by the doorway, and others again bending over the backs of the seats, listening breathlessly to what the man was saying,—with one consent turned their face upon me, waiting, without uttering a sound, to hear what would be my reply. I must say that I never felt so uncomfortable in any public meeting in my life before. What the man had said I knew and felt to be the truth. I began therefore somewhat stammeringly to utter something in self-defense, when the man at once stopped me by saying, 'There is no use in your trying to get out of the matter by saying that you have nothing to do with this opium system. Your country has. It is your nation, England, that is responsible for all this ruin caused by opium. It was the English guns that compelled our Emperor to sanction the trade, and it is through England that it may now be sold throughout the length and breadth of the land without our government being able to do anything effectual to prevent its spread throughout the kingdom.' The facts of the case were all on his side, though somewhat offensively stated. England's share in this opium question is one which no reasoning and no sophistry can turn to her honor. Whatever of greatness or of glory there may be in her history to which she can point with satisfaction, there is at least one blot upon her escutcheon which will not be easily effaced, and that is, that she was the direct means of stimulating and protecting a trade that involves a third of the human race in evils which no language can describe. I replied that as far as regarded the opium itself he and I were at one. If he condemned it, just as strongly did I; but I reminded him that if the Chinese would only cease from buying, the foreigners must of necessity stop from importing,—an argument that seemed to have such weight with him that it completely silenced him, though to myself it appeared so utterly illogical that I was heartily ashamed for having to use it. But a drowning man will catch even at a straw.

"Taking advantage of the turn affairs had taken, I glided off into another subject, and had been speaking for ten minutes or so, the man all the while listening most attentively, when something in my remarks again seemed to strike him, so he stopped me and said: 'It is not simply by your forcing your opium upon us that you manifest your hatred of us. You foreigners don't seem to be able to understand that we Chinese have any natural affection. You come amongst us and you separate husband from wife, and children from parents, and you break up the family relationships, and you leave many a family in mourning and misery.' I was utterly astonished at this charge, not having the remotest idea at what he was driving. I endeavored to stop him for an explanation, but his indignation was again hurrying him along at a pace it was impossible to control. At last, at one of his breathing spots, I managed to make him hear that he must stop, for I could not allow him to go on. 'Oh, indeed, you insist that I shall stop, do you? You think you can come here to teach us, and the moment we begin to speak of the wrongs your country has done us our mouths must be stopped! Pretty teachers of morals you are, indeed!' I assured him I did not understand his charge, and that I stopped him simply to get an explanation, not to silence him. My custom in the chapel had ever been to allow all fair discussion, and he had but to explain himself to get a fair and honest hearing. A few words from him enabled me to perceive that he referred to the coolie traffic which some years ago had been carried on in this place. Of the iniquities of this traffic in its earlier stage it would be impossible to speak in strong enough terms. Many a home had indeed been made desolate,—many a family had been bereaved by the man-stealer, and throughout this region the connection of the foreigner with it had engendered a feeling which is even now only beginning to subside. Indeed, only a week previously I had seen the lifeless trunk of a man carried by who had been beheaded an hour before for decoying persons away to be shipped to the south as coolies. Fortunately his accusation was stronger than the present state of the case would sanction, and I proceeded to show him that the evils he described did not now exist. The English government had made such arrangements for emigration that not only must a man's consent be obtained for his going abroad to an English colony, but also that the agreement entered into with him by English subjects must be faithfully adhered to in the very letter. After sitting a few minutes longer he rose from his seat and left the chapel.

"The above is a brief description of a scene of which I have a very vivid but at the same time a very painful recollection. Of course I have given the substance of his remarks in my own words. To have reproduced his exact language would have been both impossible and indiscreet. As I have already hinted, he spoke in the most offensive way. He did not stay to choose his words, and what he did say was of so strong and pungent a nature that, accustomed as I am to every variety of Chinese character, I had never met with any one that has his ability to say things in such a bitter and sarcastic way."

The narrator of this incident indulges in some piquant remarks on the theory that any attempt to elevate the Chinese must be first made through the medium of civilization. The reader is invited to ponder these sentences:

"The grievances that the Chinaman has against the foreigner are not all ideal ones,—not all the result of his intense conservatism. The Chinaman is shrewd enough to observe that whatever blessings the foreigner may bring with him, he is the cause of evils which in their present power for mischief overshadow all the effects that his good could possibly achieve. There is no one that looks upon the frightful net-work of opium shops that is spread throughout any Chinese city one visits, or that marks the fearful results in the thousands of pale and emaciated wretches that one may see issuing from these dens by day or night, but that must feel this."

That this view of the case is amply sustained by public opinion in China, might be clearly indicated by numerous quotations from imperial edicts and from the general literature. Who can read without a thrill of mingled pity and indignation the noble words of the Emperor who, when urged to legalize the trade in opium, said: "It is true I cannot prevent the introduction of the flowing poison; gain-seeking and corrupt men will, for profit and sensuality, defeat my wishes; but nothing will induce me to derive a revenue from the vice and misery of my people."

Without doubt, the dreadful famine which recently scourged North China was principally owing to the spread of poppy cultivation. A large proportion of the richest soils in that region has been devoted to the nurture of this plant, and in consequence the granaries were left empty, with no provision for a year of drought. This is but one fact in the ghastly train of evils that follow in the wake of a traffic which the enlightened public sentiment of Christendom will yet pronounce accursed, even as the unhappy victims anathematize both the drug itself and the hand that gave it.

Dr. Legge, the eminent missionary, now professor of the Chinese language and literature in the university at Oxford, gives it as his opinion that the reason for the seemingly slow progress of Christianity in the world, and especially among heathen nations, is not to be sought in any failure of doctrine or precept of the system itself, nor in any lack of authority and power on the part of its Divine Author. He says, "We must blame ourselves:— the divisions among Christian Churches; the inconsistencies and unrighteousness of professors; the selfishness and greed of our commerce; the ambitious and selfish policy of so-called Christian nations. I cannot illustrate what I mean better than by telling you, as my last word, of a conversation with His Excellency Kwo Sung-tao, the former Chinese embassador, soon after he arrived in London in 1877. 'You know,' he said to me, 'both England and China. Which country do you say is the better of the two?' I replied, 'England.' He was disappointed, and added, 'I mean looking at them from the moral standpoint;—looked at from the standpoint of benevolence, righteousness, and propriety, which country do you say is the better?' After some demur and fencing, I replied again, 'England.' I never saw a man more surprised. He pushed his chair back, got on his feet, took a turn across the room, and cried out, 'You say that, looked at from the moral standpoint, England is better than China! Then how is it that England insists on our taking her opium?'" *

Mr. Justin McCarthy, in his recent work, gives this summary of the position he takes on the opium war, in reference to the political or international aspect of the case: "Reduced to plain words, the principle for which we fought in the China war was the right of Great Britain to force a peculiar trade upon a foreign people in spite of the protestation of the government and all such public opinion as there was of the nation." †

An able writer in a recent number of the *Contemporary Review* thus arraigns his nation for her immoral transactions with this heathen country:

"Our treatment of China seems to be, on the whole, the most criminal part of our public action during the last half-century,—I mean our opium policy. We are still involved in the guilt of this crime. The story of our shame is a continuous one to this moment. Let no one pronounce this language to be too strong till he has

---

* "The Religions of China," p. 308.
† "A History of Our Own Times," vol. i, p. 113.

looked into the undisputed facts of this miserable history. We began by smuggling opium into China. The Chinese Government, believing the use of opium to be pernicious, forbade the importation of it. That there is a great craving for it among the Chinese is not denied by the Chinese Government: it is a part of their case. The smuggling of opium became a very profitable trade, which the English authorities took no pains to check. In 1839 the Chinese made a determined effort to break up the trade, and they took steps by which they gained possession of an enormous quantity of opium, valued at nearly two millions sterling, ready to be poured as contraband goods into the country. This they publicly destroyed. We made war upon them, and at the conclusion of the war, in 1842, we extorted from them, in sheer rapacity, an indemnity of five millions sterling. Forty years ago, this war was denounced by Mr. Gladstone in these terms: 'A war more unjust in its origin, a war more calculated to cover this country with permanent disgrace, I do not know, and have not read of.' Yes, the disgrace has proved permanent in a sense beyond what he meant. In 1857 the smuggling of opium became the cause of a second war, in which we forced our way to Peking. The treaty of Peking, in 1860, included a clause which legalized the trade in opium. Opium is cultivated in India under a government monopoly, and brings in a revenue variously estimated at six millions sterling, or upward. The Chinese opposition to the sale and consumption of opium has been in some degree wearied by the long struggle; but there is evidence that, if it were possible, the use of this drug would be prohibited in China as stringently as ever. After the murder of Mr.

Margary, in Yun-nan, a convention was concluded, in 1876, under which the Chinese paid a pecuniary indemnity and sent a mission to this country. The convention was negotiated by Sir Thomas Wade, H.M. Minister in Peking. One of the clauses begins thus: 'On opium, Sir Thomas Wade will move his Government to sanction an arrangement different from that affecting other imports.' We have received the indemnity, but the arrangement which the clause goes on to describe has not been ratified. The Government were moved by Sir Thomas Wade, but they were also moved, and more powerfully, by the opium interest. Lord Salisbury, with that candor which sometimes characterized the late Government, explained the whole matter. The arrangement would have put it into the power of the Chinese to prevent smuggling. With smuggling prevented, they would have been able to raise their own internal duty on opium. 'That would be a result,' in Lord Salisbury's words, 'which practically would neutralize the policy which has hitherto been pursued by this country with regard to that drug.' No wonder that the Chinese have suspected us of a design not only to make money but to demoralize and to enfeeble their race. No wonder that the Bishop of Victoria should have been stopped, as he says, again and again, while preaching, with the question, 'Are you an Englishman? Is not that the country that opium comes from? Go back and stop it, and then we will talk about Christianity.' 'Are all my exertions,' wrote Lord Elgin, 'to result only in the extension of the area over which Englishmen are to exhibit how hollow and superficial are both their civilization and their Christianity?'"

CHAPTER XII.

PROTESTANT MISSIONS NOT A FAILURE.

A SECULAR paper published in Hong-Kong, in one of its numbers issued some time during the year 1867, stated an objection to Christian missions that may be regarded as an excellent putting of the case from a standpoint wholly mercenary and worldly; and it may serve, also, to represent a phase of thought frequently entertained by lukewarm and ill-informed friends of foreign evangelistic effort. The criticism referred to is thus given:

"In like manner we maintain that, for the sums disbursed and the number of missionaries in the field, the present Protestant missions in China are a religious failure."

This proposition certainly has the merit of conciseness. The argument is in a nutshell. We are told that for the sums expended "four thousand adult Protestant Christians is a somewhat small return"; therefore, "the missions are a failure." We must, however, withhold our assent to this conclusion, at least until the standard of success is recognized. What number of converts should we consider an adequate compensation? On the one hand, the value of money and of human effort must be computed; on the other hand, the value of truth, the worth of immortal man, must be accurately estimated. Let the balance be struck! Until this is done, it is logically unsound to draw the above sweeping conclusion.

The author of the sentiment quoted would have us consider missions "by the same tests as we apply to more mundane undertakings." Certainly there can be no reasonable objection to this. The man is but an indifferent student of history who has not learned that many of the most important of human undertakings have realized their objects only after stupendous and protracted effort, and long after superficial thinkers had placed upon them the brand of failure. Were there not a single convert to Christianity in the Chinese empire to-day, it would still be too early to pronounce unfavorably on missions. It took three centuries to subdue pagan Rome to Christ, and generations of labor passed ere the land of the Druids became Christian England. Impatient zeal, or unreasoning skepticism, may demand immediate effects; but enlightened faith will calmly wait for the latter-day triumph. Sir Frederick Bruce, in his remarkable dispatch to Earl Russell, in 1862, after animadverting upon the prevailing system of evangelism in China, and laying down a plan of his own devising, confessed that the adoption of his superior views involved "a patient pursuit of results, not perhaps to be realized by the first laborers."

Foreigners in China may be divided into three leading classes,—merchants, officials, and missionaries. It is but simple justice to say that all these classes have honestly desired to succeed, and have striven earnestly to meet the expectations of their patrons at home. They have had to encounter very similar difficulties, and have prosecuted their respective enterprises under like conditions from the beginning. What has been the result?

In point of time, the merchants have enjoyed the superior opportunity. They made their first advance in the country before either Romanist or Protestant had introduced any disturbing element into the political or religious life of China, and while as yet a friendly feeling existed toward traders from the West both on the part of the government and among the people. It will not be denied that for a time the sails of commerce were filled with prosperous breezes. We are even prepared to attest the fact that large fortunes have been acquired by lawful and unlawful traffic, and that immense hongs have long received and disbursed the valuable products of European skill; but the account of the merchants as it will sum up to-day must be considered.

The hope and expectation of being able steadily to enlarge the sphere of their operations by introducing new articles into the markets have not been realized. Attempts of this kind have been repeatedly made, followed by disappointment and great financial loss. When the northern ports had just been officially declared accessible to foreign commerce, certain traders in England were wild with excitement. A Sheffield firm sent out a large consignment of knives and forks, and declared themselves prepared to supply the whole Celestial Empire with cutlery. Chinamen, however, preferred chopsticks; and the goods were sold at prices which scarcely realized their freight. Native shops in Hong-Kong were for years afterward adorned with them, formed into various devices on their shelves like guns and spears in an armory. A famous London house sent out a vast number of piano-fortes on the supposition that, as "China was opened up," many of the women would certainly want to learn to play that instrument. But the Chinese remained faithful to their gongs and trumpets, and declined all hospitality to these accompaniments of refinement and civilization. The consignees at Hong-Kong, being greatly embarrassed, at last extricated themselves by insisting upon every European resident buying *two* instruments, the price, of course, not being exorbitant. Consequently, pianos by the best makers abounded at the various ports where foreign communities were established. The climate of these ports being either remarkably dry or indescribably humid, the music-boxes soon got out of tune and discoursed most eloquent discord. Such articles as carpets, tools, machines, beds, bonnets, crinoline, coffee, butter, cheese, etc., may be found difficult to place in the market of an open port or interior town; but it is surely as easy to introduce these things as the Christian religion.

The examples of men in the China trade who have lost money rather than made it, or who have become hopelessly bankrupt, ruining both themselves and their patrons, are certainly matters of some gravity in discussing a question of success or failure in commerce; but these are not so significant as the fact that a large proportion of the business once controlled absolutely by foreigners is now passing out of their hands. Native dealers have practically secured control of the tea market: they make the prices, and usually absorb the larger share of the profits. Native companies own many of the coast steamers, and seem destined to have the whole business in their hands.

The first Chinese steamer that ever crossed the Pacific ocean reached San Francisco in the autumn of 1880, and lay inside the Golden Gate for some time until the

Department of State could settle her status. The *Wu-Chung* is to be regarded as but the pioneer of an extensive movement that will undoubtedly bring Chinamen into more or less successful competition with our wealthiest and most enterprising merchants. They already have their agents in several of the great commercial centers of Europe and America. Beyond controversy, the golden days of commerce with China are either in the past or in the untried future.

We may next turn our attention to the class of officials, and inquire, What success has been achieved in the sphere of diplomacy? We will not assume to know the secrets of state, or comprehend certain questions of administration and civil law; but we shall not be denied the right to scan public documents and apply the test of our reason to well-known facts bearing on this subject.

It should be premised that many members of the consular branch of service, embracing representatives of all nations which trade with China, have been men of high character and superior scholarly attainments; who, also, have exercised a salutary influence in their intercourse with Chinese officials, exhibiting signal zeal and ability in serving the interests of their constituency. And the same may be said, with much emphasis, of gentlemen in the higher diplomatic circle. But our discussion turns on the question of achievement in matters of dispute and negotiation with the official representatives of traditional Chinese policy.

Sir John Francis Davis early discovered a fact that has repeatedly challenged the attention and deference of Western diplomates. "The Chinese frequently get the better of Europeans, in a discussion, by imperturbable coolness and gravity. It is part of their policy to gain the advantage by letting their opponent work himself into a passion and place himself in the wrong; hence the more than ordinary necessity of carefully preserving the temper with them."* The unwritten history of diplomatic intercourse at the ports, and even at the capital, would, if known, indicate at this very point the reason of the abrupt and unsatisfactory conclusion of more than one important negotiation.

The trade in opium, incidentally with other causes, became a bone of contention that plunged England into her first war with China. Sundry disputes and hostilities supervened from time to time, which culminated in a second and third war,—not, however, through lack of the earnest efforts of consuls and envoys extraordinary, in each case, to avert such a calamity. England has for about forty years been engaged in "opening China." To employ the expressive figure used by one writer, "The point of the wedge was entered by gun-boats and armies, and the diplomatic muscle of successive cabinets has been wielding the beetle ever since, and it is not driven home yet." The cordon of barriers which was originally drawn around the treaty ports is still invincible to the merchant, although there are signs of a voluntary movement on the part of the government toward a more liberal and enlightened policy.

The signal results of war have seldom been wisely improved by diplomacy. When Captain Elliot attacked Canton, in 1840-41, and succeeded, through the valor of English sailors and soldiers, in driving the enemy from every stronghold around the city, the British representa-

---

* Davis' "China and the Chinese," vol. i, p. 247.

tive did not use this fortunate result by entering the provincial capital at once and trampling under foot the arrogant assumption that no foreigner should be allowed to pass its gates; but he accepted overtures of peace outside the walls while actually contemplating them as limits of a forbidden precinct, withdrew his forces for a handsome pecuniary indemnity, and left the Chinese to plume themselves on their success,— a proceeding which necessitated the identical work to be all done over again, years after, at the expense of a vast amount of blood and treasure. Sir Henry Pottinger committed a similar error when, after taking various cities on the coast, and by appearing with a formidable squadron before Nanking, so terrifying the Chinese that they professed themselves ready to submit to any terms, he withdrew his forces at the moment of complete triumph and was inveigled into shifting the scene of detailed negotiations back to Canton, instead of onward to Peking, thereby losing some of the most practical benefits which should have accrued. After repeated blunders, resulting in the catastrophe of Ta-koo, Lord Elgin awoke to the fact that the effectual blow must be struck at the capital. The courage and strategy of the allied forces soon brought him there, but he was content with occupying only one gate of the imperial city, utterly throwing away the first complete opportunity that had occurred of settling the old and vexed question of a personal audience of the Emperor, the postponement of which occasioned material prejudice to all foreign interests in China.

In the English treaty of 1858, provision was made for a revision of its stipulations at the end of ten years. Early in 1868 the famous "revision controversy" began.

On the English side, the campaign was opened by a circular of Sir Rutherford Alcock, dated May 28, addressed to the British consuls in China, instructing them to put themselves in communication with the mercantile communities in their several jurisdictions, to ascertain what changes could be advantageously proposed in order that Her Majesty's government might have the best means of forming a judgment of the expediency or otherwise of demanding such a revision as would lay in the direction of expansion of privileges. In pursuance of official notification, the merchants held their meetings in a public manner and with open doors, putting their demands in the shape of resolutions, and publishing them in the papers of Hong-Kong and Shanghai. They united in asking for the breaking down of exclusiveness, the curtailment of monopolies, the introduction of railways and telegraphs, privileges of steam navigation on the inner waters, the opening of new ports, the reduction of onerous duties, the working of coal and iron mines, the privilege of inland residence, the right of owning warehouses away from the ports, etc. On the Chinese side, having the advantage of complete information as to the various points which would probably be raised by the English, secret and effective preparations were made for the final grapple by the astute manipulators of state-craft at Peking. Negotiations were protracted, but ineffectual; and instead of that real and complete opening of the empire which was anticipated, only a few petty concessions were realized, and the Chinese restrictive policy won a great victory. The coveted inland residence and privilege of trade were denied, and steamers were refused admittance to interior waters. "At the last, after tedious delay and fruitless endeavors, the treaty was signed on the 23d of October, 1869. The three years' campaign was now ended. The foreigner was beaten,— the Mongol had outmanœuvered the Saxon; the scow had got to windward of the clipper; coolie muscle was exalted above steam; the paddle-wheels had to yield the way to the old-fashioned scull; and foreign civilization had to retire, abashed, from its vain endeavor to accept the invitation of Mr. Burlingame and 'graft itself on the ancient civilization of China.'"

For several years there have been five legations in Peking, with their able and experienced ministers, their learned secretaries, and, in most instances, their talented and accomplished suites. They have all enjoyed the advantage of position and prestige, with the auxiliaries of modern science, and the illustrations of art and elegance. They have also had the advantage of dealing in more or less familiar intercourse with the most representative men of the empire. What is the measure of success? Is it commensurate with the great opportunity? If so, the fame thereof has not yet reached us.

In view of the facts, it will not be denied that China has proven a hard field to both merchants and officials,— difficult to cultivate, and yielding not very generous results. Possibly the missionary will boast of no splendid success,— of nothing more than slow and steady progress; but he will at least be willing to have us consider missions "by the same tests as we apply to more mundane undertakings," as they are exhibited in the several spheres of foreign enterprise in the Far East.

The object sought by the missionaries is the complete evangelization of China. It is an undertaking of vast import, into which must enter the element of time. We ourselves are not what we are as the result of a brief period of Christian work; and it ought not to be forgotten, in the critical survey of missions in China, that it is only a few years since that country was opened to the propagation of the Gospel. Not until some time after Dr. Morrison had completed his laborious life did the agents of Protestant evangelism find it practicable to enter more than two or three cities of the empire. They could possibly make bricks without straw, but they could not build up Churches without converts, who were to be won only as the opportunity was presented of teaching and preaching. At first, the procuring of houses to live in, the erection of chapels, the organization of schools,—in fact, almost every advance movement,—was carried on in the midst of constant peril and peculiar embarrassments. Many of the ablest men have been employed as pioneers,—the picket-guard of the advancing column. It was for them to penetrate the *terra incognita* of heathenism, to encounter and subdue novel and untried difficulties, to determine the far-reaching policy of missions, to compile grammars and dictionaries, to translate the Sacred Volume and other needed text-books, and to organize and equip all the appliances for carrying on so important a work. Although not immediately producing the fruit desired, much of this labor will not have to be performed again; and the successors of these learned and faithful men are put in possession of a vast apparatus, which cannot fail in their hands to prove formidable as against the powers of darkness.

To win the first little company of neophytes was no small thing. As each idolater was held fast by the entire force of native superstition, the conversion of one was a triumph over the whole might of paganism. As a public Christian sentiment was created, the work of propagandism went forward with greater ease and more rapid success. Bands of secret worshipers expanded into societies; congregations were assembled statedly for divine service, and the whole elaborate church organization came at length into being.

The Established Church of England and the American Protestant Episcopal Church have their diocesan fields of labor, with their bishops and native and foreign clergy. The missionaries of the London Society have instituted the Independent or Congregational order. American Presbyterianism has her Synod, with several Presbyteries. The English Wesleyans, American Baptists, the Methodist Episcopal Church of the United States, to mention no others, are also represented each by their peculiar ecclesiastical forms; all working together in much harmony, the foreign laborers being reinforced and greatly aided by an able corps of native pastors and teachers.

The Synod of China, connected with the American Presbyterian Church, met, as appointed by the General Assembly, in the mission chapel in Shanghai, on the evening of October 20, 1870. The opening sermon was preached by the Rev. J. L. Nevius, D.D., in the Ningpo dialect, on the subject of "Christian Unity." Dr. Nevius was elected moderator for the ensuing year, and Rev. S. Dodd, Rev. Tsiang Nyieng-kwan and elder Lu Kyæ-dzing were chosen clerks. The body consisted of about fifty ministers, who were divided into eight Presbyteries, including one in Japan and one in Siam. The returns were found to be incomplete, but the reports as given showed a membership of over seven hundred, with contributions to the amount of some seven hundred dollars. It was estimated that if the members were equally divided into three or four Churches, the amount of money raised would support as many native pastors, and also leave something over to give toward planting the Gospel in new regions.*

The first Chinese annual Conference of the Methodist Episcopal Church was organized by Bishop I. W. Wiley, December 20, 1877, in Tieng-Ang-Tong, or "Church of the Heavenly Rest," in the city of Foo-chow. The Bishop, referring to the time when he himself had been a missionary to the Chinese, and when, twenty-three years before, he had found it necessary to leave the city in consequence of broken health, indulged in these reflections: "Then, there was not a Church nor a native Christian; now, there are in this city three large Churches of our own mission, besides several of other missions. Then, we could not, by treaty rights, pass more than five miles beyond the city; now, our missionaries and native preachers have their districts and their circuits, reaching one hundred and fifty miles to the north and west and two hundred miles to the south and east. Now, there are over four thousand native Christians in the three missions; and in this church I now see before me eighty native Chinese preachers, and between two and three hundred native Chinese Christians, representing a church membership of more than two thousand, ready to be organized into an annual Conference!"† The good Bishop might have further reflected, that, compared with the history of his home Church, there had been a gain in

---

* The "Chinese Recorder," April 1871.
† Wiley's "China and Japan," p. 224.

China of four years in time and over eight hundred in membership.

The North China Mission of the American Board of Commissioners for Foreign Missions held their first annual meeting in Peking, in the month of February 1867; at which time there were three stations, fourteen foreign laborers, and no more than a score of converts. The annual meeting for 1880 reported six stations, forty missionaries, eight licentiates, and over four hundred native Christians. And this makes no mention of the successful and prosperous mission in South China.

General organizations, transcending denominational lines but not conflicting with them, which are a pleasant and legitimate fruit of Catholicity, and also a sure indication of healthful progress, are beginning to spring up. The Chinese Tract Society, only two or three years old, is already proposing an extended scheme of operations. It has a board of forty trustees, being composed half of foreign missionaries and half of native Christians, representing all the Churches. The object is to make known the Gospel by printed truth, for which purpose it solicits the coöperation of Christians in all lands, and especially seeks the formation of auxiliary societies among the natives. Several valuable works are in the hands of the Publishing Committee, and a large number of native Christians are enrolled as members. A Chinese preacher in the Sandwich Islands has written to know how he can forward a contribution of fifty dollars to become a life member. The Shanghai Missionary Conference, held in the month of May 1877, was composed of one hundred and twenty ladies and gentlemen, representing nearly all the foreign missionary societies laboring in China. Questions of the utmost gravity, pertaining to the one universal Church of Christ, were discussed with zeal, learning, and a high order of ability. The most fraternal spirit prevailed, and the sessions concluded with a prayer-service of phenomenal power. The faith and assurance of that body of experienced Christian workers may be inferred from the fact that when the question was asked, "Ought we not to make an effort to save China in this generation?" the answer was returned as the sentiment of all, "The Church of God can do it, if she be only faithful to her great commission."*

If it be true that the preaching of the Gospel is in reality not so much the proclamation of a doctrine as the holding up of a life, it becomes a source of eminent satisfaction that our representatives in China are establishing a personal character and influence worthy of their high calling. To a gentleman who recently visited him in Shanghai, the Hon. Geo. F. Seward, late Consul-General and United States Minister, said: "The residence of a number of missionaries in Peking, their orderly lives and their harmony, have produced a good effect upon the Chinese officials." "Their presence at the capital, then," said the visitor, "has not produced complications." "On the contrary," replied Mr. Seward, "their presence has tended to allay the prejudices existing against foreigners." During the famine in North China, in 1877-8, benevolent contributions from England and America, with the local aid, amounted to some four hundred thousand dollars. It would have been simply impossible to have extended to famishing Chinese the relief

---

* "Records of the Missionary Conference": Shanghai. Presbyterian Mission Press.

contemplated by this fund without the aid of missionaries. Nearly the whole of the work of distribution was committed to their hands, and it was faithfully and ably done. It has been estimated on good authority that in the south part of Shan-si province alone six millions of people perished. The Rev. Timothy Richard wrought in that field with such success that he was enabled to relieve much suffering and save many lives. The Chinese officers sought his aid in the emergency, and subsequently offered to erect a tablet to his memory. At one time he numbered no less than four hundred inquirers, none of whom were recipients of the bounty distributed, but who were led to think that the religion that prompted the charity must be more than human. The dire distress of the Chinese was the opportunity of many of the English and American missionaries. And when the people saw these men exposing themselves to toil and hardship, without fear of the famine fever, passing from village to village and from city to city intent on the work of charity, they said, "These foreign teachers are indeed living Boodhas!" Such incarnations of mercy, placed under their own personal observation, will surely attract many Chinese away from the service of their idol gods to a pure faith and a holy life.

It is too late to speculate on a question of the probable success or non-success of Christian missions in China. *They are succeeding.* A Church of the living God has been raised up in that land,— youthful, but rejoicing in a vigorous and growing life; with numbers few, but possessing the truth, loving the truth, and ready to die for the truth. Twenty thousand converts and six hundred native preachers, eloquent as the figures are, do not express the full measure of results. The power of the Gospel to subdue the superstition, pride and avarice of Chinamen has been abundantly demonstrated. The spirit of revival and emotional piety has, on repeated occasions, stirred their impassive Asiatic nature. Moreover, revealed truth has come in contact with many unenlightened minds; and that truth is neither imponderable nor effete. "The indestructibility of force" in the material world, revealed by modern scientific research, should teach us that the moral force expended even a generation ago in this controversy with paganism has not been lost. Our unbelief stands revealed in its weakness and folly before the sublime faith of a native Christian scholar who uttered this sentiment: "The Cross points in all directions, North and South, East and West, implying that its object is to extend far and wide, and that its influence is to be commensurate with the ends of the earth." What has been achieved may be regarded as a great prophetic fact; for if the present rate of conversion of the Chinese to Christianity should continue, by the year 1913 there will be twenty-six millions of Church members and one hundred millions of nominal Christians in the empire.

Confucianism,—the representative religion of China,—containing much that is good and little that is positively vicious, and which appears wisely designed to rectify the social system and exalt the state, has had the most unlimited scope for its development. The great teacher perfected his system and committed it to the jealous watchcare of three thousand disciples nearly five centuries before Christ, and it has been continued until this day. No form of religion in the empire has been able to supplant or even seriously to influence it. It has been nourished and defended by a long line of illustrious kings and emperors; while, during a period of two millenniums, its principles have been taught and enforced by the greatest scholars and philosophers in the land. Judging from outward appearances, no system has ever been more successfully propagated. All the culture and education is based upon it, and is fashioned by its precepts and methods of thought. "The roads to honor, to wealth, and to official preferment, all start out from the skill displayed in stating and applying the maxims of the sage and his expounders. The most powerful social class is composed of those who have been covered with literary honors for their proficiency in the knowledge of Confucius. Confucianism is really the state constitution; it is the state religion; it is the state etiquette. Confucius and his teachings are worshiped by three hundred millions of people. The words that fell from his lips form the theses of all the literary tournaments of the empire. They are graven deep on granite monuments. They are posted on the doorways of pavilions and rest-houses every year. They are written on fans that are ever in hand. They are painted on bed-curtains. They are gilded on rolls, and hung up to adorn their temples and dwelling-houses. They furnish the phraseology with which men of polite learning exchange amenities with each other; and they may be heard falling from the lips of the common people in the markets, when chaffering about the price of shrimps and snails."* It thus appears that Confucianism has enjoyed all the most favorable conditions for a perfect development. God in his wise providence has given the nation length of days, isolation from unfriendly foreign influence, with the broadest field for a vast experi-

* "A Moral Problem Solved by Confucius," by Rev. William Ashmore.

ment well calculated to show what can be accomplished by the virtue that has survived the fall. What, then, is the result? Perhaps we could give no more pertinent reply than to briefly sketch the moral condition of the Chinese, as exhibited in the various phases of national life.

The "five virtues,"—benevolence, integrity, propriety, wisdom, sincerity, with filial piety,—are inculcated for universal observance, and to their partial exemplification in the daily life of the people we may attribute their remarkable longevity as a nation, their love of fixed and orderly modes of life, their thrifty habits, and their general tendency to practice the arts of peace. It must be said, however, that although truth and honesty are recognized and commended as virtues, their very opposites are far more extensively known, and constitute the defects which are peculiar to Chinese character. The art of deceiving is studied and practiced among all classes. It is popularly regarded as an accomplishment rather than as a vice. Commercial integrity is almost wholly unknown, except where fair dealing is the most profitable rule of business. The sacerdotal orders are by no means free from the practices of deception. The holiest men of the priesthood, who spend their lives in chanting prayers and counting the rosary, will not hesitate at the most outrageous mendacity, while in the eyes of the people this fact seems to derogate nothing from their sacred character. The Chinese have succeeded in devising a wise system of laws, and no pagan country in the world could be better governed if the conduct and probity of the officers were only answerable to the institution of the government. But the ruling classes are unjust, extortionate, and thoroughly corrupt. The inferior officers constantly aim at defrauding their superiors, while these in turn deceive the supreme tribunals, and all together plot how to cheat the Prince, which they do in memorials so full of cunning, adulation, and plausible reasons, that the deluded emperor frequently takes the greatest falsehoods for solemn truths. So thoroughly organized is this system of fraud, that His Majesty rarely or never knows the state of his own exchequer, nor the real condition of any part of the empire, near or remote. Should the ruling power attempt to raise a popular loan, as is frequently done in the Western world, with promise of the payment of annual interest, the attempt would prove a total failure. No subject would buy an evidence of debt against the government at any price, simply because there is no faith in its financial soundness or integrity. There is reason to believe that even the censors are hopelessly corrupt, as their opinions are bought and sold, and their apparent boldness in denouncing errors and crimes of administration is designed more frequently to cover up the misconduct of the parties accused, or their own shortcomings, than to secure honesty in the conduct of public affairs, and so these sacred guardians of the law come to possess no better claim to that high character than a mere title or name.

Thus we have before us the startling fact that, notwithstanding the prominence given to equity and truth in the accepted system of Confucian ethics, the spirit of injustice and deception pervades the entire fabric of Chinese society. But this is not all. Possessing more virtues than most heathen nations, this people at the same time exhibit all the lineaments of a fallen and depraved nature. They are ostentatiously polite, and hold "propriety," or the rules of etiquette, in high esteem; yet, no sooner is the exterior polish off, than the rudeness, brutality and coarseness of the material is seen. With a general regard for outward decency, they have many vile and polluting habits. Their conversation abounds in filthy expressions, especially when anger or resentment are excited. The mother will address the daughter, in the hearing of her neighbors, with the most foul and revolting language. In street quarrels and public disputes the same kind of language is used, and the ears of the passer-by are frequently assailed by imprecations reeking with the very essence of bestiality and corruption. The general worship of devils, deified men, and false gods; the universal habit of lying and dishonest dealing; the widespread existence of polygamy, poisoning with its bitter waters the very fountain-head of social virtue; the practice of female infanticide, openly confessed in many parts of the country, and nowhere visited with the penalties of law; the unblushing lewdness of old and young; the barbarous cruelty of officers of justice toward prisoners, and the prevalence of all the vices charged by the Apostle Paul upon the ancient heathen world,— these conspire to place before our minds a true picture of the desolating horrors of heathenism.

In the light of these facts, then, what can we do but pronounce Confucianism a stupendous failure? It not only has been unable to discover some of the most important truths necessary to a complete system of morals, but has failed to conserve the knowledge of God handed down from the ancients. More than this: while it has proven unequal to the task of lifting man to the higher plane of moral and intellectual life, it has not even made the attempt to deliver him from the chains of superstition, nor can it furnish an antidote for the malady of sin. Here is a great and overwhelming fact, the full knowledge of which is only just beginning to dawn upon our age. China, with a teeming population embracing one-third part of the human species, stands as "the Methuselah of the nations." Proud of a vain philosophy and an empty faith, and supposing them to embody all the wealth of knowledge and wisdom, this people boastingly say, "we are rich, and increased with goods, and have need of nothing," knowing not that they are "wretched, and miserable, and poor, and blind, and naked."

Thus the "land of Sinim" appears to the Christian world, after the experiment of sixty generations, yielding an eloquent though unconscious testimony to the wisdom of God's plan of salvation. The high priests of paganism must needs have their turn first, as they vainly endeavor to call down fire from heaven; while Christianity, Elijah-like, patiently waits for the time of the evening sacrifice, and until the devotees of idolatry have become faint from their self-inflicted torture and maceration. Now she comes forward, builds her altar, and displays upon it the glorious Cross,— that hallowed symbol of the world's hope,— while God answers by pouring out his Spirit to regenerate and save a fallen race.

CHAPTER XIII.

THE TI-PING INSURRECTION.

THIS remarkable movement, which at one time excited much interest in Western lands, originated with a man named Hung Sew-tseuen, son of a humble peasant residing in a village near Canton. On the occasion of one of his visits to the provincial city, probably in the year 1833, he appears to have seen a foreign Protestant missionary addressing the populace in the streets, assisted by a native interpreter. Either then or on the following day he received from some tract-distributor a book entitled "Good Words for Exhorting the Age," which consisted of essays and sermons by Leang A-fah, a well known convert and evangelist. Taking the volume home with him, he looked it over with some interest, but carelessly laid it aside in his book-case. A few years afterward he attended for the second time the competitive literary examination with high hopes of honor and distinction, having already passed with much credit the lower examination in the district city. His ambitious venture, however, met with severe disappointment, and he returned to his friends sick in mind and body. During this state of mental depression and physical infirmity, which continued for some forty days, he had certain strange visions, in which he received commands from heaven to destroy the idols. These fancied revelations seem to have produced a deep impression on his mind, and led to a certain gravity of demeanor after his recovery and return to his quiet occupation as a student and village schoolmaster. When the English war broke out, and foreigners swept up Canton River with their wonderful fire-ships and other irresistible engines of war, and when, eventually, the treaty was published showing that trade had been resumed at Canton free from former restrictions, and that four great marts had been thrown open in the northern provinces, it is not surprising that Hung should have had his attention again attracted to the Christian publication which had lain so long neglected in his library. Curiosity to learn something of the religious views entertained by the powerful nations of the West, gave place to astonishment and a profound interest when he discovered in this book what seemed to be a key to the visions which had come to him during his sickness six years before. The writings of Leang A-fah contained chapters from the Old and New Testament Scriptures, which he found to correspond in a striking manner with the preternatural sights and voices of that memorable period in his history; and this strange coincidence convinced him of their truth, and of his being divinely appointed to restore the world, that is, China, to the worship of the true God.

Hung Sew-tseuen accepted his mission and began at once the work of propagating the faith he had espoused. Among his first converts was one Fung Yun-san, who became a most ardent missionary and disinterested preacher. These two leaders of the movement traveled far and near through the country, teaching the people of all classes and forming a society of God-worshipers. All the converts renounced idolatry and gave up the worship of Confucius. Hung, at this time apparently a sincere and earnest seeker after truth, went to Canton and placed himself under the instructions of the Rev. Mr. Roberts, an American missionary, who for some cause fearing that his novitiate might be inspired by mercenary motives, denied him the rite of baptism. But, without being offended at this cold and suspicious treatment, he went home and taught his converts how to baptize themselves. The God-worshipers rapidly increased in number, and were known and feared as zealous iconoclasts. Some of them were arrested for destroying idols, among whom was Fung Yun-San himself, who, however, on his way to prison, converted his police-guard, and they not only set him at liberty but went with him as his disciples.

During a temporary absence of the two leaders from the central assembly at Thistle-mount, the religious movement first began to assume its extreme fanatical phase.* It sometimes happened that while the people were kneeling in prayer one or another present would be seized by a sudden fit and fall prostrate, the whole body covered with perspiration. In such a state of ecstasy, moved by "the spirit," he would utter words of exhortation, reproof, and prophecy, generally in rhythm, but the words often being unintelligible. The brethren noted down in a book the more remarkable of these sayings, and presented them for inspection to Hung when that personage had returned from one of his tours. The latter "judged the spirits according to the truth of the doctrine, and declared that the words of those moved were partly true and partly false," having their inspiration both from God and from the Devil. An obscure man by the name of Yang, who had joined the congregation with much earnestness, sud-

* "The Chinese and their Rebellions," by T. T. Meadows, pp. 98-105.

denly lost his power of speech, and was dumb for a period of two months, after which he spoke in the name of God the Father, and in a solemn and awe-inspiring manner reproved the sins of the people, frequently pointing out individuals and exposing their evil actions. He was thought to possess the gift of healing, by intercession for the sick. Seaou, another inspired prophet, was accustomed to speak in the name of Jesus. The fact that Hung acknowledged these two men as communicators of the divine will is strong presumptive proof of his own sincerity, for if he had been a deliberate impostor he would scarcely have tolerated a state of things which must have threatened the divided allegiance of the people. These two proselytes were subsequently each invested with a high dignity, it being distinctly stated of them respectively that "when the Heavenly Father comes down into the world to instruct the people, his sacred will is delivered by the mouth of the Eastern Prince," and that "when the Heavenly Brother, Jesus, comes down into the world to instruct the people, his sacred will is delivered by the mouth of the Western Prince."

For a year after Hung Sew-tseuen had rejoined the God-worshipers that society retained its exclusively religious nature, but in the autumn of 1850 it was brought into direct collision with the civil magistrates, when the movement assumed a political character of the highest aims. Hung had been accustomed to assert his authority as Heaven's Commissioner and to preach against all opposition with stern vehemence. He violently destroyed a much-revered idol in Kwang-si, declaring that "too much patience and humility do not suit our present times, for therewith it would be impossible to manage this perverted generation." The demolition of a number of images by his fanatical adherents finally incensed the general population and provoked the local authorities to take measures to suppress the dangerous sect.

About this time a British squadron, near the southern extremity of the empire, had finally succeeded in driving some two thousand pirates from their predatory life on the sea to a lawless career on shore, where, combining with the banditti of southeastern China, they soon became a force sufficiently strong to take and keep the field as avowed rebels against the Manchoo dynasty. Kwang-tung, of which Canton is the vice-regal city, is composed, in part, of a high, mountainous region inhabited by tribes best known as the Meaou-tsze, who are thought to be the aboriginal race. The valleys and plains of the province constitute the portion of the country last occupied by Chinese colonists, and there appears to have been two immigrations, with an interval of time between them long enough to give rise to a distinction known to this day in the terms Pun-te, or "natives," and Kih-kea, or "strangers." The latter had been settled for several generations in the province, and although possessing numerous towns and villages, they were neither so numerous nor so opulent as the "native" Kwang-tung people. The rebel horde were nearly all Kih-keas, and it was among this distinctive class of "strangers" that Hung and his associates had made the most of their converts. Nothing could be more natural than that these parties, who were both alike pursued and threatened by the imperial forces, and who also possessed a still stronger bond of sympathy in their traditions and dialect, should bo brought together in close alliance and eventually become co-religionists.

The right to rebel is in China thought to be a chief element of national stability. So long as the occupant of the throne rules with the rectitude and goodness which are in imitation of T'een-taou, or the "way of heaven," both man and nature are held in submissive harmony. But when he violates the principles of supreme justice, the passions of men and the powers of the elements alike break away from all bounds of restraint. The disasters of war, pestilence, and famine,— even earthquakes and storms of extraordinary violence,— are but so many intimations that Heaven is about to withdraw from him the Divine Commission. Says Mr. Meadows, in speaking of the patriarchal feature of the government, "In truth, the analogy between the family and the state does not hold good on Chinese views themselves. In China, sons never have the right to resist the cruelties of the most tyrannical father: by one of the oldest and most deeply rooted of the national doctrines, the people have the distinct right to depose and put to death a tyrannical emperor. And this very departure from the strict patriarchality is one of the causes of the stability of the nation: it is thereby permitted to free itself from tyrannical government, which, if prolonged, would cause its destruction."

The Manchoo garrisons, or bannermen, who had so long held residence in the country, had greatly deteriorated in their military virtues while they still retained enough of the insolence of conquerors to awaken, on occasions, the hatred of the Chinese. The practice of selling offices of trust and honor to men who had wealth but were destitute of literary and other essential qualifications, was steadily increasing. The maxims of ancient wisdom were no longer faithfully recommended by the censors of the empire, nor were they observed in the administration. The weakness and misrule of the Tartars had subjected large portions of the country to robbery and anarchy; while their prestige was greatly shaken by the shock they had sustained from British arms. As an educated Chinese, Hung Sew-tseuen must have called to mind the teaching of the Sacred Books, that it is the duty of the people to overthrow any bad government; and it is conceivable that a man of his character and singular experience should feel a mighty impulse to add the functions of patriotic insurgent to those of religious reformer, since the call and the opportunity to do so were thrust upon him with extraordinary emphasis.

Early in the year 1853, the movement had acquired large proportions, and the continued success of the Ti-pings strengthened the conviction in their minds of the exalted character of their leader, concerning whom they were emboldened to issue the following proclamation: "Our Heavenly Prince has received the Divine Commission to exterminate the Manchoos,— to exterminate them utterly, men, women, and children,— to exterminate all idolaters generally, and to possess the Empire as its true sovereign. It, and everything in it, is his: its mountains and rivers, its broad lands and public treasuries; you, and all that you have, your family, males and females from yourself to your youngest child, and your property from your patrimonial estates to the bracelet on your infant's arm. We command the services of all, and we take everything. All who resist us are rebels and idolatrous demons, and we kill them without sparing; but whoever acknowledges our Heavenly Prince and exerts himself in our service shall have full reward,— due honor and station in the armies and Court of the Heavenly Dynasty."* At one time two noted female rebel chiefs, each at the head of about two thousand followers, joined the insurgents, after submitting to the authority of their Prince and the rules of the congregation. They were placed at a distance from the main body of the Ti-ping army, to serve as outposts, one on each side. Eight chiefs of the famed Triad Society, with their respective bands, were also received, under the covenant to conform to the worship of the true God. During the twelve months' progress of Hung from Kwang-si northward to Nanking, the accessions of strength from all sources had been such as to enable him to invest that city with at least five armies of about fourteen thousand men each.

Nothing could be more sublime than the courage and general bearing of the great chieftain, as he organized and led on the adventurous host. Styling himself the "One Man," the "Son of Heaven," to whom the "exterminating decree" had been entrusted, he demanded the implicit faith and obedience of all. He would sometimes say to his more timid and fearful generals: "The Heavenly Father has given me this Middle Kingdom. The eighteen provinces are mine. I do not depend upon you for success. I can do without you; but you cannot exist without me. Should you all forsake me, my cause must triumph. Begone! The Heavenly Father mightily reigneth, therefore my dynasty shall exist forever; the Elder Brother bears my burden, therefore the Celestial Hall shall be full of glory, forever full of glory!" In this

* Meadows' "Chinese and their Rebellions," pp. 149-50.

grandiloquent manner he asserted that the possession of the empire was with him a mere question of time; and his followers, with an enthusiastic *esprit de corps*, believed in the justice of his cause and the divinity of his mission.

Traversing the northern part of the province of Kwang-si, the whole of Ho-nan and Hoo-peh, and from Woo-chang down the Great River, a total distance of about one thousand miles, this march of the Ti-ping forces was a most remarkable military achievement. They first attacked individuals and towns which had opposed and persecuted them on account of their religion, obtaining from these needed supplies of food and clothing. When towns or cities submitted to their authority without opposition, they were treated with leniency; but indiscriminate slaughter awaited all who denied and resisted their claims. The imperial troops sent to suppress the insurrection were completely routed. Before battle, the followers of the Chinese Prophet often knelt in the open fields to invoke the protection and assistance of Heaven, and then charged upon their enemies with fanatical zeal and resistless power. City after city fell before their triumphant march, and the whole empire regarded with astonishment and dismay the progress of these conquering legions.

Seldom has history placed under our observation a more impressive exhibition of the religious sentiment dominated by error and superstition than was presented among the Ti-pings while encamped before Nanking, and for some time after they had gained possession of that important city. They professed faith in the Old and New Testament Scriptures, and an imperfect translation of these was printed and circulated gratuitously by the authorities;*

* "Ti-ping T'een-kwoh," by Lin-li, vol. i, p. 306.

the head of the insurrection distinctly announcing that, in the event of final success, the Bible would be substituted for Confucius in all public examinations for official position. Abstracts of the sacred volume, put into verse, were circulated and committed to memory. Forms of prayer to the Supreme Being were in constant use, both publicly and in private. The Sabbath was strictly observed on the seventh day, all ordinary business being suspended, and religious worship and instruction maintained both in camp and in the temples. Divine service usually opened with a doxology to God, Jesus, and the Holy Spirit, after which the following hymn was sung:

"The true doctrine is different from the doctrine of this world;
It saves men's souls and gives eternal bliss.
The wise receive it instantly with joy;
The foolish, wakened by it, find the way to Heaven.
Our Heavenly Father, of his great mercy,
Did not spare his own Son, but sent him down
To give his life to redeem sinners.
When men know this, and repent, they may go to Heaven."

Three cups of tea were placed on the altar as an offering to the sacred Trinity. The further services consisted of reading the Scriptures and a sermon, the repetition of a creed by the congregation standing, and of a written prayer by the whole congregation kneeling, when the paper containing the petition thus offered was burned, an anthem chanted to the long life of the Prince, followed by the Ten Commandments, music, and the burning of incense with fire-crackers. The clergy were chosen by competitive examination, and each minister had under his spiritual jurisdiction twenty-five families, with a church, or "heavenly hall," assigned to him in some public building. Over every twenty-five parishes there was a superior, who visited them in turn on Sabbath days; while once a month the whole people were addressed by the T'een-wong, or Great High Priest. Before seating themselves to repast, all the people in their houses and the whole army were accustomed to reverent recitation of some passage from one of their sacred books. In times of danger the females were placed in positions of safety, as far as possible, and guarded from all improper intrusions; and this was consistent with their custom of punishing with death the brutal crimes against women to which they are usually exposed in the storming of cities. An Englishman, who served as special agent of the General-in-Chief, and who afterward published the "Ti-ping T'een-kwoh," under his Chinese name, Lin-le, describing his attendance on morning prayers in the "heavenly hall" of the Chung-wong's household, which took place at sunrise, the men and women sitting on opposite sides of the apartment, says: "Oftentimes, while kneeling in the midst of an apparently devout congregation, and gazing on the upturned countenances lightened by the early morning sun, have I wondered why no British missionary occupied my place, and why Europeans generally preferred slaughtering the Ti-pings to accepting them as brothers in Christ. When I look back," he adds, "on the unchangeable and universal kindness I always met with among the Ti-pings, even when their dearest relatives were being slaughtered by my countrymen, or delivered over to the Manchoos to be tortured to death, their magnanimous forbearance seems like a dream. Their kind and friendly feelings were often annoying. To those who have experienced the ordinary dislike of foreigners by the Chinese, the surprising friendliness of the Ti-pings was most remarkable. They welcomed Europeans as 'brethren from across the sea,' and claimed them as fellow-worshipers of 'Yesu.'"*

Before the attack on Nanking, a large body of the more faithful and devout insurgents knelt in prayer, and then rose and fought with invincible courage, having refused the aid of a large body of rebels because they did not renounce idolatry and continued to allow the use of opium. The city having been carried at length, and the whole Tartar garrison put to death, Hung Sew-tseuen resolved to make this the capital of his new kingdom, and attempt the gigantic task of subjugating the empire. Four leading cities of Central China were speedily occupied, two of which, Chin-kiang and Kwa-chow, constituted together a most commanding military position, when the Ti-pings acted remorselessly on the lofty pretensions and claims of the Heavenly Prince to the persons and property of all Chinese. They seized the entire population within reach, with everything of the slightest value, and transported all to Nanking, excepting the garrisons which were left in the other three cities. The men were organized into armies and dispatched in various directions; while their aged parents, their wives, sisters, and children, were detained at the capital, and kept as hostages for the fidelity of their relatives in the field. The march from the south to Nanking was now to be exceeded in brilliancy by a movement toward the northern seat of empire. The very day on which the Ti-ping army left the banks of the Yang-tsz-Kiang, all communication with its friends and the base of supplies was cut off, with the exception of such irregular correspondence as could be maintained by disguised messengers.

* "Ten Great Religions," by James Freeman Clarke, pp. 64-67.

A strong force of imperialists followed the advancing host as it perseveringly made its way northward in spite of the inclement weather and various accumulating difficulties. Swerving first to the west, then to the east, but never turning southward, the march was maintained during a period of six months. Beleaguered by their more numerous and more efficient foes at Tsing-hai, the rebels yet maintained their position while an auxiliary army was being sent to their relief from Nanking. The united forces continued their progress toward Peking, until their near approach threatened with imminent peril the Dragon Throne itself, and spread dismay among the servants of the Emperor. But they were finally repulsed with great slaughter, the struggle leaving a wide extent of country in a state of ruin and distress, the insurgents and imperialists seeming to vie with each other in their efforts to harass and plunder the people.

Although the sympathies of the Christian world had been enlisted for this great uprising among a heathen people, so characterized at first by sincere religious sentiment, it had no more practical manifestation than a few feeble and unsuccessful attempts on the part of missionaries to reach with their influence the ill-taught Ti-pings; and finally the whole might of Western civilization was thrown in the scale against the attempted revolution. The fact that the use of opium was utterly prohibited by the government at Nanking doubtless had a strong influence in shaping the policy of the English merchants, and the European powers through their consular agents were controlled by the demands of commerce. The ports open to foreign trade became the bases of operations against the insurgents, and the imperial cause was reinforced by detachments of British and French troops. The British cruisers treated the Ti-ping junks as pirates because they captured Chinese vessels. They were also engaged in repeated transactions when these junks were destroyed, and their men shot, drowned, and hunted down; in one instance giving up a crew they had captured to be put to death. The British soldiers and navy took part in forty-three battles and massacres, in which about four hundred thousand Ti-pings were killed, and upward of two millions more died of starvation in the famine occasioned by the operations of the allied English, French and Chinese troops.* Gen. Ward, an American, drilled a force of twenty-five hundred natives after the foreign style, the organization being enlarged and rendered more effective under Gen. Burgevine, another American. The "Ever-victorious Army," commanded by Col. Gordon, of England, operating in the province of Kiang-su, and a French-drilled force in Che-kiang, dealt rapid and decisive blows at the expiring life of the rebellion.

Hoping to retrieve their waning fortunes, the rebels at one time endeavored to take possession of the coast provinces and avail themselves of the advantages of the commerce of their ports. They were so far successful as to occupy both Shanghai and Ningpo, but were compelled by English troops, aided by the Chinese, to abandon those cities. Notwithstanding their intercourse with and treatment by foreign nations might have justly embittered their minds and given rise to resentment and retaliation, foreign residents in Ningpo and foreign travelers who visited them in the interior were almost invariably received with cordiality, and treated with respect and kindness.

* "Intervention and Non-intervention," by A. G. Stapleton.

Driven out of every other stronghold, the insurgent forces retired to Nanking, when the doomed city was completely invested by an immense army. In July, 1864, the last hope of the Ti-ping, or "Universal Peace" dynasty, was extinguished in the fall and destruction of its capital. Three days were given up to the dreadful work of slaughter; nevertheless, many who escaped the edge of the sword fled to different parts of the country and joined predatory bands, or returned to their peaceful homes in the South. Hung Sew-tseuen, the rebel chief, had committed suicide, but his remains were exhumed from the ruins of his palace, the head severed and exposed for public inspection, and the remainder of the body cut in pieces and afterward burned. The "Young Lord," Hung Fu-teen, who had succeeded to the dignity of his father, encircled himself with a funeral pile, intending to fire it when the city fell; but finally, amid the general confusion, effected his escape with a number of followers. He was afterward captured and condemned to suffer a slow and ignominious death in the provincial city of Kiang-si.*

The august head of the Empire made no acknowledgment in his public decrees of the foreign assistance he had received, but piously ascribed the success of his armies to the gods of the hills and streams, who had given their efficient protection and guidance. Announcing the overthrow of rebellion in a formal edict, the youthful sovereign thus revealed to his faithful subjects the anxiety that had long oppressed the imperial mind.

"At the period when His Majesty the late Emperor came to the throne, it happened that the Canton rebels had risen in insurrection and spread devastation through

* "Autobiography of the Chung-wong," translated by W. T. Lay, pp. 83, 103.

many cities. The army was at once put in motion in order to carry out the dictates of Heaven; but, although many desperate rebels were extirpated, nevertheless their influence diffused itself around, and it was found impossible at once to put them down. Our Imperial Sire was filled with anguish and care day and night, and His thoughts were ever occupied with the extermination of the thieves and the comfort of His people. In mournful anxiety He looked forward to the announcement of victory.

"When in the eleventh year of Heen-fung, He sped upward on the dragon to be a guest on high. In His last decree and testament, He even then adverted to the state of disquiet still prevalent in the Southeast, and that His people were being driven hither and thither and compelled to fly in all directions. The sainted anxiety was ever troubled.

"On Our accession to the important charge laid upon Us, We cried unto Heaven in bitter agony, and day by day did We watch for the annihilation of the great ring-leader, that so the boundaries of the empire might be restored to peace, and the yet unfulfilled will of Our Imperial Sire be accomplished. The two Empresses Dowager gave their disinterested attention to the numerous state matters, and instructed and nurtured Ourself. They were ever looking for victorious news, from night till morning and from morning till night successively.

"Kuan-wun and Tsung Kwo-fan having now, on the 29th of this month, announced a victory and the recovery of Nanking, We feel grateful to Our departed Sire for the means left behind him, which have stimulated Us to complete this great work, and to celebrate the fame of Our ancestors. But in the midst of Our joy and gratitude We are weighed down with excessive grief. We had purposed to proceed Ourself to the sarcophagus of the departed Emperor and there pour out Our tribute of grief and affection over the departed remains; but the Empresses Dowager fearing that, as the Autumn crops are now in a flourishing state, and that the number of carriages, etc., forming Our escort along the Imperial path, will be sure to tread down the people's labor, and moreover, that the repair and filling in of the road will seriously disturb the people, have directed Us to appoint the Prince of Shun, Yi-huan, to proceed to the Shrine of Glorious Happiness, the resting-place of the coffin, and before the communion table in front of it perform the necessary ceremonies on Our behalf, and respectfully announce the victorious news."

CHAPTER XIV.

OCCIDENTAL LIFE IN THE ORIENT.

CANTON is more widely known in the West than any other city of the Celestial Empire. Dotted all over with temples and pagodas, containing many palatial residences and extensive warehouses, adorned with private and public gardens in which the floral art displays a profusion of unique and wonderful skill, presenting to the habitant as also to traders from the country and visitors from abroad her places of amusement and gilded dens of vice, displaying in her restaurants tempting viands alike to the hungry traveler and the leisurely gormand, with a population much given to pleasure and folly, this great emporium has long been recognized as the "Paris of China." It is the oldest and, even to this day, the most difficult center of missionary operations in the whole country. Here as nowhere else prejudice has developed against the foreigner, because here the greatest wrongs have been perpetrated against the people and the government, and the worst examples of Christian civilization have for generations been placed under the daily observation of all classes of native society.

When the treaty of 1858 was made, French influence artfully gained the insertion of a proviso that all sites formerly possessed by Catholic missions should be restored. Whereupon, from among the numerous deeds of trust and conveyances of land forthcoming from the Vatican was one of the former purporting to prove that a plot of eighteen acres in the heart of Canton had once been possessed by the agents of the Church. The Chinese authorities were naturally astounded at this, as the site in question had been occupied by the Government House from time immemorial, and they immediately entered their solemn protest. But the French commander said, "If you have no power to give it, I have power to take it"; and he proceeded to occupy the premises with a military force. Already reduced to a heap of ruins by the fortunes of war, all that remained of the Chinese structure soon disappeared, and on this very spot arose in process of time a Roman Catholic Cathedral, towering in solitary state over the flat-roofed city. So far from being impressed with the beauty and sacred character of the edifice, the Chinese generally look upon it as a monument of robbery and a constant reminder of their duty to cherish the feelings of hatred and revenge.

On a low, flat island outside the city walls, in the midst of a dense suburban population, but entirely separated from the natives by the river and a canal, is the far-famed "Shameen," or foreign settlement. Here are the residences and warehouses of the merchants, the consular and other official buildings, and the homes of some of the missionaries. The whole place is fitted up in a costly and attractive manner, appearing to the European observer like "an oasis of civilization in a desert of barbarism." The anchorage for foreign shipping is at Whampoa, a reach in the river twelve miles below. In former years ships from almost every great mart in the world were found in these waters, where the exchange of merchandise was conducted on a large scale; but as the neighboring Anglo-Chinese city has grown in magnitude and importance, Canton has diminished in relation to foreign trade.

Near the southeastern extremity of the Chinese empire, and about one hundred miles from the famous capital of Kwang-tung province, lies the small and mountainous island of Hong-Kong. When taken possession of by the British, in 1841, it was inhabited by a few native fishermen and smugglers; but in the lapse of a quarter of a century European capital and enterprise have wrought great changes. The city is officially known under the name of Victoria, although the old Chinese appellation of Hong-Kong is usually given to the whole island and settlement. It is one of the most unique and beautiful of oriental cities. The streets are remarkably clean and neatly finished. Everything here is under strict police and military surveillance. A hundred thousand Chinese on the island, most of them concentrated in Victoria, are under a large controlling foreign presence. The harbor is one of the finest in the world, and floats an immense commerce. In 1866 the writer counted at one time, from the flat roof of the Stag Hotel, a hundred and fifty steamers and sailing vessels; these being exclusive of the almost innumerable fleet of native craft, all of which are duly numbered and registered. according to police regulations. The "san-pans" are long, narrow, shallow and flat-bottomed boats, being propelled by paddles, or a kind of oar, and capable of carrying from two to twenty persons, with a limited amount of baggage. Europeans frequently apply to the smaller class the term "barber boat," but the Chinese name, signifying "three boards," from the simple form of construction, is also in constant use.

These tiny vessels may be seen at any hour of the day out on the harbor and along the bund, passing and repassing like cabs in the streets of London or New York.

The population of Victoria includes representatives from many parts of the world,— English, American, French, Portuguese, Indian, Malay, Arabian, and Persian. The Parsees form a considerable community, and some of them are successful and wealthy merchants. In the morning, and even at high noon, there is not much stir in the city, except in the purely Chinese quarter; but, as the day advances, the principal streets gradually assume a more lively aspect, until late in the afternoon and well into the night, when a vast tide of human life is seen pouring through each main avenue. There are people of almost every nationality and color, in costumes odd, antique, and many-hued: on foot, on horseback, in sedans, in phaetons; here and there a military or naval officer, proudly bearing the insignia of his rank, with groups of common soldiers and jolly jack-tars sauntering in and out of the curiosity shops, or bantering with fruit-venders; now and then a foreign lady, dressed *à la Parisienne*, riding in an open carriage, or in her chair, borne by men in uniform; some hurrying to and fro, as if pursuing important business engagements, some walking leisurely, with cane in hand; haughty Parsees, worshipers of the sun, sporting the Persian habit, and distinguished by their tall glazed hats; half-naked coolies, carrying heavy burdens with their bamboo poles, in contrast with the Celestial gentry, who appear in long robes, gracefully waving the ever-present fan; and native women in gay apparel, attracting public attention by their various arts,— painted courtesans, whose shameless presence in the light of day and in the glare of the street-lamp but too plainly uncovers the leprous spot of Hong-Kong society. Over all this strange scene, more fantastic and heterogeneous than perhaps any other city in the world can present, the air is resonant with the jargon of many languages, the twang of the banjo, the song of the minstrel, the indescribable plaint and whoop of burden-bearers, the cries of men hawking their wares, the din of countless rattle-boxes, and the rush of wheels,— sounds mellifluous, discordant, and ear-splitting.

Victoria has been called "the city of palaces," from its extensive hongs and numerous and elegant residences. The men who principally hold its commerce in their hands are real merchant-princes. They furnish their mansions at great expense, and in the style of the home aristocracy. Their tables abound with every native and foreign luxury, and a liberal hospitality is dispensed toward casual visitors from distant parts of the world. The daily newspaper, theatricals, libraries, reading and lecture associations, billiard-rooms, fives and racket clubs, with other sources of culture and amusement, are accessible to every foreigner of position and means. Religion is not wholly neglected, as divine service is held each Lord's Day in the English cathedral, and stated worship is maintained in a dissenting chapel whose pulpit has long been supplied by able divines. Protestant evangelism among the native population is carried on with vigor, but not with marked success. One important agency of the London Mission is a publishing house, which does excellent work, from the making of a matrix to the printing and binding of a book. Foreign residents do not forget that they are exiles from home, as one may see from the words of Solomon, cut in large letters on the arch over the main entrance to the Post-office: "As cold waters to a thirsty soul, so is good news from a far country."

In the rear of the city rises a mountainous ridge, crowned by Victoria Peak, which is a thousand feet high. Kennedy Road, a beautiful drive on the side of this elevation, affords many magnificent views of the harbor; while the summit commands an exquisite prospect of mountains, islands, and land-locked seas on every hand. A part of Happy Valley, a picturesque ravine, is devoted to the inevitable English race-course. Here, also, are the six cemeteries,— Roman Catholic, English Protestant, Mohammedan, Jewish, Portuguese, and Zoroastrian. In the latter may be seen the small "Towers of Silence" in which the bodies are exposed to be devoured by birds of prey. Several of these cities of the dead are beautifully laid out and adorned with luxuriant tropical trees, plants, and flowers. Not without significance should we regard these burying-places of many nationalities grouped together in this "Happy Valley." The strange mixture of life in the busy mart, and the various races sleeping quietly at last without prejudice and without hatred, side by side, when life's fitful dream is o'er, may appear to us as emblematic of a common hope and a common destiny which the Universal Father will yet bestow upon all.

Shanghai reposes on the banks of a small stream which disembogues its turbid waters near the mouth of the Yang-tsz-kiang. The foreign city is composed of the English, American, and French "Concessions," separated from each other by narrow creeks. Two thousand vessels clear this port yearly, and as many as three hundred steam and sailing craft have been known to lie in the harbor at one time. A street called "the bund" trends along the curve of the river for three miles, being open to the water front for that distance and lined on the opposite side with many imposing structures built in the finest style of European architecture. Several of the consular establishments are on a scale worthy of the great nations they represent. The Church of England has a costly cathedral, quite throwing into the shade the Presbyterian edifice and the Union Chapel. A splendid Club House and Masonic Hall are among the notable features of the place. Gas lamps adorn and illumine the fine streets. A well-paid and efficient body of police, selected from the London constabulary, maintain order among the more than seventy thousand Chinese who live within the foreign precincts. Municipal affairs are conducted by a Council elected annually from among the residents; and the importance of the trust committed to their charge is indicated by the fact that the budget presented for acceptance at a yearly meeting in 1872 exhibited a total of estimated receipts for taxes, dues, licenses, post-office, etc., of over three hundred thousand dollars. About every conceivable means of amusement and recreation are here enjoyed; while the press and the library, with reading and lecture associations, minister to the intellectual taste.

There are fourteen ports or depots, exclusive of Hong-Kong, where foreigners have taken up their residences for purposes of commercial intercourse. Eleven of these are situated at intervals along a coast line of eighteen hundred miles, and three on the river Yangtsz. At some of the ports settlers have acquired land for building purposes as opportunity may have offered;

and, consequently, their dwellings and hongs lie in isolated and scattered positions. At others, a particular site has been set apart within which foreign merchants are permitted to acquire property and build, subject to a small rental to the Emperor as lord of the soil. At others again, the later acquired ports more especially, a concession has been made to the British crown of a special tract subject to a trifling rental to the Chinese government, and this has been divided into convenient lots to suit purchasers.

The necessity of giving employment to large numbers of Chinese servants, and the various exigencies of trade, have demanded an easily-acquired medium of oral communication. This has been provided in the "Pigeon-English," a barbarous and childish dialect that has become the almost exclusive language in business intercourse between natives and foreigners at the open ports. The uncouth and ridiculous jargon is made up mostly of English words in a modified or corrupted form, with an admixture of Portuguese and Chinese, wrought into local idioms. The term "business" is a very important and frequently-recurring word, but the Chinaman is utterly unable to pronounce it,— his efforts yielding a sound somewhat resembling the word *pigeon*. So the accommodating foreigner takes the liberty of adopting the modified form of expression, and the "Pigeon-English" comes to mean simply the Business-English. The word *my* is arbitrarily made to stand for the different cases and numbers of the first personal pronoun, *you* for the second, and *he* for the third. The whole dialect is exceedingly meager, containing, perhaps, only a few hundred words, and both foreigners and natives learn to speak it quite fluently in a few months, making it answer very well all practical purposes. Some American resident has taken the pains to translate a poem of Longfellow's into this rude speech, the first lines of his "Excelsior" being made to read as follows:

"That nightey time begin chop-chop,
     One young man walkey — no can stop.
 Maskee snow! maskee ice!
 He carry flag with chop so nice —
          Topside-galow."

The Rev. Arthur E. Moule has celebrated in "Pigeon-English" verse the utility of the bamboo, and his effusion we here transfer for the delectation of our readers:

"One piecee thing that my have got,
     Maskee that thing my no can do.
 You talkey you no sabey what?
          Bamboo.

"That chow-chow all too muchey sweet
     My likee; what no likee you?
 You makee try, you makee eat
          Bamboo.

"That olo house too muchee small,
     My have got chilo, wauchee new;
 My makee one big piecee, all
          Bamboo.

"Top-side that house my wanchee thatch,
     And bottom-side that matting, too;
 My makee both if my can catch
          Bamboo.

"That sun he makee too much hot
     My makee hat (my talkey true)
 And coat for rain, if my have got
          Bamboo.

"That Pilong too much robbery
    He makee; on his back one, two,
He catchee for his bobbery
                  Bamboo.

"No wanchee walk that China pig,
    You foreigner no walkee you,
My carry both upon a big
                  Bamboo.

"What makee san-pan go so fast?
    That time the wind so strong he blew,
What makee sail and rope and mast?
                  Bamboo.

"My catchee everything in life,
    From number one of trees that grew,
So muchee good my give my wife
                  Bamboo.

"And now, man-man, my talkee done,
    And so my say chin-chin to you;
My hope you think this number one
                  Bamboo."

Foreign merchants and traders in China, with frequent and most honorable exceptions, are not in sympathy with the work of Christian missions. Many of them are engaged directly or indirectly in the opium traffic, which even the most ignorant native does not fail to regard as of doubtful morality, but which traders are unwilling to abandon because of the immense profits. Living in the midst of inferior races, where the restraints of home-life are frequently laid aside, they sometimes indulge their passions without regard to divine or human law. The holy Sabbath is little heeded, either in diplomatic or business circles. The missionary, wholly occupied in the peculiar work to which he is sent, has no time to labor for their spiritual well-being, but cannot always suppress his indignation; and, seeing iniquity in those from whom he had reason to expect righteousness, he denounces the cupidity and vices of his own countrymen, who in turn denounce him; and, unhappily, innocent parties are sometimes involved. The latter are generally in almost total ignorance of the work and success of the men they execrate,—never going where the chapels are thronged with eager worshipers, never entering the orphanages and hospitals where the abandoned are cared for and the afflicted are ministered to in the name of the Good Physician, and never visiting the training schools, where intelligent and enthusiastic youth are being prepared for the sacred ministry and other spheres of usefulness. This breach is constantly widening, the effect being to multiply a peculiar class of difficulties always to be accounted formidable. Nor is the evil confined to this empire. The merchant-marine, the naval squadrons visiting Chinese waters, and strangers who are making the tour of the globe, often receive their impressions from ignorant, prejudiced, or impassioned sources, and they return home to create a public sentiment adverse to foreign missions. Something should be done to heal this breach between missionaries and merchants, and the case calls for serious consideration on the part of Bishops, Secretaries, and other leaders of the great evangelizing movement in pagan lands.

The contact of Western civilization with Chinese conservatism is beginning to tell upon the latter. With none of the ill-considered haste manifested in the Japanese tendency to all things foreign, the government and the commercial classes of the empire yet evince a purpose to adopt such European ideas as seem to them safely progressive. The movement may perhaps be regarded as slow and hesitant, but it has reached a volume and momentum which may be characterized as national.

The revenues derived from the trade conducted in foreign bottoms at the various open ports are collected by a numerous body of officials, consisting of foreigners and natives, the former controlling. The system was introduced at Shanghai, in 1855, as a safeguard against the corruption of native customs officers; and, under the superintendence of Robert Hart, it has become one of the most efficient customs establishments in the world. That light-houses have been erected on the coast is owing chiefly to the influence of this distinguished foreigner, who probably brings into the Imperial Treasury a larger annual revenue than any other servant of the Emperor.

An extensive arsenal has been created at Kiang-nan, near Shanghai, where some of the ablest practical engineers Europe and America can produce have for years been engaged in introducing machinery and imparting instruction. In 1866, pursuant to a contract between Mr. P. Giquel and Viceroy Tso, of Fooh-kien province, the former was made sole director of the projected Foochow arsenal, and almost immediately left for Europe to engage teachers for the schools, workmen for the shops and foundries, and to purchase engines, machinery, etc., being amply supplied with funds for the purposes named. The ground selected for the site of the arsenal was a paddy field near Pagoda Anchorage. To make it available it was found necessary to raise the whole five feet by filling in with dirt, and 13,718,350 cubic feet of earth were deposited over an area of some forty acres. The work on the arsenal proper commenced in October 1867, and was prosecuted with great vigor. In 1869 the foreign employés numbered fifty-seven in all,— including one director, one civil engineer, one surgeon, five professors, two secretaries, two accountants, two draughtsmen, thirteen foremen, and twenty-eight artisans,— a large majority being Frenchmen. The schools of engineering and of theoretical and practical navigation were taught in English; while the designing school, the school of naval construction, a chronometer school, with the department for apprentices in the various workshops, were taught by six French professors and their assistants. The preparation of the ground was an immense work, and the erection of temporary buildings involved much expense and labor, and the results achieved in so brief a time showed wonderful enterprise on the part of Mr. Giquel and the chief mandarins in charge. In the year above mentioned the temporary arsenal comprised a workshop in which models were made, several steam-saws, a machine-shop, a foundry, a forge with thirty-one fires, a boiler and copperware manufactory, a brick-kiln, a lathe-shop, a great forge with two furnaces, a steam-hammer of two tons weight, and an iron rolling-machine capable of rolling plates an inch thick,— all in active and successful operation. Besides, there were four slips for ship-building, residences for the director and teachers, warehouses, buildings for foreign and Chinese laborers, etc. In addition to one hundred and twenty Chinese sailors in the service, and five hundred soldiers occasionally detailed from the camp near by, no less than fifteen hundred native carpenters, smiths and coolies were employed on the premises. The total average expenditure of the works amounted to fifty thousand taels, or about seventy thousand dollars, per month. The first transport was launched on the 10th of June, and in six months a gun-boat followed. Since the completion of the permanent buildings, unless the expectations of the director have been disappointed, the government works at Foo-chow have been able to furnish each year three engines and as many ships. There is a third and somewhat smaller arsenal at Tien-tsin.

That nothing may be left undone in the effort to make the Celestials an effective war power, foreign drill-masters are called in, who, in training their soldiers, resort to the use of words of command in the English tongue. Bishop Wiley states, in his "China and Japan," that when he entered the city of Foo-chow he met a number of soldiers returning from their drill, and was surprised at hearing them shout to each other in our own language, "Shoulder arms," "forward march," etc.

By means of its peculiar educational system, the Chinese government in some sense monopolizes and directs all the talent of the nation. "Employ the able and promote the worthy," is a maxim long held in high repute, and is something more than a mere theory. A talented and industrious man may raise himself from the most obscure position in society to the head of a viceroyalty or the presidency of one of the supreme tribunals at Peking. Preliminary examinations are held in each district town, and the successful students are all duly entered for the decisive trial before the literary chancellor of the province. Those who are so fortunate as to secure the bachelor's degree are considered in a fair way to win further honors and official position; but they must soon face the triennial examination for the next degree before two Imperial

Commissioners. The names of the graduates are published by a crier at midnight from the highest tower in the city, and next morning lists of the successful competing licentiates are hawked about the streets and sent by couriers to all parts of the province. The third degree is conferred at Peking, when the new-made doctors are introduced to the Emperor and do him reverence, the three who possess the most signal merit receiving rewards from His Majesty. They are all inscribed upon the list of candidates for promotion by the Board of Civil Office, to be appointed as vacancies occur. The fourth and highest degree of *Hanlin*—"Scholar Laureate of the Empire"—is a very great dignity, and all who attain it are enrolled as members of the Imperial Academy and receive salaries.

The Chinese have the original patent for civil service reform, and, with at least all due ceremonies and apparent even-handed justice to aspirants for place and honors under the empire, they have maintained their educational system for more than two thousand years. Not only are the candidates for civil office promoted according to their examinations, but when men come for forty successive years with a view to government promotion, although unsuccessful, they pass into a certain honorable position. As a result, they have scholars who can, in some respects, mock the wisest men we are able to produce. The native classics, with the comments on them, make a mass of knowledge equal in volume to some of our largest commentaries on the Bible; yet the Emperor never lacks for scholars who can repeat every word of them from memory.

Notwithstanding their proud distinction as a literary people, the Chinese aspire to Western learning. Inferior schools have been established by the government at Canton and Shanghai, the former under Dr. Happer, and the latter presided over by Rev. Dr. Y. J. Allen; the object of these institutions being to raise up a class of young men for the public service possessing the advantage of both foreign and native culture. The University of Peking, with Rev. W. A. P. Martin, LL.D., at the head, and possessing a corps of eleven professors, seven of whom are foreign, has for a number of years successfully carried on the work of imparting instruction to students from various sections of the country. A printing-office with six presses has been erected in connection with the college for the purpose of publishing scientific works. The full literary and scientific course of study extends over eight years,—the first three being given exclusively to foreign languages, and the remainder to the acquisition of scientific and general knowledge through the medium of those languages.

Not satisfied with these experiments at home, the government appointed a Royal Commission to visit the different civilized nations of the world with a view of selecting some place to establish a Chinese Educational Mission; and, after much deliberation, the United States was chosen, and Hartford, Conn., selected as the city in which to erect the school. Grounds were purchased and suitable buildings completed at a cost of over fifty thousand dollars. The pupils, who now number one hundred and twelve, were selected in China according to their literary attainments or capabilities, and are to be taken through a term of fifteen years. The school is in charge of two Imperial Commissioners, a translator and interpreter, and two teachers, whose prescribed duty it is to see that these students possess the advantages of a thorough English and Chinese education. The government of China has thus set before the American republic a conspicuous example of that policy of civil service reform which wisely seeks to educate the servants of the state for the discharge of their peculiar and important functions. Yung-wing, of the embassy in Washington, has established, in connection with this institution, a school for the training of Chinese telegraph operators, which is the advance step in a plan conceived among high officials of the empire to erect telegraph lines between all the large cities of China. The annual expenditure on this remarkable mission is over one hundred thousand dollars.

One writer boldly asserts that the Chinese "have adopted every manifest improvement which has presented itself for these many centuries." In proof of his position, he states that, "At the commencement of the Christian era they adopted the decimal system of notation introduced by the Boodhists; and changed their ancient custom of writing figures from top to bottom for the Indian custom of from left to right. Every dynasty has improved the calendar according to the increased light obtained from Western astronomers. This holds particularly true of the present epoch. When the Tartars obtained possession of Peking, the native mathematicians and astronomers hastened to present the new governors with the ancient calendar '*fully revised and corrected.*' An eclipse was near at hand. The Emperor commanded a competition. The calculations of the Roman Catholic, Father Schaal, alone were correct, and thereupon he was appointed president of the Board of Astronomy. In the seventeenth century, the Emperor, Kang-hi, adopted movable copper types for printing his *magnum opus*, an illustrated encyclopædia of ten thousand books, in three hundred volumes; and to this day movable types of wood are used for printing the daily *Peking Gazette*. Chinese farmers in the south and north almost simultaneously naturalized the cotton plant; the former had it from Batavia, the latter from Bokhara. The northern people have universally adopted Indian corn, or maize, as also the potato, from Central Asia. Tobacco was introduced by the Manchoo dynasty, and opium, alas! by foreign merchants.

"The same disposition prevails at the present moment in a marked manner among certain prominent literary men. The translation of Herschel's great work on Astronomy has been well received, and its teaching will doubtless prevail. Tsun Kwo-fan, the great mandarin who has been so prominently before the European public of late years, has republished all the works of Euclid, consisting of the first six books translated by Matthew Ricci, and the remaining nine recently translated by Mr. Wylie. Li Hung-chang, the famous general of world-wide celebrity, has republished Whewell's *Mechanics*, translated by Mr. Edkins, with a large supplement upon Hydrostatics and Conic Sections, taken from the Almanak which used to be issued yearly by that gentleman. The father of Yeh, the former viceroy of Canton and the hero of the late Canton troubles, has republished the works on medicine, natural philosophy, and astronomy, given to the Chinese by Dr. Hobson. Tsun Kwo-fan's brother, Tsun Kwo-chein, formerly governor of Che-kiang province, has likewise published all the works of the native mathematician, Li, who has been so much indebted to the Protestant missionaries, and who has this spring (1870) been called to Peking by the Emperor, and appointed professor of mathematics in the new Anglo-Chinese college at the capital."*

Their liability to misunderstandings and consequent collisions with nations of the West have produced a disposition on the part of the Chinese to become acquainted with our conventional rules of international law; and, accordingly, Wheaton's standard work on that subject has been translated by Dr. Martin and printed at the Emperor's expense. Nor have they been insensible to the good deeds of Western philanthropy. Hospitals, it is true, have existed among them for many centuries; but, without doubt, such institutions received a vast impulse first from Roman Catholic and later from Protestant missions; until foundling hospitals and asylums for the sick and aged, and societies for providing coffins and food for the poor, have been established in many of the leading cities. Mr. Pearson successfully introduced vaccine inoculation; although the pamphlet accompanying his invaluable present, containing some necessary directions for the use of the virus and stating the discovery to have been English, was so mutilated by the native publishers as to give no trace by which it could be known that the discovery was other than Chinese.

It may be true that "a very populous and ancient nation like the Chinese is slow to turn to an unaccustomed stand-point," but it is quite evident that among their most intelligent men there are those who are quick to see the value of improvements and who readily become ac-

---

* Williamson's "Journeys in North China," vol i, pp. 33-35.

customed to changes. Among the most progressive men of the empire is Li Hung-chang, some time viceroy of the province of Chih-li, in which is situated the Imperial city of Peking. Clinging tenaciously to the time-honored institutions of his country, he is nevertheless cautiously effecting important changes. He has connected with his office an American, and several Chinese who received their education in the United States, with still others who studied at Cambridge University and in various cities of Europe. Prominent articles relating to Chinese affairs contained in the leading newspapers of the world are translated for his information; and he is consulted by the supreme government upon every important point arising with foreigners. He believes in Krupp guns, Remington rifles, English torpedoes, and American dredges. The supervision of all the arsenals is confided to his care. He is the possessor of a beautiful steam barge, kept for his own purposes of travel up and down the Pei-ho. Once, when impressed with the beauty and genius shown in some imported instruments, he exclaimed, "How wonderful! How comes it that such inventions and discoveries are always foreign?" It is probably owing mainly to the influence of this man that the Emperor's permission was recently granted to construct a telegraph line twelve hundred miles in length from Shanghai to Tien-tsin; and when this enterprise is completed the government at Peking will be in immediate communication, by electricity, with all the courts of Europe and the Executive at Washington.

When Mr. Hart was appointed Inspector-General of Customs, it was made a condition of his appointment, by Sir Robert Bruce and Mr. Burlingame, that he should not occupy a quasi-diplomatic position, but should reside at the treaty ports. He was subsequently retained at Peking, however, by the consent and approval of these foreign ministers, probably because they found it expedient to have him as an intermediary agent; and it soon became evident to observing foreigners that he had acquired a powerful influence at court. Taking advantage of his opportunity in official and friendly intercourse with the chief mandarins, Mr. Hart frequently urged upon them the necessity for the establishment of a resident mission at the court of every Treaty Power. His motive in pressing this policy he states in these words: "I regarded representation abroad as of paramount importance, and as, in itself, progress; for, while I thought that I saw in it one of China's least objectionable ways of preserving freedom and independence, I also supposed it would constitute a tie which should bind her to the West so firmly, and commit her to a career of improvement so certainly, as to make retrogression impossible." In the latter part of October, 1867, Mr. Burlingame went to the yamun to pay his farewell visit; when, in the course of a conversation with Prince Kung, he inquired whether he could be of any service to the Foreign Office on the present occasion of his departure from China and return to America. The Prince replied by some such jocular remark — with possibly a touch of sarcasm — as, "Why, you might just as well be our Embassador at once!" The idea thus broached rapidly grew to be considered as a serious question, receiving the cordial support of Mr. Hart, and finally culminated in the formal appointment of the now celebrated Commission. Although the establishment of Missions abroad had been urged upon the government for years, the selection of Mr. Burlingame may be said to have been spontaneous: that is to say, he did not solicit the appointment, it naturally growing out of what at first was a mere pleasantry.* He was placed at the head of the Embassy, and two Chinese officials of high rank associated with him, the *attachés* consisting of two foreign secretaries, one English and one French, six Chinese student interpreters, two of whom spoke French, two English, and two Russian; besides twenty subordinate officers, valets, physicians, and servants. The brilliant career of these representatives of China through America and Europe, and their success in opening up a more intelligent intercourse between the East and the West, are all familiar matters of history.

In February, 1873, the empresses dowager resigned their powers as regents of the empire into the hands of Tung-chi, who, having passed his minority, assumed the reins of government. This long-expected event was seized upon by the foreign ministers to urge the right of audience with the Emperor. Their united and determined purpose in taking this step, added to the logical necessities of the case since the adoption of the foreign policy inaugurated in the Burlingame mission, rendered their movement successful.

The audience took place on the 29th of June, eight hundred mandarins in splendid costume gracing the occasion with their presence. The embassador of Japan was received first, a separate interview being accorded to him. When he had retired, the ministers of the United

---

* Note on Chinese Matters, by Robert Hart, in "North China Herald," dated Peking, June 30, 1869.

States, Russia, Great Britain, France and the Netherlands, entered the presence in a body, and, without the usual servile ceremonies, were permitted to gaze upon "the sacred countenance." M. de Vlangally, the Russian minister and dean of the diplomatic corps, read an address to the Emperor in French, which Herr Bismarck, secretary and interpreter of the German legation, repeated in Chinese. Each minister then deposited his credentials on a table in front of the throne. This ceremony over, the Emperor delivered, in the Manchoo dialect, his reply to the address. Prince Kung, kneeling by the footstool of His Majesty, interpreted the Emperor's words in Chinese. At the close of the audience, the embassadors were escorted to their chairs with great ceremony, by members of the Tsung-li yamun.

One significant fact, in connection with the late Emperor's accession to power, may be here appropriately referred to. Returning from his journey to the tombs of his ancestors, which had been undertaken in accordance with a custom of the dynasty, the shops of Peking were allowed to remain open and the streets were not cleared of people as the imperial *cortége* passed along. This public disregard of the ancient usage on such occasions, together with the important concession of the audience question, may be contemplated as precursory to yet more startling events in the mental awakening which has already touched with subtle and resistless power those chief centers of influence,— the Temple and the Throne.

The foreigner is strongly intrenched in China. He is there with his colonies, his concessions, his municipal council, his courts of justice, his temples of learning, his newspapers, his religions, his philosophies, and his commerce. If it were possible to expel him in person, the influence he has begotten would still remain to exercise a resistless and controlling power over the forces destined to subvert and re-create that ancient empire.

As one has said, "That East which men have sought since the days of Alexander itself now seeks the West." What should be the attitude of America toward her government and people? In view of our immense missionary and commercial investments in China, and in view of a trade which, during the few years immediately preceding 1868, rose from eighty-two millions to three hundred millions, and which is capable of sufficient expansion to be felt in every workshop in the civilized world, do not a broad philanthropy and a wise statesmanship unite in pointing out a policy of peace and good will? If we must limit and control the Chinese immigration, let it be so; but the genius of our republican institutions and the spirit of our Christianity will forever protest against the war of races inaugurated on our Pacific coast.

APPENDIX.

THE TREATIES WITH CHINA.

THE following is the text of the two treaties signed at Peking on September 17, 1880, by the Commissioners-Plenipotentiary of the United States and China respectively. The first, which provides for the future regulation of Chinese immigration, is in these words:

I.

Whereas, In the eighth year of Heen Fung, Anno Domini 1858, a treaty of peace and friendship was concluded between the United States of America and China, to which were added, in the seventh year of Tung Chih, Anno Domini 1868, certain supplementary articles to the advantage of both parties, which supplementary articles were to be perpetually observed and obeyed; and

Whereas, The Government of the United States, because of the constantly increasing immigration of Chinese laborers to the territory of the United States, and the embarrassments consequent upon such immigration, now desires to negotiate a modification of the existing treaties, which shall not be in direct contravention of their spirit:

Now, therefore, the President of the United States of America has appointed James B. Angell, of Michigan, John F. Swift, of California, and William Henry Trescott, of South Carolina, as his Commissioners-Plenipotentiary, and his Imperial Majesty the Emperor of China has appointed Pao Chun, a member of his Imperial Majesty's Privy Council and Superintendent of the Board of Civil Office, and Li Hung Tsao, a member of his Imperial Majesty's Privy Council, as his Commissioners-Plenipotentiary; and the said Commissioners, having conjointly examined their full powers, and having discussed the points of possible modification in existing treaties, have agreed upon the following articles in modification.

ARTICLE I. Whenever, in the opinion of the Government of the United States, the coming of Chinese laborers to the United States, or their residence therein, affect, or threaten to affect, the interests of that country, to endanger the good order of the said country, or of any locality within the territory thereof, the Government of China agrees that the Government of the United States may regulate, limit, or suspend such coming or residence, but may not absolutely prohibit it. The limitation or suspension shall be reasonable, and shall apply only to Chinese who may go to the United States as laborers, other classes not being included in the limitation. Legislation taken in regard to Chinese laborers will be of such a character only as is necessary to enforce the regulation, limitation, or suspension of immigration, and immigrants shall not be subject to personal maltreatment or abuse.

ART. II. Chinese subjects, whether proceeding to the United States as teachers, students, merchants, or from curiosity, together with body and household servants, and Chinese laborers, who are now in the United States, shall be allowed to go and come of their own free will and accord, and shall be accorded all the rights, privileges, immunities, and exemptions which are accorded to the citizens and subjects of the most favored nation.

ART. III. If Chinese laborers, or Chinese of any other

class, now either permanently or temporarily residing in the territory of the United States, meet with ill-treatment at the hands of any other persons, the Government of the United States will exert all its power to devise measures for their protection, and to secure to them the same rights, privileges, immunities and exemptions as may be enjoyed by the citizens or subjects of the most favored nation, and to which they are entitled by treaty.

Art. IV. The high contracting powers having agreed upon the foregoing articles, whenever the Government of the United States shall adopt legislative measures in accordance therewith, such measures will be communicated to the Government of China. If such measures, as enacted, are found to work hardships upon the subjects of China, the Chinese Minister at Washington may bring the matter to the notice of the Secretary of State of the United States, who will consider the subject with him; and the Chinese Foreign Office may also bring the matter to the notice of the United States Minister at Peking, and consider the subject with him, to the end that mutual and unqualified benefit may result.

In faith whereof, the respective plenipotentiaries have signed and sealed the foregoing at Peking, in English and Chinese, being three originals of each text, of even tenor and date, the ratifications of which shall be exchanged at Peking within one year from the date of its execution.

Done at Peking, this 17th day of November, in the year of our Lord 1880, Kuang Tsu, sixth year, tenth moon, fifteenth day.

JAMES B. ANGELL. [Seal]
JOHN F. SWIFT. [Seal]
WM. HENRY TRESCOTT. [Seal]
Signatures of Chinese Commissioners. [Seal]

II.

The commercial treaty reads thus:

The President of the United States and his Imperial Majesty the Emperor of China, because of certain points of incompleteness of the existing treaties between their two Governments, have named as their Commissioners-Plenipotentiaries, that is to say, the President of the United States: James B. Angell, of Michigan, John F. Swift, of California, and William Henry Trescott, of South Carolina; his Imperial Majesty the Emperor of China: Pao Chun, a member of his Imperial Majesty's Privy Council, and Superintendent of the Board of Civil Office, and Li Hung Tsao, a member of his Imperial Majesty's Privy Council, who have agreed upon and concluded the following articles:

ARTICLE I. The Governments of the United States and of China, recognizing the benefits of their past commercial relations, and in order still further to promote such relations between the citizens and subjects of the two powers, mutually agree to give the most careful and favorable attention to the representations of either, or to such special extension of commercial intercourse as either may desire.

ART. II. The Governments of China and of the United States mutually agree and undertake that Chinese subjects shall not be permitted to import opium into any of the ports of the United States, and the citizens of the United States shall not be permitted to import opium into any of the open ports of China, to transport it from one open port to any other open port, or to buy or sell opium in any of the open ports of China. This absolute prohibition, which extends to vessels owned by the citizens or subjects of either power, to foreign vessels employed by them, or to vessels owned by the citizens or subjects of either power, and employed by other persons for the transportation of opium, shall be enforced by appropriate legislation on the part of China and of the United States, and the benefits of the favored nation clause in existing treaties shall not be claimed by the citizen or subject of either power, as against the provisions of this article.

Art. III. His Imperial Majesty the Emperor of China hereby promises and agrees that no other kind or higher rate of tonnage dues or duties for imports or exports on coastwise trade shall be imposed or levied in the open ports of China upon vessels wholly belonging to citizens of the United States, or upon the produce, manufactures, or merchandise imported in the same from the United States, or from any foreign country, or upon the produce, manufactures or merchandise exported in the same to the United States, or to any foreign country, or transported in the same from one open port of China to another, than are imposed or levied on vessels or cargoes of any other nation, or on those of Chinese subjects. The United States hereby promise and agree that no other kind or higher rate of tonnage dues or duties for imports shall be imposed or levied in the ports of the United States upon vessels wholly belonging to subjects of his Imperial Majesty, and coming either directly or by way of any foreign port from any of the ports of China which are open to foreign trade, to the ports of the United States, or returning therefrom, either directly or by way of any of the open ports of China, or upon the produce, manufactures or merchandise imported in the same from China, or from any foreign country, than are imposed or levied on vessels of other nations which make no discrimination against the United States in tonnage dues or duties on imports, exports, or coastwise trade, or than are imposed or levied on vessels and cargoes of citizens of the United States.

ART. IV. When controversies arise in the Chinese Empire between citizens of the United States and subjects of his Imperial Majesty which need to be examined and decided by the public officers of the two nations, it is agreed between the Governments of the United States and China that such cases shall be tried by the proper official of the nationality of the defendant. The properly authorized official of the plaintiff's nationality shall be freely permitted to attend the trial, and shall be treated with the courtesy due his position. He shall be granted all proper facilities for watching the proceedings in the interests of justice. If he so desires, he shall have the right to present, to examine and to cross-examine witnesses. If he be dissatisfied with the proceedings, he shall be permitted to protest against them in detail. The law administered will be the law of the nationality of the officer trying the case.

In faith whereof, the Plenipotentiaries have signed and sealed the foregoing at Peking, in English and Chinese, etc.

Signatures of the Chinese Commission.

JAMES B. ANGELL.
JOHN F. SWIFT.
WILLIAM HENRY TRESCOTT.

BOOKS PUBLISHED BY
S. C. GRIGGS & COMPANY
CHICAGO.

ANDERSON—AMERICA NOT DISCOVERED BY COLUMBUS. A historical Sketch of the Discovery of America by the Norsemen in the 10th century. By Prof. R. B. ANDERSON. With an Appendix on the Historical, Literary and Scientific value of the Scandinavian Languages. 12mo, cloth, $1.

"A valuable addition to American history." — *Notes and Queries*, London.

ANDERSON—NORSE MYTHOLOGY; or, the Religion of our Forefathers. Containing all the Myths of the Eddas carefully systematized and interpreted; with an Introduction, Vocabulary and Index. By R. B. ANDERSON, Prof. of Scandinavian Languages in the Univ. of Wisconsin. Crown 8vo, cloth, $2.50; half calf, $4.00.

"Prof. Anderson's work is incomparably superior to the already existing books of this order."—*Scribner's Monthly*.

"The exposition, analysis and interpretation of the Norse Mythology leave nothing to be desired."—*Appleton's Journal*.

ANDERSON—VIKING TALES OF THE NORTH. The Sagas of Thorstein, Viking's Son and Fridthjof the Bold. Translated from the Icelandic by Prof. R. B. ANDERSON; also TEGNER'S FRIDTHJOF'S SAGA, translated by GEORGE STEPHENS. One vol. Cloth, $2.

"Prof. Anderson's book is a very valuable and important one."—*The Nation*.

"A charming book it is. Your work is in every way cleverly done. These quaintly delightful sagas ought to charm many thousands of readers, and your translation is of the best."—*Prof. Willard Fiske, Cornell University*.

ANDERSON—THE YOUNGER EDDA,—also called Snorre's Edda, or the Prose Edda. With an Introduction, Notes, Vocabulary and Index. By Prof. R. B. ANDERSON. Crown 8vo, cloth, $2.

"The most complete and literally faithful English version yet produced of Snorre's Edda."—*The Scotsman*, Edinburgh, Scotland.

BLANC—THE GRAMMAR OF PAINTING AND ENGRAVING. Translated from the French of Charles Blanc by Mrs. KATE N. DOGGETT. With the original illustrations. 8vo, cloth, $3.

"We know of no other work which can quite take its place in the hands of those who, without any artistic training, desire to acquire clear ideas concerning the elementary principles of art."—*Appleton's Journal*.

☞ *Books will be mailed postpaid on receipt of price.*

BARBOU — VICTOR HUGO; His Life and Works. From the French of Alfred Barbou, by Miss F. A. SHAW. With Portraits and *fac-simile* letter. Cloth, $1.

"Filled with delightful personal details."—*Baltimore Gazette.*

"A concise and reliable account of the life of one of the most celebrated men of the day."—*Boston Courier.*

BREDIF — DEMOSTHENES — POLITICAL ELOQUENCE IN GREECE. With extracts from his orations, and a critical discussion of the "Trial on the Crown." From the French of L. BREDIF, of the University of France, by M. J. MACMAHON, A. M. 8 vo, cloth, gilt top, $3.

"One of the grandest studies ever made of the great orator."—*Le Pays*, Paris.

"Fascinatingly clear and forcible."—*Sat. Evg. Gazette*, Boston.

"Essentially Gallic, epigrammatic — not diffuse, nor yet too terse — brilliant and sparkling, clear in arrangement, logical in deduction."—*The Critic*, New York.

BROWN — WIT AND HUMOR. A choice collection. By MARSHALL BROWN. Illustrated. 12 mo, cloth, $1.50.

"There is an enormous amount of laughter in the pages of this book."—*New York Evening Mail.*

BURRIS — THE TRINITY. By Rev. F. H. BURRIS. With an Introduction by JOSEPH HAVEN, D.D., LL.D. 12mo, cloth, $1.50.

"One of the most unique, sincere and thorough discussions of the subject of the Trinity which we have ever seen."—*American Wesleyan*, New York.

CAREW — TANGLED. A Novel. By RACHEL CAREW. Square 16mo, cloth, $1.

A beautiful and sparkling tale of an Alpine watering place.

CONE — TWO YEARS IN CALIFORNIA. By M. CONE. With fifteen fine Illustrations, a map of California, and a plan of the Yosemite Valley. 12mo, cloth, $1.50.

"It abounds in information practical in character, and is stored with facts which will be new to the vast majority of our people."—*Albany Evening Journal.*

CROSS — ECLECTIC SHORT-HAND. A new system adapted both to general use and to verbatim reporting. By J. G. CROSS, A.M. 12mo, cloth, $2.

"So simple as to make it possible for a person to acquire it without the aid of an instructor, and in a comparatively short time."—*Hartford Post.*

DEMENT — INGERSOLL, BEECHER AND DOGMA. Positions of Mr. Ingersoll and Mr. Beecher considered. By R. S. DEMENT. 12 mo, cloth, $1.

"Mr. Dement's trenchant diction is well matched by his potent logic. An earnest, honest, hearty and healthy book for the times."—*Standard*, Chicago.

FAWCETT—HAND-BOOK OF FINANCE. With over eighty Tables and Diagrams. By W. L. FAWCETT. 12mo, cloth, $1.75.

"As a full and very complete collection of monetary statistics it has never been equaled or even approached. A storehouse of facts."—*Philadelphia Press.*

FORESTIER—ECHOES FROM MIST-LAND; or, The Nibelungen Lay revealed to Lovers of Romance and Chivalry. By AUBER FORESTIER. 12mo, cloth, $1.50.

"The simplicity and directness of the ancient chronicle are admirably preserved in the version, and the work forms a unique addition to our store of sterling fiction."—*New York Home Journal.*

FOSTER—PRE-HISTORIC RACES OF THE UNITED STATES. By J. W. FOSTER, LL.D. Illustrated. Crown 8vo. Cloth, $3; half-calf, gilt top, $5; full calf, gilt edges, $6.50.

"It is full of interest from beginning to end."—*Popular Science Monthly.*

"Literally crowded with astonishing and valuable facts."—*Boston Post.*

"One of the best and clearest accounts we have seen of those grand monuments of a forgotten race."—*The Saturday Review*, London.

FREEMAN—SOMEBODY'S NED. A Novel. By Mrs. A. M. FREEMAN. 12mo, cloth, $1.

"Aside from its deep interest as a story, it presents social problems worthy the most earnest consideration. The author writes with a most noble purpose, and makes her story plead with powerful eloquence."—*Boston Home Journal.*

HOLCOMB—FRIDTHJOF'S SAGA. A Norse Romance. By ESAIAS TEGNER, Bishop of Wexio. Translated from the Swedish by THOMAS A. E. and MARTHA A. LYON HOLCOMB. 12mo, cloth, $1.50.

"The translation is exceedingly well done."—*Harper's Magazine.*

"No one can peruse this noble poem without arising therefrom with a loftier idea of human bravery and a better conception of human love."—*Inter-Ocean*, Chicago.

HUDSON—LAW FOR THE CLERGY. A compilation of the Statutes of the States of Illinois, Indiana, Iowa, Michigan, Minnesota, Ohio and Wisconsin, relating to the duties of Clergymen in the solemnization of Marriage, the organization of Churches and Religious Societies, and the protection of Religious Meetings and Assemblies; with notes and practical forms, embracing a collation of the Common Law of Marriage. By S. A. HUDSON. 16mo, cloth, $1.

"It contains what every preacher should have. It is a safe guide in securing deeds and titles to property, to churches, etc."—*Religious Telescope*, Dayton.

JONES—THE MYTH OF STONE IDOL. An Indian Love Legend of Dakota. By W. P. JONES, A.M. Small 4to, gilt, $1.

"We read it through, beguiled by its melodious lines and the pathos of its simple tale. Its descriptions are fine pictures."—*Zion's Herald*, Boston.

JANSON—THE SPELL-BOUND FIDDLER. A Norse Romance. By KRISTOPHER JANSON. Translated. By AUBER FORESTIER. With an Introduction by R. B. ANDERSON. 12mo, cloth, $1.

"It contains more about Ole Bull than has ever been published at any one time in English, comprising incidents that have never before appeared in print."—*San Francisco Post.*

"The story is a graphic and poetic description of one side of the peasant life of the North well worth reading. We commend it to all lovers of the romantic, and to all lovers of Norse life and literature."—*Christian Register*, Boston.

JOUSSET—CLINICAL LECTURES. From the French of P. JOUSSET, Physician to the Hospital Saint-Jacques, Paris. Translated by Dr. R. LUDLUM, of Chicago. 8vo. Cloth, $4.50; Half Morocco, $5.50.

"It contains about 500 pages octavo, of the very best and most reliable clinical experience in the practice of homœopathy of any work extant in the profession."—*A. E. Small, M.D., in Chicago Tribune.*

KIPPAX—CHURCHYARD LITERATURE. A choice collection of American Epitaphs, with remarks on Monumental Inscriptions and the Obsequies of various nations. By JOHN R. KIPPAX, LL.D. 12mo, cloth, $1.50.

"A collection remarkable for quaintness and eccentricity."—*New York Daily Tribune.*

LIE—THE PILOT AND HIS WIFE. A Norse Love Story. By JONAS LIE. Translated by Mrs. OLE BULL. Cloth, $1.50.

"Most absorbingly interesting. . . . In realism, picturesqueness and psychological insight, 'The Pilot and His Wife' leaves very little to be desired. Every one of the dramatis personæ is boldly conceived and elaborated with great skill. We have none of the stale repetitions of the usual well-worn characters of fiction, which is indeed no mean praise. . . . A delightful and entertaining book."—*Scribner's Monthly.*

LIE—THE BARQUE FUTURE. By JONAS LIE. Translated by Mrs. OLE BULL. 12mo, cloth, $1.

"Its pictures of life in the far north—the fishermen of Norway, the lonely trading-ports on the Fjord, the habits of the people—are full of a simple and rare beauty. The impression which the book makes is altogether delightful, and we commend it to our readers in the strongest terms.—*Literary World*, Boston.

LORIMER—"ISMS." OLD AND NEW. By GEORGE C. LORIMER, D.D. 12mo, cloth, $1.50.

CONTENTS.—*Agnosticism — Atheism — Pantheism — Materialism — Naturalism — Pessimism — Buddhism — Unitarianism — Spiritualism — Skepticism — Liberalism — Formalism — Denominationalism — Mammonism — Pauperism — Altruism.*

IN PRESS. Ready in October, 1881.

MATHEWS—GETTING ON IN THE WORLD; or, Hints on Success in Life. By WILLIAM MATHEWS, LL.D. 12mo, cloth, $1.50; the same, gilt edges, $2.00; half calf, gilt top, $3.50; full calf, gilt edges, $5.

"It is a book of facts and not of theories. The men who have succeeded in life are laid under tribute and made to divulge the secret of their success. They give vastly more than 'hints'—they make a revelation.—*Christian Era*, Boston.

MATHEWS—THE GREAT CONVERSERS, and Other Essays. By WILLIAM MATHEWS, LL.D. 12mo, cloth, $1.50.

"One will make the acquaintance of more authors in the course of a single one of his essays than are probably to be met with in the same limited space anywhere else in the whole realm of our literature."—*Chicago Tribune*.

MATHEWS—WORDS, THEIR USE AND ABUSE. By WILLIAM MATHEWS, LL.D. 12mo, cloth, $1.50.

"We heartily recommend the work as rich in valuable suggestions to those who desire to cultivate accuracy in speaking and writing."—*The Lutheran Quarterly Review*.

MATHEWS — HOURS WITH MEN AND BOOKS. By WILLIAM MATHEWS, LL.D. 12mo, cloth, $1.50.

"A rare *entrepot* of information conveyed in a style at once easy, lucid and elegant. Any one desirous of cultivating an acquaintance with the leading thinkers and actors of all ages, and to have in a compendious form intelligent opinions on their lives and works, will find herein the result of deep research and sound reflection.—*Sheffield Post*, England.

MATHEWS — MONDAY-CHATS. By C. A. SAINTE-BEUVE. With an Introductory Essay on his life and writings by the translator, WILLIAM MATHEWS, LL.D. 12mo, cloth, $2.

"The translation is excellent throughout."—*New York Evening Post*.

"No essays of the kind in modern literature are superior, if equal, to these masterly portraitures, in which philosophy and elegance are happily combined."—*Boston Daily Globe*.

MATHEWS — ORATORY AND ORATORS. By WILLIAM MATHEWS, LL.D. Cloth, 12mo, $2.

"Covers the whole field in a thorough and masterly manner."—*Boston Globe*.

"A sort of concentrated biography of the great orators, presented in the mosaic of their most brilliant wit and invention."—*N. Y. Home Journal*.

MATHEWS — LITERARY STYLE; and Other Essays. By WILLIAM MATHEWS, LL.D. 12mo, cloth, $1.50.

"Exquisitely entertaining."—*Advance*, Chicago.

"Its influence is excellent and ennobling."—*Standard*, Chicago.

"Sparkling with the clear light of thought."—*Home Journal*, New York.

"Can be dipped into anywhere with the certainty of finding something good and something worth remembering."—*Boston Transcript*.

MORRIS — BRITISH THOUGHT AND THINKERS: Introductory Studies, Critical, Biographical and Philosophical. By GEORGE S. MORRIS, A. M. 12mo, cloth, $1.75.

"It presents wise reflection, entertaining speculation, valuable literary criticism, and a large amount of interesting biographical matter, given with the skill of a practiced writer and the force and authority of an able and powerful mind. It is a book of great value and deep interest." — *Boston Courier.*

MILLER — WHAT TOMMY DID. By EMILY HUNTINGTON MILLER. Illustrated. 16mo, paper covers, 50 cents; cloth, $1.

"If there is any other way in which fifty cents will purchase as much sustained and healthful amusement as is offered by this little book we should be glad to know it." — *John Habberton, in the Christian Union.*

MISHAPS OF MR. EZEKIEL PELTER. Illustrated. $1.50.

"If it be your desire 'to laugh and grow fat,' you will find The Mishaps of Ezekiel Pelter a great help." — *American Christian Review,* Cincinnati.

ROBERTSON'S LIVING THOUGHTS. A THESAURUS. Selected from Robertson's Sermons, &c., by K. B. TUPPER. With introduction by W. C. RICHARDS, Ph. D., and an Analytical Index. 12mo, cloth, $1.25.

"This volume contains the cream of his writings." — *Boston Transcript*

"Full of things for the perusal of which one can hardly fail to be the better." — *New York Graphic.*

ROBERT — RULES OF ORDER, for Deliberative Assemblies. By MAJOR HENRY M. ROBERT, Corps of Engineers, U. S. A. Pocket Size. Cloth, 75 cents.

The Standard Parliamentary Authority in the United States.

"The best book extant." — *Hon. J. W. Husted, late Speaker N. Y. Legislature.*

"Superior to any of the Manuals now in use." — *Hon. T. A. Cowgill, Speaker of Ohio House of Representatives.*

"I find it the most conspicuous and comprehensive embodiment of the rules observed in American assemblies that I have ever seen. It should be studied by all who wish to become familiar with the correct usages of public meetings. — *Bishop Haven, late Chancellor of Syracuse University.*

ROGERS — THE WAVERLEY DICTIONARY. An Alphabetical Arrangement of all the Characters in Sir Walter Scott's Novels, with a Descriptive Analysis of each Character, and Illustrative Selections from the Text. By MAY ROGERS. 12mo, cloth, $2; half calf, gilt top, $3.50; full calf, gilt edges, $5.

"The selections are made with excellent judgment, and form a worthy musterroll of the most immortal of all the Scottish clans." — *Appleton's Journal.*

SMITH — PATMOS; or, The Kingdom and the Patience. By J. A. SMITH, D.D., Editor of *The Standard.* Cloth, $1.25.

"No one can read this volume without receiving a new inspiration to faithful service in the cause of Christ." — *Zion's Advocate.*

TAYLOR — SONGS OF YESTERDAY. By Benj. F. Taylor. Beautifully illustrated. Octavo, with handsomely ornamented cover in black and gold. Full gilt edges, $3; morocco, $6.

"The volume is magnificently gotten up. . . There is a simplicity, a tenderness and a pathos, intermingled always with a quiet humor, about his writings which is inexpressibly charming. Some of his earlier poems have become classic, and many of those in the present volume are destined to as wide a popularity as Longfellow's 'Village Blacksmith' or Whittier's 'Maud Muller.'"—*Boston Transcript.*

TAYLOR — BETWEEN THE GATES. By Benj. F. Taylor. Illustrated. 12mo, cloth, $1.50.

"Benj. F. Taylor gives us another of his charming volumes of pen-pictures. Every fact is so pictorially stated, and with so exuberant a fancy, that the book has all the charm of fiction.—*Harper's Magazine.*

TAYLOR — SUMMER SAVORY. By Benj. F. Taylor. 12mo, cloth, $1.

"A series of pen pictures of the most versatile and charming character. One is delighted with the thought-surprises, and again you pause to admire the word-wonders with which the book is so full. The lines smell of fragrant herbs, and shimmer with sunbeams, and are gay with flowers."—*Methodist Protestant,* Baltimore.

TAYLOR — IN CAMP AND FIELD. By Benj. F. Taylor. 12mo, cloth, $1.50.

"Each of these sketches is a gem in itself. One may search the annals of war from Tacitus to Kinglake and not find anything finer."—*Inter-Ocean.*

"The description of Hooker's battle 'above the clouds' is one of the grandest pieces of word-painting in the English language."—*Peoria Transcript.*

TAYLOR — OLD-TIME PICTURES AND SHEAVES OF RHYME. By Benj. F. Taylor. Illustrated, small quarto, silk cloth, price $1.50; the same, full gilt edges and side, $1.75.

"I do not know of any one who so well reproduces the home scenes of long ago."—*John G. Whittier.*

TAYLOR — THE WORLD ON WHEELS, and Other Sketches. By Benj. F. Taylor. Illustrated. 12mo, cloth, $1.50.

"One of the most elegant, as well as pungent and rich, specimens of wit and humor extant."—*New York Illustrated Weekly.*

"Brings you very near to nature and life in their pleasantest moods wherever you may happen to be."—*E. P. Whipple, Esq., in the Boston Globe.*

"Few equal Mr. Taylor as a word-painter. He fascinates with his artistic touches, and exhilarates with his sparkling humor, and subdues with his sweet pathos. His sentences glisten like gems in the sunlight."—*Albany Journal.*

WHEELER — THE FOREIGNER IN CHINA. By L. N. WHEELER, D. D. With introduction by PROF. W. C. SAWYER, Ph. D. 12mo, cloth, $1.25.

The simplest, clearest and most complete statement of the relations of China and the Chinese to Western civilization to be found in the English tongue. Ready in Sept., 1881.

WINCHELL — PREADAMITES: or, A Demonstration of the Existence of Men before Adam; together with a Study of their Condition, Antiquity, Racial Affinities, and Progressive Dispersion over the Earth. With Charts and other Illustrations. By ALEXANDER WINCHELL, LL. D., Prof. of Geology and Palæontology in the University of Michigan; Author of "Sketches of Creation," etc. 8vo, cloth, $3.50.

"A remarkable and powerful contribution to the reconciliation of the Bible and modern science."—*Literary World*, Boston.

"One of the most noteworthy contributions to an important branch of the great controversy of our day that has been given to the world in either hemisphere."—*Montreal Gazette*.

"The work is popular in its best sense—attractive in style, clear in exposition, and eminently instructive. . . . It is not too much to say that it settles the controversy."—*Popular Science Monthly*.

"It is not too much to say that there is no single work in our language which brings together so much of the latest investigations concerning the tribes of men inhabiting our planet, and their distribution over the continents."—*The American Naturalist*.

WINCHELL — SPARKS FROM A GEOLOGIST'S HAMMER. By ALEXANDER WINCHELL, LL. D., Professor of Geology and Palæontology in the University of Michigan, Author of "Pre-Adamites," "Sketches of Creation," etc. Illustrated. 12mo, cloth, $2.

A progressive series of papers adapted to convey to the general reader, in attractive style, the fullest and latest results of scientific investigation with reference to the history of our planet. Ready in October, 1881.

www.ingramcontent.com/pod-product-compliance
Lightning Source LLC
Chambersburg PA
CBHW031940230426
43672CB00010B/1993